Acclaim for Martin Dugard's
THE LAST VOYAGE of COLUMBUS

"A journey rich in drama and incident. . . . A story told with brio and panache. . . . Dugard weaves a powerful narrative of tension and suspense. . . . He has a keen eye for interesting detail. . . . He evokes the wonders of the exotic and extraordinary New World. . . . His retelling of the tale is masterly, as brisk and bracing as a stiff nor'easter. . . . Those content to sit back and enjoy the voyage will be richly rewarded and entertained."
— Neil Hanson, *Los Angeles Times Book Review*

"In a rich, fluent account, Dugard offers both a gripping naval adventure and a revealing history. . . . His detailed reconstructions rely on ships' logs, journals, letters, and other contemporary accounts, letting the participants describe these extraordinary adventures themselves."
— Ben Sisario, *New York Times Book Review*

"Vivid. . . . This lively and engaging work captures the essence of Columbus's era. . . . This voyage was so extraordinary and harrowing, and the telling of it so compelling, that it is bound to capture the imagination of readers. Strongly recommended."
— Margaret Atwater-Singer, *Library Journal*

"Dugard's narrative brings this drama alive in vivid terms. . . . A valuable addition to the understanding of this critical turning point in history."
— David Hendricks, *San Antonio Express-News*

"Riveting. . . . Like all good storytellers, Dugard knows that pacing and context matter, and he manages to keep a handle on both for much of this rich, compact tale. . . . His book breathes life into that futile, unquenchable, 500-year-old dream. There's adventure for you."

— Ben Cosgrove, *San Francisco Chronicle*

"Astonishing adventure stories are interwoven with personalized accounts of dazzling characters, the first of which is Columbus himself. . . . Dugard vividly describes the delicate relationship between the Spanish explorers and the various natives. . . . Using firsthand accounts from ships' logbooks, fellow travelers, and the explorer's own journal, Dugard often steps back to let the historical figures speak for themselves. . . . The book succeeds in bringing great historical events to life."

— Monika Kugemann, *Pittsburgh Post-Gazette*

"Vivid. . . . Dugard weaves a compelling narrative set neatly against a colorful historical background. . . . Plenty to digest for the history-minded reader who enjoys a bracing story of courage and adventure on the uncharted high seas."

— *Kirkus Reviews*

"A veritable page-turner. . . . Dugard is right in his element, vividly bringing to life close encounters with hurricanes, waterspouts, tidal waves, flash floods, hostile natives, bloody mutinies, shipwreck, and the cramped and highly unhygienic life below-decks on a tiny caravel. . . . If you know as little about the great man as I do, *The Last Voyage of Columbus* is a darn good place to begin your education." — Hans Werner, *Toronto Star*

"This new book is the epic tale of the captain's fourth expedition and is anything but dull. Filled with swordfights, shipwrecks, lust for gold, war, hurricanes, and discovery, the only thing that seems to be missing is Douglas Fairbanks Sr."

— Larry Cox, *Tucson Citizen*

"This swashbuckling tale makes for exciting reading. . . . Dugard is generous in providing riveting accounts of ship life and foreign conquest. There is also a remarkable human element to his story. . . . A heady read."

— Carol Herman, *Washington Times*

"Dugard sprinkles eyewitness accounts throughout and repeatedly brings to bear a modern assessment of the great captain's infirmities. . . . We think we know our icons, but thanks to Dugard, this man from Genoa manages to surprise us still."

— Jim Frisinger, *Knight-Ridder Newspapers*

"Martin Dugard adds considerably to our knowledge of the explorer and his deeds. . . . A historian and scholar, Dugard is also a writer and storyteller of considerable skill."

— Norman N. Brown, *AP Weekly Features*

"While the main events of history paint the picture of our past in broad strokes, it is often the lesser known stories that fill in the details and enrich our understanding of events. *The Last Voyage of Columbus* is of the latter variety, and in it we find a figure who, while familiar, is more human and thus more interesting than the Christopher Columbus we know from history textbooks. . . . Remarkable."

— James Neal Webb, *BookPage*

ALSO BY MARTIN DUGARD

Chasing Lance
Into Africa
Farther Than Any Man
Knockdown
Surviving the Toughest Race on Earth

THE LAST
VOYAGE
of
COLUMBUS

*Being the Epic Tale of the Great
Captain's Fourth Expedition, Including
Accounts of Mutiny, Shipwreck, and Discovery*

MARTIN DUGARD

BACK BAY BOOKS
LITTLE, BROWN AND COMPANY
New York   Boston

Back Bay Books / Little, Brown and Company
1271 Avenue of the Americas
New York, NY 10020

Originally published in hardcover by Little, Brown and Company, June 2005
First Back Bay paperback edition, May 2006

Library of Congress Cataloging-in-Publication Data
Dugard, Martin.
    The last voyage of Columbus : being the epic tale of the great captain's fourth
expedition, including accounts of swordfight, mutiny, shipwreck, gold, war,
hurricane, and discovery / Martin Dugard. — 1st ed.
        p.   cm.
    Includes bibliographical references and index.
    ISBN 0-316-82883-1 (hc) / 10: 0-316-15456-3 (pb) / 13: 978-0-316-15456-7 (pb)
    1. Columbus, Christopher — Travel — America.   2. America — Discovery and
exploration — Spanish.   3. Explorers — America — Biography.   4. Explorers —
Spain — Biography.   I. Title
E118.D84 2005
970.01'5'092 — dc22   2004024725

10 9 8 7 6 5 4 3 2 1

Q-FF

Design by Renato Stanisic

Printed in the United States of America

For Callie, again

CONTENTS

A DEBT OF GRATITUDE TO ALL WHO MADE THIS BOOK POSSIBLE, PARTICULARLY ERIC SIMONOFF, GEOFF SHANDLER, LIZ NAGLE, RICKIE HARVEY, ALEX DISUVERO, AND JUNIE DAHN

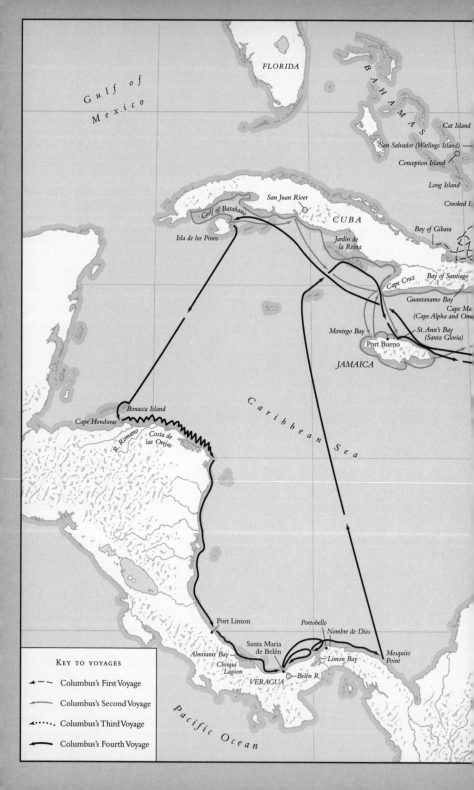

FLORIDA

Gulf of Mexico

BAHAMAS

Cat Island

San Salvador (Watlings Island)

Conception Island

Long Island

Crooked I.

San Juan River

CUBA

Bay of Gibara

Gulf of Batabano

Jardín de la Reina

Isla de los Pinos

Cape Cruz

Bay of Santiago

Guantanamo Bay

Cape Ma
(Cape Alpha and Ome

Montego Bay

St. Ann's Bay
(Santa Gloria)

Port Bueno

JAMAICA

Caribbean Sea

Bonacca Island

Cape Honduras

R. Romano

Costa de las Orejas

Port Limon

Portobello

Nombre de Dios

Santa Maria de Belén

Almirante Bay

Chiriqui Lagoon

Belén R.

Limon Bay

Mosquito Point

VERAGUA

Pacific Ocean

KEY TO VOYAGES

◄ – – Columbus's First Voyage

——— Columbus's Second Voyage

•••••• Columbus's Third Voyage

━━━━ Columbus's Fourth Voyage

The Voyages
of
Christopher Columbus

Atlantic Ocean

Caicos Islands
East Caicos
— Grand Turk Island

Inagua (Babeque)

Monte Cristi

0 Miles   100   200

0 Kilometers   200

dad   La Isabela

LA ESPAÑOLA (HISPANIOLA)

VIRGIN
ISLANDS

Azua   Santo Domingo

PUERTO
RICO

Saba   St. Eustatius

St. Croix

Mona Island

St. Kitts
Nevis   Antigua

Mona Passage

Redonda

Alta Vela

Montserrat   Guadeloupe

Marie
Galante

Dominica

Path of hurricane

Martinique

Caribbean Sea

L E S S E R   A N T I L L E S

Parian
Peninsula

Margarita   Guiria   Bocas del Dragon

TRINIDAD

Gulf of Paria

Point Arenal   Boca de la Sierpe

SOUTH AMERICA

Orinoco River

THE LAST
VOYAGE
of
COLUMBUS

In Chains

October 1500
Santo Domingo

The sun was rising over Santo Domingo, the city named for his father, as Christopher Columbus woke to yet another morning in prison. It was eight years, almost to the hour, since he had discovered the New World. Armed guards stood outside the thick wooden door. His ankles and wrists had long ago been rubbed raw by iron shackles. Even lying flat on his back, he could feel their heaviness against his flesh and anticipate the manacles' noisy clank as he threw his feet over the edge of the bed.

Columbus was alone in the bare cell. A verdant morning breeze wafted in through the window, on its way from the green mountains of Hispaniola out to the Caribbean's turquoise waters. The fragile gust was yet another reminder that the freedom of wind and open sea — the freedom that had defined his life — beckoned less than a half mile away.

He was forty-nine in an era when most men died before thirty; widowed, crow's feet darting across his temples, the father of one son by marriage and another out of passion. His red hair had gone gray years before. The long freckled face with the aquiline nose, so ruddy at sea, had assumed an alabaster pallor during his confinement. Ailments common to lifelong sailors slowed his movements, blurred his sight, ruined his kidneys: rheumatism from the damp and chill, ophthalmia (inflammation of the eyes) from gazing too long at the sun, hereditary gout made worse by a shipboard diet heavy on wine, garlic, cheese, salted beef, and pickled sardines.

At almost six feet tall, Columbus would always be something of a giant, standing half a head taller than most of his crew. It was the explorer's public stature that had been diminished. Though too proud to admit it (even to himself), Columbus was a far cry from the rascal who had once enchanted a queen and even farther from the swashbuckling hero whose exploits galvanized Europe into seeing the world from an astonishing new perspective. Like a great performer lingering too long on stage, Columbus was beginning to make all who watched him uncomfortable — not that he had much of an audience beyond those four dirty walls.

"The Admiral of the Ocean Sea," as Columbus was formally titled, had not yet been sentenced. Given the impulsive nature of Santo Domingo's judiciary system, it was anyone's guess what might happen next. He had already been deposed as governor and viceroy of Hispaniola, an island he had discovered in 1492 and on whose southern shores Santo Domingo was located. At the very least, the stripping of his other New World titles and claims would also come to pass. At the very worst, he would be hanged. Santo Domingo had two very prominent gallows situated along the muddy banks of the Ozama River. They had been built, ironically enough, on Columbus's orders.

The rangy explorer swung his legs over the side of his small, wood-framed bed. "God is just," he rationalized. "He will in due course make known all that has happened and why." Sinking to his knees, Columbus prayed for redemption.

As he did so the lock turned in his door. It swung open. An emissary of the acting governor stepped inside the cell. Alonso de Vallejo ordered Columbus to pick up his chains and follow him.

A terrified and slightly pathetic Columbus did as he was told.

Love and Hope and
Sex and Dreams

CHAPTER ONE

The Voyage the Whole World Remembers

1492
The New World

Columbus's problems began, ironically, with his greatest success. It was summer when Columbus first sallied forth across the ocean blue — or ocean dark, as Spain's more timid sailors called that vast unknown beyond the Pillars of Hercules. He was a forty-one-year-old Italian vagabond who had seduced the most powerful woman in Europe into paying for his outrageous journey. Spain's hierarchy-obsessed nobility considered him a nothing, a no-account foreigner. Somewhere, Columbus had promised, not so far over the western horizon, lay the wealth to finance Spain's wars of unification and conquest. The voyage could end either in death and disgrace or in a most sublime glory.

Columbus was a cheerful, confident man, prone to the occasional boast. Those traits belied a deep intensity: Columbus's focus was so great while sailing or praying that he was oblivious to events going on around him. Yes, the world was round — of that he had no doubt. But often his world was nothing more than himself. He was sure he would succeed.

Commanding a fleet of three small caravels — the *Niña,* the *Pinta,* and the *Santa Maria* — he departed Spain a half hour before sunrise on August 3, 1492.

Just three days out, the *Pinta's* rudder floated loose, the result of sabotage by her fearful owner, who it turned out had been cowed into supporting the journey. The little *Niña,* spry and lithe but designed for coastal sailing, was coltish on the high seas. The fleet limped into port in the mountainous Canary Islands for an unscheduled, month-long layover. The *Pinta's* rudder was refastened. A bowsprit was added to the *Niña,* and her sail configuration changed from a triangular lateen to square-rigged so she would handle easier with the wind as it came from behind.

Columbus hoisted sail from the Canaries on September 6. Over the thirty-three days that followed, the crews, more accustomed to short Mediterranean trips, pleaded for him to turn back. When he refused, they threatened mutiny. Through it all, Columbus did not deviate from his westerly course. At 10 p.m. on October 11, vesper prayers still fresh on his mind, Columbus spied a light bobbing in the distance. Four hours later a lookout confirmed that it was not a lamp or fire on some distant ship but the white sands of what would be labeled the New World a year later, reflected by a dazzling moon. At dawn Columbus climbed carefully over the side of the swaying *Santa Maria,* into a waiting longboat. He was rowed ashore, where he claimed the land for the Spanish sovereigns. Before the voyage was over, he would claim several other islands for Spain.

He might as well have been claiming them for himself. Columbus received a royal reward of ten thousand Spanish maravedis (a maravedi being the modern-day equivalent of twelve pennies) for being the first among his crew to sight land. But that was really just the beginning. The Spanish sovereigns had been so desperate to best their Portuguese neighbors (many of whom, thanks to the intimacies of royal lineage, were also their cousins and distant relations) that they practically handed the New World to Columbus. Indeed, a pair of treaties dreamed up a decade earlier and brokered with Ferdinand and Isabella four months prior to his voyage had given the charismatic Genovese explorer an enviable financial stake in his discoveries. The so-called Capitulations of Santa Fe pledged Columbus control over lands "discovered or acquired by his labor and industry," elevated him to the rank of admiral, and named him viceroy and governor-general of all lands in his new domain. Columbus, or a chosen subordinate, would be the sole arbitrator in all disputes between his new lands and Spain, particularly in reference to shipping traffic.

He would also receive one-tenth of all royal profits (including gold, pearls, spices, or gems) from his discoveries; the right to purchase an eighth percentage of a ship sailing to the new lands, in exchange for a further one-eighth profit from any goods said ship procured; and one-third of any profit due him from his new title as Admiral of the Ocean Sea. Spain, after fronting all the money, had effectively entered a partnership with the perseverant Genovese rather than gaining a colony outright. Columbus had lived on the financial bubble his entire life. Now he was about to become rich.

Or so he thought. On his journey back to Europe aboard the *Niña* in March 1493 (the flagship *Santa Maria* having foundered off the coast of Hispaniola and the lesser members of its crew sent ashore to build a fort in which to live until a relief ship arrived), a cyclone shredded his sails. The *Niña* was too crippled to make it all the way to Spain and limped into Lisbon for repairs. Portuguese King João II — João the Perfect, as he was known — had long kept Columbus at a distance. A decade earlier, he had twice turned down Columbus's proposals for a New World voyage. But he now hastily cleared his calendar to receive the explorer. The king was bearded and sloe-eyed, with long delicate fingers that in March 1493 looked girlish. He was revered for his intellect and physical strength but also feared for his ruthlessness. Once, when a brother-in-law threatened his power, João ordered his relative's immediate execution. When another later tried the same thing, João strangled the misguided relation with those deceptively fragile-looking hands.

João congratulated Columbus on his prescience and achievements and regaled him as a conquering hero. A knowledgeable, passionate advocate of nautical exploration, trained in its nuances, João listened with fascination and a growing rage to descriptions of the new lands Columbus was calling the Indies. Little did Columbus know, but he had stumbled into a diplomatic trap.

João's great-uncle Henry the Navigator had begun Portugal's crusade for maritime greatness, but it was João who had built an empire for his tiny nation. João recognized that Portugal lacked a limitless supply of natural resources and would eventually become Europe's poor stepchild if it didn't acquire colonies to provide trade goods. It was João's maritime advisory committee, the Junta dos Matemáticos, that sent Diogo Cão farther south than any Portuguese ship had ever traveled when he was ordered to explore Central Africa in 1482. So after their meeting, as João bade Columbus farewell (over the objections of his advisers, who thought Columbus an insolent braggart and called for his execution), he knew as well as anyone the new shape of the world — and its implications.

Columbus sailed from Lisbon's enclosed harbor, down the Tagus River into the Ocean Sea, then south along the Portuguese coast on his way back to Spain. Meanwhile, before Columbus could so much as breathe a word of his find to Ferdinand and Isabella, João made the outrageous pronouncement that the Indies belonged to Portugal. Spain was trespassing. João's argument was based on the Eighth Article of the 1479 Treaty of Alcaçovas, giving Portugal control of all lands south of the Canary Islands and opposite the African coast. Columbus's bold new discoveries lay six degrees south of the Canaries; they were twenty-six hundred miles due east — a distance greater than the width of Europe — but south, nonetheless.

King Ferdinand and Queen Isabella had both ratified the Treaty of Alcaçovas, yet they howled in protest. Proving that they were João's equal in gamesmanship, the Spanish sovereigns immediately invoked a Crusades-era statute permitting seizure of heathen lands by Christian rulers for the propagation of the Catholic faith. Columbus, being a devout Christian, had accomplished just such a thing, they argued. Then, instead of settling the matter through the give-and-take of traditional diplomacy (a give-and-take that could have cost Spain chunks of the New World), and well aware that Portugal's naval might dwarfed that of Spain (which could allow the Portuguese to simply sail to the New World and take what they wanted), Ferdinand appealed to the one man whose opinion was beyond reproach: the pope.

The visionary, calculating Ferdinand had seen a heady future for himself at a young age, one with power extending far beyond the small provinces whose rule he inherited. Now he foresaw a great Spanish empire, transcending the Iberian Peninsula, extending west to Columbus's New World and east to Italy. In taking his case to Rome, Ferdinand was seeking out a man who might share that same vision — or at the very least, be so corrupt that he might be swayed on the sly.

Pope Alexander VI was the ideal choice. Born Rodrigo Borgia, the sixty-two-year-old pontiff was Spanish by birth and patriarch of the infamously corrupt Borgia clan. Alexander had uttered the Roman Catholic priest's mandatory vow of celibacy at a young age but viewed it as mere formality to procuring fortune and sway. Alexander had fathered seven children out of wedlock. His current mistress was forty years younger than himself. He had not been selected pope in 1492 because of his piety or in the best interests of the Catholic Church but because he had purchased the position. Then, rather than change his hedonistic ways while following in the footsteps of St. Peter, Alexander delighted in orchestrating lavish bacchanals of food and sex within the Vatican palace. At one particular bash servants were ordered to keep track of each man's orgasms; those satyrs displaying the most virility were awarded colorful silk tunics before stumbling back to their homes and wives.

To say that Alexander VI was morally pliable was an understatement. Add a deep affection for his ancestral roots (when Ferdinand and Isabella routed the Moors at Granada, Alexander defamed St. Peter's Cathedral by staging a Spanish bullfight in its still-uncompleted courtyard), and the sovereigns had the perfect ally.

The decision of the pope, per custom, would be final.

CHAPTER TWO

The Passage

On May 3, 1493, Alexander handed down his swift verdict. The ocean blue — and the rest of the world, for that matter — was split in two. In a series of papal bulls, Alexander VI drew a line down the globe from North Pole to South. This line of demarcation lay one hundred leagues west of Portugal's Cape Verde Islands colony. With the exception of those nations already governed by a Christian ruler, everything to the east of that invisible boundary — the Canaries, the Azores, the entire African continent, Madagascar, and Saudi Arabia — belonged to Portugal. Everything to the west belonged to the newly unified and ascendant Spain. So far as the world knew, the newly decreed Spanish holdings amounted to nothing more than a gaggle of sandy tropical islands inhabited by seminude natives — discovered, of course, by Columbus. It was testimony of the Spanish sovereigns' great faith in those findings that they would willingly cede so much of the world to a rival nation based on the tantalizing hope of something much greater to be discovered later.

Papal decisions could not be appealed. Nevertheless, the

headstrong João immediately disputed Alexander's bulls —
not because he was naive enough to believe a corrupt Spanish
pope would rule against the Spanish sovereigns, but because
João sought a compromise that would bring at least a taste
of the New World's booty to Portugal. João had a hunch that
a large, unknown continent lay south of Columbus's discoveries, directly opposite Africa — and he was determined to
own it. João was betting that the Spanish sovereigns were so
enamored of the New World opposite Europe that they
would agree to his terms.

He was right. The Treaty of Tordesillas, brokered without the aid of Rome, amended the bulls. The Spanish sovereigns signed on July 2, 1494, and João II on September 5.
The treaty required Portugal to formally recognize that
Columbus's discoveries belonged to Spain. In return, Ferdinand and Isabella agreed to move the line of demarcation
farther to the west. João, who was already sending ships east
to find the Indies, had got the better of Ferdinand. His manipulations would pay off years later, giving Portugal a
foothold in South America and control of Brazil's considerable wealth, in addition to total command of the eastward
route to the Orient.

So it was that the growing Spanish dreams of empire lay
solely on the broad Italian shoulders of Christopher Columbus and his westward passage to India. Based on the premise
that the world was round — an ancient point of view that
lay fallow in Europe during the Dark Ages — sailing far
enough west brought a traveler to the east. Or in Columbus's way of thinking, India did not just lie east of Spain, it
also lay very, very far to the west.

The seeds of Columbus's logic had been sown in Baby-
lon, six centuries before the birth of Christ. A cartographer
whose name has been lost by history carved the first known
world map on a clay tablet. Of course cultures throughout
the world had drawn maps for ages. The Chinese sewed

them onto swatches of silk. Islanders of the South Pacific wove plants and shells together to depict their region. Eskimos carved maps on ivory. But each of these maps was regional, displaying the rivers and landmasses vital to a single culture's daily existence. The Babylonian map was a breathtaking cartographical leap forward, but deeply flawed nonetheless. The earth, for example, was shown not round like a ball but circular and flat — a medieval Frisbee, floating on a large, blue ocean.

The idea of a flat earth was widely accepted at the time. One theory even supposed the horizontal sphere rested atop the backs of four elephants, all balanced atop the shell of a mighty tortoise. Both these notions troubled the Greek philosopher Aristotle, for they made no sense. When a ship sailed out to sea, its hull disappeared over the horizon before its sails. A flat earth would mean both hull and sail would diminish from view together. Just as illogically the earth cast a circular shadow on the moon during eclipses. The world, Aristotle concluded, was most obviously round. His theory was soon accepted, and as Greek and Roman cartographers mapped this new worldview, east-west and north-south lines were added, and the terms "latitude" and "longitude" given them.

In the second century AD, Claudius Ptolemy, a scholar at Egypt's Alexandria library, undertook his comprehensive study of the cosmos, *Geography*. Ptolemy evinced a certain arrogance, fortified by his immense knowledge. He once wrote a tome on mathematics with a lengthy title that he shortened to *Almagest* — the "Greatest." He was just as zealous about propagating his world knowledge in *Geography*. Ptolemy ruminated over the text, exhaustively analyzing and rejecting many widely held theories about the earth in his attempts to make the book definitive. The final result was a work of genius that still influences mankind nineteen centuries later. It includes a world map, more than two dozen regional maps, and a comprehensive listing of the earth's known cities by latitude and longitude. His world map was the first to be oriented north and showed a planet of three continents: Asia, Africa, and Europe.

Ptolemy's map of the world, however, was also horribly flawed. The Atlantic and Indian oceans were too small. The Pacific was nonexistent. Asia was shown to be far broader than in actuality, covering more than half the world. The coast of China ran south and west until it connected with the African coast, totally enclosing the Indian Ocean. Grievous mistakes all, based on speculation and the deductions of "world" travelers. Ptolemy's map, however, was accepted as fact.

When the Roman Empire fell, the Alexandria library was looted, and its museum destroyed. In AD 391, a mob of Christian agitators, believing all things secular and intellectual to be evil, burned the library's contents. *Geography* was among the books lost. A copy had been spirited away before the fire, which was a lucky break for later generations, for as Europe settled into the Dark Ages, cartography became a dead science. Ptolemy's work was dismissed as pagan propaganda and then forgotten altogether. Once again it became popular for Europeans to believe that the world was flat. Most maps drawn during this time were speculative, more interested in showing pilgrims the way to Paradise than serving as an accurate outline of land and sea.

Even after the Dark Ages came to an end, the route to Eden remained a fixture of world maps. In keeping with a passage from the book of Genesis — "And the Lord God planted a Garden eastward in Eden" — it was always shown in the east. The seventh-century writings of Isidore of Seville presented these theories as fact. More than seven hundred years later, Sir John Mandeville reinforced the notion. The well-meaning, if self-aggrandizing and misinformed, Englishman's *Travels and Voyages* was an account of his various journeys, real and imagined. Based on what he had learned, Mandeville gave clues to Eden's earthly location. "Of Paradise can I not speak properly, for I have not been there," he wrote. "This paradise lay near the Orient." Four mighty rivers — the Nile, Ganges, Euphrates, and Tigris — flowed from its center. He spoke of 7,549 islands nearby, populated by savages.

But the cartographic focus on the east wasn't solely because of Eden. In 1271 a seventeen-year-old Venetian named Marco Polo traveled to China via ship and camel. By the time he returned home twenty-four years later, Polo had ample knowledge of a part of the world known to few Europeans. The following year Genoa conquered Venice, and Polo was thrown in prison. There he dictated the story of his travels. Completed in 1298 and copied by hand as it was distributed throughout Europe, *The Book of Ser Marco Polo* told of a land with such ingenious devices as paper money, coal burned for fuel, and a pony express–style mail service. More important to Columbus, Polo vividly described the topography of Asia.

Meanwhile, *Geography* was quietly making its presence felt in the non–European world. Throughout the centuries Muslim Arabs had used it to produce their own detailed maps of Africa and the Indian Ocean. In the fourteenth century, just as cartography began a European revival, a Benedictine monk came across a rogue copy of *Geography* while prowling through a used-book store in Constantinople. He purchased the book and took it back to Europe, where, despite the astonishing amounts of forgotten knowledge on its yellowed pages, it languished for another century. In 1478 it was rediscovered yet again and translated into Latin. Thanks to the birth of the printing press, it was finally disseminated throughout Europe. Polo's writings, which had quietly endured as a travel classic for two centuries, also underwent a surge in popularity as they were printed en masse and widely distributed for the first time.

For mariners like Columbus, who had seen the dawn of maritime maps that showed the European coastline in minute detail, *Geography*'s long lost guide to the planet was a godsend. That its information dovetailed with Polo's accounts gave *Geography* the gravitas of biblical truth. Also, thanks to his work as a chart maker, Columbus's knowledge of the most modern concepts of the design and construction of maps put him at the forefront of medieval knowledge. He could cite specific references rather than merely speculate. And by his reckoning his voyages across the Atlantic had confirmed his theories. His knowledge was encyclopedic. He considered Cuba to be the Chinese province of Mangi. His impromptu colony of La Navidad was located on the outlying island of Cipangu. Coincidentally, by the time he returned to Spain in 1493, a German navigator and merchant named Martin Behaim had produced a twenty-inch-wide globe showing Ptolemy's ideas. Although mankind had long considered the world round, that was an abstract intellectual ideal on par with concepts like social equality and the Holy Trinity. Behaim's globe allowed thinkers and commoners alike to see the world in tactile, three-dimensional fashion — to wrap their hands as well as their minds around Columbus's theories. The Atlantic was narrower on Behaim's globe than Columbus knew from first-hand experience, but China was exactly where he had thought. Even the northern tip of Cuba angled in the same direction indicated by Behaim and Ptolemy.

The 1492 voyage had convinced Columbus and the sovereigns that his theories were correct. Clearly this New World, based on all existing knowledge of the planet earth, was actually the outer fringes of the Asian continent. The decision was crucial. Ferdinand and Isabella were not as interested in a new world as in the riches of an old world, the Oriental world. The wealth they sought was not just gold and pearls, but something far more precious: pepper.

And pepper was found only in the East.

CHAPTER THREE

Good Taste

Spices of all kinds were a medieval fixation, but they had been a part of daily life for millennia. In 2600 BC Egyptians fed spices to slaves building the Cheops pyramid. Wealthy Romans slept on pillows scented with saffron to ward off hangovers. A spice market on Via Piperatica — Pepper Street — was vital to the lifeblood of ancient Rome. It was the Romans who invaded Arabia over the cost of pepper and whose legionnaires — rugged men fond of marching into battle wearing perfume — introduced spices to northern Europe and Britain. In addition to aesthetic qualities, salt, pepper, and other spices concealed the aroma of spoiled food and helped preserve slaughtered meat, sometimes for months. As spices became a functional part of all levels of societies, it was only natural that they also became a powerful economic force.

Spices weren't indigenous to Europe, though. They came from a tropical belt spreading from the monsoon-drenched Asian subcontinent east to the fragrant islands of Malacca, Ceylon, Java, and Sumatra. The journey from there to European palates was long and involved. Arab merchants traveled to India and the "Spice Islands," then filled their dhows with cargoes of pepper, allspice, cinnamon, cassia, cloves, nutmeg, and vanilla. Then they sailed west again, riding the trade winds across the Arabian Sea to the Horn of Africa and into the Red Sea, that saber-shaped inlet bordered by northern Africa on one side and the Arabian Peninsula on the other. The cargo was offloaded in Syria, near the isthmus that would someday become the Suez Canal. It was then hauled overland by mule and camel caravans into Egypt. After being loaded aboard a new fleet of ships in Alexandria, the spices were shipped northwest across the Mediterranean to Venice, where wholesalers waited to purchase them for disbursement to the apothecary shops and kitchens of Europe. Thanks to an exclusive arrangement between the Arabs and the merchants of Venice dating to the seventh century, the Venetians were the sole European outlet for India's pepper and spices.

Controlling Europe's leading commodity allowed Venice to control Europe. When the demand for pepper increased, the Venetians raised prices but artificially reduced supplies. Egypt drove the cost higher by levying a 30 percent tariff on all pepper passing through their ports. Making matters worse, the lone overland route was shut down in 1453, when the Ottoman Turks captured Constantinople. This ensured the Venetian and Egyptian stranglehold on the market. The price of pepper increased thirtyfold in the fifteenth century. Venetian merchants flaunted their prosperity by building opulent marble mansions.

By 1492, however, Europeans could not imagine life without spices. Those with the money paid willingly, and those without it found a way to pay. It was a turning point in history, a time when the medieval world's fixation on the hereafter was being replaced by the Renaissance's sensual focus on the here and now. Spices were the currency of that transition. One pound of nutmeg was equal trade for seven fattened oxen. One method of preparing rabbit called for cloves, ground almond, saffron, cypress root, sugar, cinnamon, and nutmeg, while one recipe for stag demanded that the entire animal be roasted in a fireplace, then drawn and quartered and slathered in pepper sauce. Fruit was often boiled and then topped with vinegar, pepper, and cinnamon. People floated spices in their wine or served them on small platters as an after-dinner condiment.

Social position could even be judged by the amount and types of spices served to company. A peasant might offer guests veal seasoned with salt and local spices, but a member of the ruling class would go a step further, adding exotic pepper, nutmeg, and cinnamon. An individual's status was discernible to the palate, giving rise to a new definition of "taste." No longer did it refer merely to flavor but also to pedigree and class.

For those with great taste, nothing was more esteemed than pepper. Six and a half million pounds were consumed annually in Europe. The gritty black berry was used to pay debts, bequeathed in wills, and presented as gifts of state. A man would willingly marry below his social position if the bride's dowry included enough of the spice. Pepper and power were synonymous. As Venice accumulated more and more wealth, it became clear to other nations that breaking Venice's grasp on the spice trade would make those riches theirs. This desire was foremost on the Spanish sovereigns' minds, and Columbus knew they might lose faith in his theories should he return empty-handed. So when he was unable to find traditional black pepper on that maiden journey to the New World, he came up with an ingenious hoax: he brought back a quantity of brightly colored dried chilies and rechristened them "red" peppers in his presentation to the sovereigns.

"He who is lord of Malacca," it was said of the small island where spices grew like weeds, "has his hand on the throat of Venice." Columbus's deceit bought him time, but it also whetted the appetites of the Spanish king and queen. They now could reach India via the Atlantic. The era of the Venetians was over, they thought. But Venice's would not be the only throat they attempted to squeeze.

CHAPTER FOUR

Power

Columbus was not a simple man, nor was he a stranger to court intrigue. But as a traveler of the known world, forced to trust strangers in lands from Africa to Iceland, he took it on faith that a man's word was binding. A signed contract meant evermore. Thus when Ferdinand and Isabella started to reverse the balance of power in their partnership — indeed, began a sly campaign to reverse the Capitulations of Santa Fe and rob him of all claims in the New World — Columbus's faith that no such thing would ever occur was almost childlike. But within two months of his return from the first voyage, they commenced an ongoing effort to make their Admiral of the Ocean Sea — also quietly referred to as the Genovese, the outsider, the commoner, and even per rumor, the Jew — expendable. As with all deceptions it began in a most plausible fashion. And as with the many involvements of Ferdinand and Isabella, the primary characteristic of the plot was its ruthlessness.

The two rulers had married in 1469. Isabella was by far the more attractive of the two: petite and beautiful, with auburn hair, calm blue eyes, and a gracious nature. Her devout Catholic character and worldly intellect made her the better of many men — including Ferdinand. She was polished and insightful, an advocate of the arts and literature. Yet she was also a warrior, with battle armor tailored to her boyish physique. Isabella was firm and even ruthless when matters of state demanded, yet loving and maternal to her five children. In many ways that affection extended to all the people of Spain. Her reign was not defined by acts of self-glorification but by acts that glorified her nation.

Their desire to see Spain prosper financially and to see it rise from a fragmented assortment of kingdoms to become the most dominant nation in Europe — if not the entire world — was the most powerful bond between Isabella and Ferdinand. Although something of an egomaniac, Ferdinand was no less committed to Spain's greatness. Ferdinand was only slightly taller than his diminutive bride, with a ruddy face, bushy auburn eyebrows, and male pattern baldness that accentuated his forehead. His teeth were small and crooked, and he spoke in rapid bursts. Ferdinand was fond of one-upmanship, whether through war, diplomacy, or intrigue.

Ferdinand and Isabella's marriage had been arranged. She was heir apparent to the mighty Crown of Castile. With its population of six million, Isabella's massive kingdom cut a swath through the heart of Spain, stretching from the Portuguese border on the west, south to the Mediterranean and Atlantic coasts, north to the Bay of Biscay, and east as far as San Sebastian and Cartagena. The Moorish kingdom of Granada lay at the southern edge of Castile, a heathen dagger in the heart of her Catholic homeland. It was the only vestige of the Muslim invasion of Spain seven centuries earlier, and Isabella deeply resented the alien incursion. Even in the early days of her reign, the reconquest of Granada was never far from her thoughts.

Ferdinand's Aragon was elfin in comparison. The lands

from the eastern border of Castile to the French border in the Pyrenees were subdivided into the four kingdoms of Navarre, Aragon, Catalonia, and Valencia — their combined population was a fourth of Castile's total. Yet Ferdinand was a larger-than-life figure, not cowed by Isabella's more expansive landholdings. He had first proved himself on the battlefield at the age of twelve and had fathered three children out of wedlock soon after. The first time he met Isabella was on October 14, 1469, in Valladolid. Her emissaries had escorted him there, straight from presiding over the Aragon parliament in Zaragoza. Five days later they married. Ferdinand was seventeen. Isabella was just a year older.

Juan of Aragon, Ferdinand's father, advised the young royals that their true power lay in working together. It was advice that they never forgot. In an arrangement undertaken by few monarchies before or since, Isabella and Ferdinand ruled equally as king and queen. Their likenesses appeared together on coins, and all public documents contained both signatures. Through warfare and diplomacy, Ferdinand and Isabella transformed a land (divided by kingdoms) — characterized by civil war, vigilante justice, and corruption — into a unified country whose powerful influence was felt from Rome to London. Their youngest daughter, Catherine of Aragon, would become the first wife of Henry VIII, a marriage aligning Spain and England until long after Isabella's untimely death finally separated Ferdinand and Isabella.

They demanded total obedience from the Spanish nobility, installed a code of laws and a judicial system, and ordered that every Spaniard be considered a free man — no serfs or slaves. Additionally, Isabella and Ferdinand reformed the corrupt Spanish clergy, put an end to the sexual debauchery that once defined the royal court, and established a militia to arrest the thieves overwhelming Spain's highways. And all this was done with an air of frugality. Ferdinand and Isabella preferred to spend the nation's riches on improving Spain, not on themselves.

Yet for all that progressive brilliance, the sovereigns sometimes seemed mired in the Dark Ages. What became known as the Spanish Inquisition, their ethnic cleansing of Spain that began in 1478, was a revival of the secretive, thirteenth-century papal court that investigated suspected heretics and forced them to change their beliefs. The Spanish Inquisition's original goal was not to prosecute Jews or Muslims but to determine whether Jews and Muslims who had converted to Catholicism — conversos — were backsliding to their prior faith. Those reverting or practicing Judaism in secret were called Marranos — "pigs" — a reference to the Mosaic laws against pork consumption.

Isabella was the more devout of the two sovereigns, yet she strenuously protested the Inquisition. Ferdinand would hear none of it. He had a bigot's heart and considered foreigners and heretics the root of all evil. Unifying the Iberian Peninsula and eradicating heresy had been his pet project since becoming king. Ferdinand was so convinced of the need for the Inquisition that even the Catholic Church, in his eyes, could not be trusted to handle such a delicate spiritual matter.

For proof Ferdinand needed only point to Sixtus IV, pope at that time. Sixtus was much more comfortable in the secular world than the spiritual, so given to immoral lapses that the church went to the unusual extreme of sanctioning him for nepotism when he named an eight-year-old grand-nephew archbishop of Lisbon and for the attempted murder of two prominent rivals during High Mass in Florence.

In 1481, at Ferdinand's urging, Sixtus transferred control of the renewed Inquisition from the Catholic Church to the Spanish government. As Ferdinand knew it would, the capitulation of Sixtus carried the weight of doctrine. When Isabella expressed doubts in her daily trips to the confessional about the morality of persecuting the Jews, the priests convinced her that the Inquisition was not really a form of persecution but a right and just means of discipline in the eyes of the Lord. To believe otherwise, they warned her, was akin to heresy.

One of these priests was a Dominican monk named Tomas de Torquemada — ironically, he was the descendant of conversos (his father was of Jewish lineage) but was convinced that Jews and Muslims were the sticking point in the sovereigns' drive for Spanish unity. Fernando was impressed with Torquemada's dogmatism and decreed that the monk should serve in the newly created role of inquisitor general, giving him such absolute power that soon even the most ardent Catholics feared for their lives. Suspected Marranos were stripped of personal property and possessions, imprisoned, interrogated, and tortured in a most heinous fashion. More than six thousand Spaniards would be burned at the stake. Between thirty and sixty thousand Jews would be banished from Spain. The Inquisition became so successful in the eyes of the Catholic Church that it lasted until 1834, embedding an environment of secrecy and fear in Spain's already idiosyncratic culture — all because of Ferdinand's longing for power.

CHAPTER FIVE

In Which Ferdinand and Isabella Realize Their Great Mistake

May 1493–June 1496

Columbus knew of the Inquisition. There was no escaping its horrors and the way it cowed Spain's people into telling lies about friends and neighbors, all in the hope that such lies would not someday be directed at them. But he owed his success to the sovereigns and was, above all, deeply loyal. Selectively oblivious to the horrors of the Inquisition, he was completely unaware that Ferdinand was increasingly bothered by his very presence. The New World held great potential, and Ferdinand's regrets over signing the Capitulations of Santa Fe had been gestating since the moment Columbus's whimsical theories proved real. To have handed over such lands to a subject would have been foolish enough, Ferdinand was realizing, but ceding them to a foreigner was an embarrassment.

On May 20, 1493, in a calculated power grab eerily reminiscent of his self-serving decision to annihilate Spain's Jews and Muslims, Ferdinand began whittling away at the Capitulations. He appointed a loyal Spanish member of the royal court to represent the sovereigns in all financial matters relating to the New World. The act was innocuous on the surface, a simple act of designation, as if the Indies were a minor aspect of Ferdinand and Isabella's realm. But the mandate given Juan Rodriguez de Fonseca, new royal auditor of the Indies, was nothing of the sort. He was to record all expenses and income from the New World. Every speck of gold, every pepper seed, every slave was to be tallied. Cargoes and crews would be scrutinized in his customhouses. Accountants in his employ would sail with each ship to ensure compliance. Fonseca would be nothing less than overlord of the Indies — a title Columbus mistakenly thought belonged to him alone. Every aspect of the Admiral of the Ocean Sea's New World travels now fell under the domain of the obsequious, calculating, land-loving, and decidedly unadventurous Fonseca.

Ferdinand had many abhorrent traits, but he was unmatched at realpolitik. He had intended to stifle and steal Columbus's power before it subsumed the burgeoning Spanish empire. In Fonseca he had found the ideal man for the job.

Perhaps it was inevitable that Columbus and Fonseca would become enemies. They were born in the same year, but age was all they shared. Columbus, of course, was but an Italian commoner. Fonseca was a Spaniard through and through, born in Toro, near the splendors and power of Seville. He was the second son to a powerful father slain while fighting for Castile, whose official position had been lord of the towns of Alaejos and Coca.

Fonseca's family selected his clerical career before he was born. Since his older brother Antonio would inherit the family titles, Juan was educated as a priest, much like his uncle Alfonso, who had served as archbishop of Seville. Alfonso had accumulated so much wealth in the position that he built a massive fortress in Segovia, the Castillo de Coca, with prominent embattlement and three sets of brick walls that were each two-and-one-half-feet thick. Though such a massive castle may have seemed an overblown form of protection for a man of the cloth, the Fonseca family would go on to maintain it for several centuries.

Fonseca, then, was simply carrying on the family legacy passed on from Alfonso. Those family connections earned him a spot at the royal court at a young age, working for one of Isabella's confessors.

Columbus labored his entire adult life, sailing the Mediterranean, Atlantic, and African ports, making his living as a sailor, captain, and chart maker. At one point he was so deeply in debt that he was afraid to enter Portugal, knowing he would be thrown in prison until his creditors were repaid. Fonseca, on the other hand, was granted a series of church benefices that made him rich. This fortune allowed him the leisure to postpone his ordination until April 6, 1493, at the age of forty-two — three weeks after being present in the royal court as Columbus briefed Ferdinand and Isabella about his first voyage.

The predestined clash between the unctuous cleric and the visionary Columbus took place immediately. For his second voyage to the New World, Columbus longed to perform an all-encompassing exploration of the Indies. He had dreams of a speedy, state-of-the-art fleet specifically designed for that purpose. Fonseca was adamant that colonization be the priority. The ships he had in mind would be large and bulky, suitable for carrying men and cargo but not exactly ideal for exploring. Columbus raged, but Fonseca — acting with the tacit agreement of the sovereigns — overruled him. The gambit was deliberately haughty, a pointed reminder that Columbus's interests would now come second to the Crown's — and to Fonseca's. "There arose," Fernando Columbus wrote of Fonseca's feelings toward his father, "a mortal and unceasing hatred of the Admiral, and everything to do with him. He was chief of the plotters who secured the Admiral's disgrace with the Sovereigns."

On September 25, 1493, just five months after returning from his first foray into the New World, Columbus set
sail on his second voyage, this time leading a convoy of seventeen ships loaded to the gunwales with Spanish colonists.
Salvos of cannons, a cavalcade of trumpets, and gaily colored ceremonial flags bid Columbus farewell as he sailed
from the port of Cádiz. Twelve hundred official passengers
and three hundred stowaways packed the decks. Some were
sailors, but many more were adventurers, artisans, farmers,
craftsmen, and ex-convicts, all off to start a new life in a
new land. Not a single woman was on board, but each boat
had a horse or two stabled in the hold, soon to be joined by
fowl, pigs, sheep, and goats when the fleet stopped for
wood and water in the Canary Islands. Columbus's young
sons, Diego and Fernando, both of whom would serve as
pages to the royal court in his absence, looked on proudly
from the quay.

Once a colony had been established, it was Columbus's
intention to put the newcomers to work digging for gold
and then continue his search for pearls, spices, and that all-
important passage to India. Although he had hopefully
named the inhabitants of the islands he discovered "Indians," he was painfully aware that he had not yet set foot on
that country's fragrant shores.

That blustery autumn day marked the public high point
of Columbus's career, greater even than discovering the
New World. The founding of a colony in the New World
would clearly signal the dawn of a new age in world history — and Spanish power. Little did Columbus know,
however, that the downward spiral that would land him in
prison had already begun.

The very next day, September 26, 1493, Pope Alexander VI was prodded into issuing yet another papal bull. The
bull, *Dudum siquidem,* clarified his previous edicts at the request of Ferdinand and Isabella. Spain, Alexander con-

firmed, was entitled to all lands discovered by sailing west or south toward the Orient.

It was a subtle proclamation but one that would have long-term effects on Columbus. The pope and Catholic sovereigns were acknowledging that the New World might contain a great number of undiscovered landmasses. If that were true, it was clearly too much of the globe for one explorer to discover. Yet based on the Capitulations of Santa Fe, Columbus controlled all lands "discovered or acquired by his labor and industry." The explorer took this to mean all of the New World. In Columbus's mind, he was the only man allowed to explore it — no matter how large. For three years the sovereigns had acted as if that were their reading of the document, too, by not sending any other voyages of exploration to the Indies. *Dudum siquidem* would change that — in favor of Spain.

On April 10, 1495, while Columbus was still in the Indies, two years into his epic second voyage (a tour de force of exploration that saw him discover and chart almost every single island in the Caribbean, including Puerto Rico, the Virgin Islands, Jamaica, Cuba, and a tempestuous strait between Puerto Rico and Hispaniola known as the Mona Passage), Fonseca made his move. In a unilateral decision that had Ferdinand's unspoken blessing, the bishop and royal auditor declared that Columbus would no longer be the only explorer in Spain's New World. The government would henceforth be allowed to enter into contracts with private adventurers of Spanish extraction. They were to share a fourth or fifth of all profits, depending upon their reputation, with the Crown. Fonseca also created a customs department that would inspect all New World cargoes and demanded that all individuals wishing to travel to the New World obtain a special governmental clearance.

Even Columbus.

The Admiral had no recourse but to plead his case to

the sovereigns upon his return to Spain, in June of 1496. Ferdinand and Isabella craftily sided with Columbus, but only up to a point. The sovereigns amended Fonseca's original mandate. Columbus was still entitled to profits from all lands he had discovered up to April 1495. But they now stuck to the letter of the Capitulations. He would no longer receive wealth from all the New World. In addition to wealth from Hispaniola, his share would be limited to lands discovered before that date, unless — and this was a most important technicality — Columbus discovered them himself. If some other explorer arrived in the Indies first, Columbus would get nothing.

The stage was set for a race to find the passage. More than ever before, Columbus needed to get to India first.

It was not to be.

CHAPTER SIX

The Unexpected Portuguese Triumph

I n Lisbon — that balmy seaside city of tangled streets perched atop seven terraced hillsides — Columbus's quest for the Orient was not taken lightly. The Portuguese were incensed by Spain's newfound interest in exploration, which chafed at the very core of their nation's being. Their forefathers were explorers, starting with the Phoenicians, who first sailed up the 626-mile-long Tagus in the twelfth century BC (the citizens of Portugal were so enamored of nautical wanderers that they liked to claim Lisbon was not founded by the Phoenicians but by the great Ulysses).

Over the centuries Lisbon had become one of the world's premier ports. The skyline changed from the functional to the palatial as the city's rich denizens built grand towers, churches, and homes. Its harbor had room for five hundred ships and was often filled. The Praça do Comércio, the city's great square on the quay, was overcrowded with sailors, travelers, and merchants. Shipments of cork, salted fish, olive oil, wine, and resin were loaded onto Portuguese vessels bound for London, Paris, Genoa, and Cairo. Portugal was a nation that faced the sea, literally and metaphorically.

Not surprisingly, it was only a matter of time before the Portuguese had begun seeking their own passage to India. Portugal spent the better part of the fifteenth century trying to find a way to get there. While Spain's nautical community was busy with fishing, piracy, and import-export merchants, Portugal ventured farther and farther south down the African coast, into lands no non-African had ever seen, raising maritime discovery to new heights. The Portuguese had even designed a special ship for voyages of exploration. Known as the caravel, it was small and versatile, with a hull that drew little water, making it possible to venture up rivers or over shoals. The sails were lateen — like the shark fin–shaped sails first used by ancient Greeks and still in use in the twenty-first century by Arab traders — which made it easier for these ingenious vessels to sail close to the wind. No two caravels were exactly alike because savvy shipwrights kept all the plans in their heads, lest the competition steal them. The average size, however, was seventy feet long and twenty-five feet wide. Caravels were nimble and cost-effective, requiring able crews of two dozen or fewer. This allowed the holds to be used primarily as storage space for additional supplies instead of as crew quarters. Even the haughty Venetians, who had a keen eye for seagoing vessels, marveled at the caravels. One Venetian navigator referred to them as "the best ships that sailed the seas."

Thanks to the caravel and a very talented corps of commanders, Portugal soon had a trade monopoly along the West African coast. Ships laden with slaves, gold, ivory, and an African strain of pepper sailed home to Lisbon in such quantities that whole regions of Africa were named for the goods they produced. Centuries later, monikers such as the Ivory Coast and Gold Coast would still be in use.

By the time João II ascended to the throne, in 1481 at the age of twenty-six, Portugal had added a westward push into the Ocean Sea to their exploration oeuvre. They controlled the island chains of Madeira and the Azores and were always searching for more. Columbus, coincidentally, had been a Portuguese resident during the early years of João's reign. He had arrived there through the most random act of fate: a Genovese ship on which he served was destroyed during a naval battle in May 1475. As he treaded water, awash in the stench of battle and the horrific awareness that shipmates had just died, Columbus clutched a piece of debris bobbing nearby, then began kicking to shore. He washed up on a beach in Lagos, of all places, the southernmost tip of Portugal and epicenter of Portuguese navigation (the legendary Henry the Navigator once held court there).

Columbus had sailed back to Genoa soon afterward, seeking the succor of home. He had been born in that Mediterranean port, in 1451. The Italian metropolis was nestled in the north, near the French border. Its waterfront streets were narrow and winding, leading upward from the docks of its perfect natural port into the steep green Apennines. For the sailor approaching her shores for the very first time, Genoa appeared to have had been carved out of the mountainside by a master craftsman.

Life revolved around the sea, though not in the hand-to-mouth manner of some small fishing villages. "A truly regal city," was how Petrarch, the great Italian poet, described the city-state a century before Columbus's birth. The Romans had first settled the city in AD 200 and soon designated it the headquarters of their Mediterranean fleet. When the Roman Empire fell two centuries later, Genoa's residents maintained their focus on the Mediterranean, only in a more commercial manner. By the era of the Crusades, Genoa had become the most powerful mercantile hub in all the Mediterranean and was quick to wage war on other naval cities to maintain that power.

To live by the sword, however, is to die by the sword. A

series of failed wars with Venice, beginning in 1380, eroded Genoa's dominance. By the time Columbus was born, Genoa lacked the vitality and wealth of Venice, but was by no means impoverished. The Genovese were still entrepreneurs of the highest order, with an abiding passion for squeezing every last ducat from the goods and services their ships carried to and from the rest of the world. There were spices from India by way of Venice (after markup); slaves from Africa; olive oil, almonds, and textiles from the Iberian Peninsula. Its waterfront was a bustling, raucous place, where the accents and languages of foreign sailors mingled with the smell of salt air and freshly caught fish. The two most esteemed professions were banking and shipbuilding, with slave trading a close third.

The Genovese were also explorers, discovering the Canary Islands, charting Africa's Gambia and Senegal rivers, and settling the Cape Verde Islands. A certain visionary sensibility also led them into colonial administration and financing. So it was that nations like Portugal, with grandiose dreams but small pocketbooks, often found the money to pay for their voyages of exploration via the bankers of Genoa.

This was the heritage of the man who would one day discover the New World. History would remember him by the Latin version of his name, and during the second half of his life, he would go by the Spanish translation — Cristóbal Colón — but he was born Cristoforo Colombo, son of Domenico Colombo, a wool merchant and minor cog in Genoa's political machine. Columbus's mother, Susanna Fontanarossa, bore five children who lived. Cristoforo was the oldest. He — along with his brothers Bartolomé and Diego — was taught from a very young age that loyalties to family and Genoa were paramount. Those lessons would never be forgotten.

Columbus's formal education began at age five, with

the basics of reading and writing learned in a grammar school on busy Pavia Street. In later adolescence he was schooled in accounting, cartography, Latin, and the mathematical basis of navigation — a vital piece of knowledge for aspiring sailors and businessmen alike in Genoa. Ambitious and restless, Columbus first went to sea in his teens. By 1492 he had been a sailor for a quarter century, working his way up through the nautical ranks from ship's boy to commander; marking his life by storm, calm, sun, and gale; enduring countless midnight watches, navigational headings, depth soundings, log entries, and ports of call. Thousands of sailors were, of course, just like him, men who had seen the known world from the swaying, creaking deck of a small merchant sailing ship. But Columbus was one of the few eager to venture from the known into the unknown and the only one who had devoted his entire adult life to finding a westward passage to India. He was sure it was out there, waiting to be found. To ignore that reality and merely pass his days as a merchant captain was to settle for mediocrity — an outcome unacceptable to the bold Genovese.

In 1492 a friend described Columbus as being "a man of fine appearance, well built, taller than most, and with strong limbs. . . . His hair was very red and his face was ruddy and freckled. He spoke well, was tactful in his manner and was extremely talented. He was a good Latinist and a very learned cosmographer, gracious when he wished but hot tempered when he was crossed." Columbus also had the patience of Jeremiah. For eight trying years he had groveled in the courts of Spain and Portugal (both chosen for their seafaring nature and curiosity about Atlantic exploration) seeking funding for his risky voyage.

All that lay in the future when Columbus returned home from Portugal in 1475, only to find that Genoa had entered into a period of daunting political strife. The French had crossed the border, seeking to annex Genoa by force. Columbus had stayed just long enough to stroll the dockyards, whose smells and panorama he knew so well, and then shipped out immediately. He spent the next year sailing on merchant vessels to Iceland, Ireland, and England. But by the fall of 1477, he was back in Portugal. He settled in Lisbon, where Bartolomé had a burgeoning career in one of the world's sexiest new occupations: nautical chart making. To know the seas in the age of exploration was to hold a map of the known universe. It was knowledge that men and nations were willing to pay handsomely for.

The key to success was up-to-date knowledge. This made the Columbus brothers the ideal pair. Not only did they care deeply for each other, with a loyalty shared by few great brothers in history, but both men were also well-traveled sailors, and both were capable of drawing charts. While one went off to sea, perfecting and updating their maps of the ocean and coastline, the other stayed behind to run the business. It was in Lisbon, scrutinizing charts day after day, taking a glass of wine with fellow mariners, and absorbing the nuances of the world's three continents and the vast uncharted spaces in between, that Columbus began wondering about a voyage into the unmapped regions. All he lacked to make it a reality were the finances and political clout to command such a voyage. Thus the vision lay fallow.

Columbus sailed home to Genoa again in the summer of 1479. There he saw his parents for the last time (his mother would die the following year; his father would live almost two more decades), perhaps told them of his intention to marry soon, and then sailed away from Genoa on August 26, never to return. He went back to Lisbon, where he had been keeping the company of a young woman by the name of Felipa Perestrelo y Moniz, who was living in a convent near his chart-making shop. She was the daughter of Madeira's former governor, and some time in late September or early October of that year, the two wed. The

Monizes were wealthy and influential, one of Portugal's noble families. Columbus's societal status was instantly elevated by the marriage. No longer was he a mere sailor and chart maker. Through Felipa's late father's political connections, Columbus now had access to Portuguese royalty.

Columbus left Bartolomé and the chart business and went off to make a life with his new bride on Porto Santo, the smaller of Portugal's Madeira Islands. In 1480 Felipa gave birth to a son, Diego. Columbus provided for his growing family by working on Portuguese vessels that were sailing to Africa's Gold Coast to explore. Those were pivotal years, for he learned how to properly steer a caravel on the high seas and along a rugged coastline — skills he would one day refine to an art.

All that came to an abrupt end in 1484, when Felipa died of unknown causes. Young Diego in tow, Columbus sailed back to Lisbon, buried his wife in a church overlooking the city, and rejoined Bartolomé in the chart-making shop. But by now mapmaking was just a stopgap occupation. Perhaps emboldened by the newfound realization that life can be very short, Columbus began dedicating himself to his voyage of discovery. He pursued this ambition with a boldness and passion he had never before displayed.

Through Felipa's powerful family connections, Columbus had long possessed the means to seek an audience with João II. But it was only after Felipa's death that he did so. The two men met later that year. Columbus, four years older than the ruthless king, clutching rolls of maps to prove his arguments, promised João that he would find land and riches by sailing west. As reward, the would-be explorer wanted grants of nobility and knighthood, to be named Admiral of the Ocean Sea, named viceroy and governor of any lands he might discover, and receive a tenth of all income from those new lands. João, appalled, turned him down flat. He thought Columbus's manner was overly zealous, his proposal greedy,

and his arguments about a westward route to India uncon-
vincing. In the opinion of João and his junta, Columbus
greatly underestimated the width of the Ocean Sea. The
devastated, debt-ridden widower and the infant Diego
slunk from Portugal and the chart-making business. They
traveled east, into Spain, where Columbus began anew his
search for a visionary financial backer. Bartolomé was not
long behind.

João, however, had been more intrigued by Columbus's
ideas than he acknowledged. He secretly ordered two of his
caravels to sail west to find the Orient. When they returned
in failure, João's doubts about Columbus's theories were
confirmed. He ordered yet another Portuguese fleet to sail
down the African coast, seeking an eastward passage to India.
That fleet, led by a dogged navigator named Bartolomeu
Dias, set sail in 1486. But when Dias hadn't returned two
years later, João reconsidered Columbus's ideas. The king
summoned the would-be explorer, who was having little
success in Spain, back to Lisbon, granting him special protection from his creditors so he wouldn't be cast into debtors'
prison the instant he crossed the border. In a savage coincidence, Dias's fleet sailed back up the Tagus in December
1488, just as Columbus prepared to meet with João. Adding
insult to injury, João invited the devastated Columbus to listen in as Dias briefed the king on his journey. The news was
nothing short of incredible: Dias had become the first man
in history to sail around the southern tip of Africa. An eastward passage to India was now a possibility. In fact, Dias insisted, he would have sailed all the way there if his crews
hadn't pleaded with him to turn back.

João's interest in a westward passage abruptly vanished.
A chastened Columbus fled to Spain once again, where he
pleaded his case to Isabella for four more years — ultimately with success.

In 1495, while planning the voyage that would finally

take Portugal's men and ships to India, João was stricken with uremia, a painful blood poisoning caused by his body's inability to eliminate waste products through urination. He was just forty years old when he died. He had fathered a bastard but left no legitimate heir. João's successor was his twenty-six-year-old cousin, Duke Manuel, an unremarkable young man whom João had disliked immensely. In the eyes of many, Portugal's nautical prowess was destined to become a thing of the past.

But Manuel would prove himself João's better. His daring would soon affect Columbus's life in a most direct way.

Manuel ignored those nearsighted advisers who suggested he set aside voyages of exploration. On July 8, 1497, four Portuguese ships hoisted sail from Lisbon, bound for India, per João's original plan. The crew numbered 170 of the nation's finest sailors. Its leader was a heavyset young man of twenty-eight named Vasco da Gama. Columbus was in Spain at the time, wrangling financing and approval for a third expedition. In yet another coincidence that defined the close rivalry between the Spanish and Portuguese exploration communities, da Gama's maps and charts were provided by Diogo Ortiz de Vilhegas, a Junta dos Matemáticos member who had voted against Columbus's voyage plans in 1484.

Da Gama had sailed the West African coast before and was wary of the Gulf of Guinea's tricky currents and harsh weather. To avoid them he sailed southwest until he very nearly reached the coast of a still-undiscovered Brazil before turning east toward the bottom of Africa and a place Dias had named the Cape of Good Hope. When da Gama finally made it, he had gone ninety-six days without seeing land. No sailor had ever done such a thing. "We returned to the land," a weary da Gama scribbled in the ship's log on Tuesday, November 7.

After resting eight days in a clean bay he named

St. Helena, da Gama pushed on. The voyage seemed interminable. His storeship was having trouble, so da Gama ordered it broken up and its cargo and crew transferred to
other ships. The currents along East Africa were severe,
pushing his ships backward as if they were trying to sail up a
river. The men developed scurvy. Arab traders along the
coast threatened the Portuguese with war when they tried
to put ashore. Finally, on May 20, 1498, just a week and a
half before Columbus finally began his third voyage, da
Gama sailed the *Sao Gabriel* into port at Calicut, on India's
southwest coast. He was greeted enthusiastically by the local
ruler, a silk-wearing tyrant known as the Zamorin. The
Zamorin's Arab advisers, sensing the end of their trade monopoly, soon turned him against da Gama. The Portuguese
explorer and his crew were treated with contempt throughout their three-month stay, and at times da Gama feared his
life was in danger.

Nevertheless, the *Sao Gabriel*'s holds were soon filled
with enough pepper to pay for the cost of the voyage sixty
times over. Da Gama paid his respects to the Zamorin one
last time before sailing. Da Gama, who would one day return and ruthlessly overthrow the Zamorin, foreshadowed
the act with an audacious request: a pepper stalk, to be re-
planted in Portugal.

The Zamorin was unfazed. "You can take our pepper,"
he boldly told da Gama in granting the request, "but you
will never take our rains." It was well known that the double
monsoons off the Indian Ocean gave Calicut's pepper its
superior quality. Unaware he had just delivered the perfect
argument in favor of Portugal seizing his kingdom, the
Zamorin bade da Gama farewell.

On September 8, 1499, da Gama sailed up the Tagus
and joyfully laid eyes on the hills of Lisbon once again. News
of his voyage had already reached Portugal, thanks to a sister ship that had sailed ahead. When he stepped ashore, da

Gama was mobbed in the Praça do Comércio. King Manuel pronounced him to be admiral of the Indian Ocean — a sharp poke at Spain and Columbus — with a regal salary and a feudal kingdom to match the title. A church was built along the Tagus as thanks for the bounty and power da Gama's accomplishment would forever bring to tiny Portugal. Commemorative gold coinage was struck. Messages went out to Europe's monarchs, boasting of the new trade route.

Da Gama had been gone two years and two months, lost two ships, and endured the loss of his brother, but he had sailed to India and back. An aquatic passage to the Orient had been found. Thanks to the Treaty of Tordesillas, it belonged to Portugal — and Portugal alone. With Portugal set to reap the rewards of this discovery, and Spain about to be shut out, the pressure was on Columbus to find his westward passage.

CHAPTER SEVEN

Mouth of the Serpent

1498
Paria

Columbus's troubles had been gathering steam since 1492. The grand triumph of his first voyage had been followed by the perceived failure of the second, brought on by Fonseca's emphasis on colonization over exploration. Whatever awe his first voyage to the New World had inspired was long gone. In its place was the recognition that journeys from Spain to the New World were commonplace. Spanish caravels now made the voyage regularly, ferrying supplies and colonists. At the same time Columbus was nearing fifty — old age. He had begun to focus less on his immediate financial status and more on his estate and was determined to leave his heirs a sizable financial legacy. The vagaries of exploration and the rush of discovery were no longer his primary reasons for sailing. In their place was a desire to govern Hispaniola and enhance his riches. That shifting emphasis, along with Fonseca's ongoing campaign to reduce the explorer's stature in the eyes of the sovereigns, accelerated Columbus's fall from royal grace.

Columbus's problems came to a head during the summer of 1498, on his third expedition of discovery. Every one of his voyages had a nickname, and the third was known as the *rumbo austral,* or "southern voyage," because his intended route dipped toward the equator. Regardless of the Treaty of Tordesillas's prohibitions about just such an endeavor, Columbus was heading south to explore João II's hunch that an uncharted continent existed opposite Africa. More germane to Columbus's aims, the land was specifically thought to lie opposite the African region of Guinea, where the Portuguese had discovered gold. Based on the teachings of Aristotle, like latitudes produced like commodities. Discovering gold would ensure continued good standing in the Spanish royal court. By now Ferdinand and Isabella were getting impatient for a return on their investment in the New World. They had invested men, money, and ships in the venture for six years and had little wealth to show for it. It was bad enough that Portugal, thanks to da Gama, was on the verge of becoming awash in riches, but the realization that the Spanish half of the world was impoverished made the sovereigns doubt Columbus's abilities. "He saw that his signal services were held of slight value," sniffed one observer, "and that suddenly the reputation that these Indies at first had enjoyed was sinking and declining, by reason of those who had the ear of the Sovereigns."

Columbus had other agendas. One was a return to the island of Hispaniola. He had been gone two long years, and to the transient Columbus, who had spent his life moving from country to country, city to city, Hispaniola was more than just a port of call; it was a home. He had discovered the Caribbean's second-largest island, planted its colonies, fostered their development at the expense of his reputation and exploration career, shared its revenues with the sovereigns, and ruled Hispaniola as governor and viceroy. In much the same way a feudal knight lorded over his share of a larger kingdom, so Columbus ruled Hispaniola. He longed for it to prosper. The holds of his vessels were filled with corn, wine, and meat to fortify the island's colonists.

The other hidden agenda was to quietly search for a westward aquatic passage to India. That elusive goal was still the tent pole propping up his career. Finding it would complete his life's work with a flourish and make da Gama's achievements seem irrelevant except as historical curiosity.

Columbus set sail from Sanlúcar de Barrameda, on the southern coast of Spain at the mouth the Guadalquivir River, on May 30 with a fleet of six ships. He directed the caravels *Garza, La Gorda,* and *La Rábida* to sail directly for Hispaniola, to join the *Niña,* which had already gone ahead. They carried new settlers as well as foodstuffs. It made no sense for them to join the exploration segment of the voyage.

The other three vessels — the caravels *El Correo, La Vaqueños,* and his flagship, the *Santa María de Guía,* a hundred-ton vessel he referred to only as *la nao,* "the ship" — set a course south from Spain, paralleling Africa. Spain was at war with France, and Columbus suspected that French spies in Spain's dockyards had tipped off the enemy about his voyage. The prospect of being taken prisoner by French privateers was very real, and Columbus sailed cautiously toward Madeira, where he had not been since Felipa's death, more than a decade earlier. He arrived without incident and sent his men ashore to refill the fleet's water casks and cut firewood for the cooking. He later put in at the Canary Islands to do the same. Then, after a stop for salted goat meat and fresh water at the Cape Verde Islands, three hundred miles off the West African coast yet choked by airborne Sahara dust, Columbus went hunting for the hidden continent.

The southerly route was nearly his undoing. Columbus had navigated the icy black waters of the northern climes as a young man but found the withering heat of the equatorial latitudes far more daunting. It was the first time during his voyages of discovery that Columbus sailed into what was then known as the Atlantic Ocean, which had been defined since 1387 as the sea off the coast of Africa (it would be 1601 before that name would be given to the whole ocean). The name was a reference to Atlas, the titan from Greek mythology who upheld the pillars of heaven.

To Columbus, however, the Atlantic was a decidedly hellish place. He referred to its waters as "the burning seas." His ship's decks — those creaking, swaying platforms on which his men worked, slept, and dined — became so hot from the summer sun that Columbus feared that spontaneous combustion would set them ablaze. Making matters worse, the fleet was becalmed for eight days in the doldrums. "The wind stopped so suddenly and unexpectedly and the supervening heat was so excessive and immoderate that there was no one who dared go below to look after the casks of wine and water, which burst, snapping the hoops of the pipes; the wheat burned like fire; the bacon and salted meat roasted and putrefied," he wrote. Concerned about the lack of fresh water, Columbus abandoned the southern route and steered northwest, toward Hispaniola.

On July 31 lookout Alonso Perez spied a green island with three prominent mountains looming over its southwest tip. It had been Columbus's intention to name his first landfall Trinidad, in thanks to the Holy Trinity for the fleet's deliverance. The three peaks lent that choice the air of predestination. His sailors broke into a chorus of the Benedictine hymn "Salve Regina." The words were in Latin, a language few peasants understood, and the sailors' gruff voices were described by one listener as a "confusion of bawlings." Yet Columbus found the performance inspirational and wrote that his crew's song of worship "glorified the divine bounty."

"I had already called the island Trinidad. The harbor would have been very good if we could have found bottom.

There were houses and people and fine cultivated land, as green and lovely as the orchards of Valencia in March. I was sorry we could not enter the harbor," Columbus recorded. "Next day I continued on my course looking for a harbor where I could repair the ships, take water, and supplement the corn and scanty provisions I was carrying."

Twenty miles off the port bow lay another chunk of land. Columbus, not knowing it was a fourth continent, simply called it Gracia — "thanks." He didn't bother making landfall.

On August 2, after replenishing his fresh water on Trinidad, Columbus continued along the island's coast, encountering a most unusual estuary. "I saw some lines of waves crossing this estuary with a great roaring sound, which made me think that there was a reef here with rocks and shallows that would prevent us from entering. Beyond this line of waves was another and yet another, which made a great noise like a sea breaking on a rocky beach." All around him the sea rushed in and out "like the Guadalquivir in flood." The river was actually the mighty Orinoco, emptying fresh water into the Caribbean through four reef-lined channels. Columbus dropped anchor to ponder the best course of action.

Columbus's dilemma was whether to sail forward or go back. If he turned around, the powerful waves might actually broach his vessels, flipping them sideways into the surf and then crushing them on the rocks. If he sailed deeper into the estuary, they stood a chance of getting stranded in shallow waters. His ships, their hulls stuck fast on sand and coral, would then be torn apart by the current. No easy choice was available for Columbus to make. One way or the other, it was a gamble.

Columbus analyzed the situation for two days and nights. He was a fastidious observer of the ocean, sun, and stars and prone to insomnia when a new phenomenon captivated his attention. On August 4 he made his decision. Under a waning moon Columbus ordered his small fleet to weigh anchor and sail forward into the estuary. He would take his chances in the shallows.

Based on his previous voyages, Columbus knew the New World was filled with phenomena unfamiliar to Europeans. One was the mud volcano. Also known as sedimentary volcanoes, these oddities are caused in part by the explosion of trapped methane gas and can indicate underground petroleum deposits. Though much smaller than their magmatic cousins, mud volcanoes erupt in the same manner, spewing deadly high-pressure bursts of mud and flames from conical vents. They are powerful enough to cause earthquakes and tidal waves. Columbus was unaware that the estuary into which he had led his fleet was ringed by one of the largest concentrations of mud volcanoes on earth. They surrounded him on all sides, lining the beaches and ocean floor like nature's version of unexploded ordnance, capable of detonating without warning at any time.

On the night of August 4, 1498, one of them did.

"Standing on the ship's deck, I heard a terrible roaring which came from the southward toward the ship. And I stood by to watch, and I saw the sea lifting from east to west in the shape of a swell as high as the ship, and yet it came toward me little by little, and it was topped by a crest of white water which came roaring along with every great noise," Columbus wrote of the killer tidal wave. A terrified Columbus forced himself to stay calm. He barked a series of loud orders so he could be heard above the tidal wave's approaching groan. The night watch frantically scurried to comply. They were joined by their off-duty shipmates, who had awoken to what was now a thunderous roar and the painful sensation of tumbling across the deck as it pitched sharply upward. Columbus's deft commands guided the fleet toward an egress into the placid waters of the gulf beyond.

The three ships darted through the passage, away from the mud volcanoes. A damage inspection was immediately ordered, and roll called. Amazingly, not a man was missing or hurt. The only item broken was a cable on *La Vaqueños,* which had snapped. "Even today," Columbus would write months later, "I can recall my physical fear that the ship might be swamped when it [the wave] broke over her." He would later name the slot between Trinidad and the mainland Boca de la Sierpe — "Mouth of the serpent" — for the way it nearly swallowed his fleet whole.

The next day Columbus sailed north into a deep gulf. Trinidad was to his right. Gracia was behind and to his left, curving around until it formed a peninsula that loomed directly before the fleet. "The further I went the sweeter and fresher I found the sea water," he observed. "I anchored and sent the boats to land."

Thus Europeans set foot on the fourth continent for the first time. Columbus was not among them.

"I found some of the most beautiful country in the world, which was thickly populated," he noted of what would become known as Venezuela. "I reached it in the morning, at nine o'clock, and, on seeing this green and beautiful country, anchored in order to meet its people." At first Columbus was unsure of what he had found. But then he wrote: "I have come to believe that this is a mighty continent which was hitherto unknown." The Indians told him the land was named Paria. Columbus, usually so fond of ignoring Indian names and calling new lands after sovereigns and saints, chose to call it that, too.

Paria was mountainous, the jungles choked with fertile black soil, brightly plumed birds, and great hordes of monkeys. The local people, much to Columbus's relief, were mostly friendly. "Great numbers came to the ships in their canoes," he recorded. "Our men who landed found them very pleasant and were very well received."

Most pleasing of all to Columbus, the natives wore bracelets woven from pearls and heavy necklaces of gold and were eager to trade with him. This fourth continent — this Paria — was everything he had hoped it would be.

CHAPTER EIGHT

In the Shape of a Woman's Breast

August–October 1498
Santo Domingo

Columbus thought a section of the new land was Eden — not an, but *the* — which he was convinced lay on the fringes of the Orient. In thinking so he was following several theories in vogue at the time. Among other things he noted the similarities between the mighty river flowing into the Gulf of Paria and a biblical description of Adam and Eve's domain. "A river flowed out of Eden, to water the garden," he quoted from Genesis. "And there it divided and became four rivers." But this conclusion meant, at least for now, an end to his exploration. "I believe the earthly paradise lies here, which no one can enter except by God's leave," he concluded before turning around and heading back to sea.

Later, when it came time to write letters to the sovereigns detailing all he had seen, Columbus devoted a lengthy passage to the earthly paradise. But beyond the heavenly, he was just as enchanted by the region's potential wealth, so casually displayed by the locals. In his letters he assured Ferdinand and Isabella that his latest discovery would be yet another New World treasure trove. "These Indians, as I

have said, are all very well built, tall and with finely propor-
tioned limbs. Their hair is very long and straight, and they
wear woven cloths around their heads, which look from a
distance like silk and resemble, as I have said, Moorish
scarves," he wrote. "They all wear some jewel round their
necks or on their arms, in the local fashion. Many of them
have pieces of gold hanging round their necks . . . I inquired very carefully where this gold came from, and they
all pointed to a land bordering on theirs to the west, which
was very high and not far away. But they all told me not to
go there because the inhabitants ate men . . . I also asked
them where they got their pearls, and they again pointed
to the west and to the north as well, to show that it was
beyond their own country." Columbus drew a map to accompany the letter so the sovereigns could see the exact location of his new find. As further proof he planned to
include a large supply of pearls.

Columbus longed to linger and probe deeper into the
Orient, searching for India. But the food in the holds was
spoiling, and shipworms were eating away at his hulls.
Columbus himself was going blind from a withering combination of insomnia, navigating by the sun, and the simple
act of squinting at the horizon hour after hour, scrutinizing
each abnormality for signs of land, ships, or some hidden
shoal. Later generations of navigators would have the tele-
scope to aid their vision. Still later generations would filter
ultraviolet rays with the darkened lenses of sunglasses. But
no such devices existed in Columbus's day; he didn't even
have the luxury of a long-billed cap. And thus, even as his
eyes grew tired, watery, and so red-rimmed that they appeared to be bleeding, Columbus peered into the distance.
He had endured the same optical exhaustion on the second
voyage and knew that only rest on land, away from the dazzling glare of the sea, could cure him. It was time to make
haste for Hispaniola.

On August 15, 1498, Columbus's fleet sailed from Paria, into the uncharted heart of the Caribbean. He was traveling from a newly discovered land whose latitude and longitude were still not precisely known to a brand-new city whose exact location he did not know, through waters no man — European or otherwise — had ever sailed. Columbus had no knowledge of local currents, winds, or landfalls. Given the conditions and his painful ophthalmia, he was sailing, literally, blind. And yet Columbus confidently set a course northwest by north, sure he had plotted Paria's location correctly. The moon was dark, so he sailed only during the fifteen hours of daylight. At night the ships were allowed to drift with the current as lookouts kept a sharp eye for uncharted reefs and islands. Despite the vagaries of wind, drift, and ship's boys who forgot to turn the hourglass (time being a vital aspect of navigation), after seven days Columbus made landfall just one hundred miles west of Santo Domingo. It was as if he had innately followed the loxodromic curve of the earth — the rhumb line — the shortest, most direct path from one point on the globe to another. A lesser navigator might have been chuffed by such a heady accomplishment, but Columbus, a perfectionist at sea, was disappointed. He concluded that the hundred-mile error was the result of currents "which here are very strong, setting toward terra firma and the west." It would not be the last time those currents bedeviled the Admiral.

It was August 31 when Columbus first sailed up the Ozama River into Santo Domingo. In many ways he was at the zenith of his accomplishments. On his first voyage of discovery, he had found the New World. On his second he had begun its settlement. On his third he was expanding the known parameters of not just the New World, showing it to be more than a mere scattering of islands in the middle of a mighty sea, but of the entire earth. His instincts about the ocean were so prescient that many said he navigated by scent. The opposite — that he was as much a man of calculation as of native cunning — was true, too: Columbus's mathematical third-voyage observations about the North Star's odd position in the sky were so acute that he was certain it was making a smaller earth orbit in southern latitudes. Based on that, Columbus theorized that the world was not actually round, as history would so famously remember him believing, but "something like a woman's breast."

He was right. In a single summer of sailing, he had discovered a new continent and divined the true shape of the earth, two discoveries that refuted centuries of scholarly thinking. On land, whether in Spain or Hispaniola, Columbus's thought process was muddled and impulsive. It led him to conceive great notions and dream fantastically but just as frequently led to lapses in judgment. But at sea Columbus was an unparalleled genius, fueled by focus and challenge. History is rife with examples of explorers burdened by this duality — James Cook, David Livingstone, and Richard Francis Burton, among the many. The difference between Columbus and the others was that they preferred the unknown to civilization, recognizing the unfinished spots on the map as their true domain. Columbus was the opposite. Greatness on the seas was overwhelmed by a passionate desire to rise above his station. As he got older he no longer ached to return to the unknown but to return *from* the unknown.

As a result, Santo Domingo was not a stopover, but a conclusion. Columbus had done almost all he had set out to do on the third voyage. Now it was time to turn his attention to the tenuous prosperity of his fiefdom.

Santo Domingo marked Columbus's third attempt at establishing a vibrant colonial city. The first had been founded by accident on Christmas Eve 1492. Columbus's flagship the *Santa Maria* ran aground on a coral reef close to shore and was beyond salvage. "So softly that it was not felt," Columbus wrote of the calamity, "nor was there wave nor wind." The vessel was stripped, and the contents were rowed to a Taino Indian village on the marshy coast. Like Columbus and his crews, the Taino were of a seafaring bent. They were an offshoot of the Arawak tribe, who had migrated from the coast of South America to islands throughout the Caribbean some 2,500 years earlier. Their mode of transport was to paddle *canoas* — boats carved from tree trunks. After Columbus encountered the Taino during his first landfall in 1492 (and on every subsequent voyage), he took descriptions of what would become known as the canoe back to Spain with him, having no knowledge that this simple watercraft would someday save his life.

The Taino, whose total population throughout the various islands was roughly half a million, were a peaceful people — but only to a point. When threatened, they reacted with deadly fury. It was a matter of survival. The Taino were regularly subjected to raids by the cannibalistic Carib tribe and had a ready arsenal of bows and arrows, spear throwers, swords made from palm trees, and war clubs. Somewhat ingeniously, they also disarmed foes by heating pepper in clay pots, producing a noxious gas that could be used as a weapon when the pots were hurled at the enemy.

Their leader was a hereditary chief known as a cacique. A group of nobles known as *nitainos* were one step down and directed the working class — the *naborias* — who were responsible for the farming, hunting, and fishing so necessary to their survival.

Somewhat notably, the Taino were a clothing-optional society. Married women were expected to wear a small cotton apron; rulers and spiritual leaders wore feather mantles and clothes on ceremonial occasions, but otherwise total nudity was common.

Columbus didn't think he or his men had anything to fear from this tribe of seemingly guileless people. Their relations thus far had been friendly. So, with his fleet reduced from three ships to two, Columbus selected thirty-nine nonessential personnel — the master-at-arms, ship's boys, an interpreter, able seamen not pulling their weight, a painter, a secretary, two surgeons — to remain behind. He provided them with a year's supply of food and solemn instructions to spend their days searching for gold and to not fondle the native women — a daunting order, given the Taino's friendliness and the unmarried women's habit of walking around without a stitch of clothing. Columbus christened the sailors' new home La Navidad, for the day of its founding.

Relationships between the colonists and the Indians quickly grew strained. To protect themselves the Spaniards built a small fort out of planks from the *Santa Maria*'s hull. No record of what happened next exists. But when Columbus returned eleven months later, the fort was burned to the ground. The men had been massacred. Their corpses still littered the ground, spread out over a radius miles wide.

This was something of a shock to Columbus, but even more so to the fifteen hundred new settlers he had brought with him from Spain. Volunteers all, anxious about making a life in the great unknown, this complement of farmers, friars, and craftsmen was deeply disturbed by this introduction. "A sadness and profound grief seized their hearts," observed one eyewitness. Columbus thought it best to give the Taino a wide berth. He established his second colony a hundred miles to the east, near the Bajabonico River, and named it for his patron. La Isabela seemed an ideal location, with fresh water in steady supply, fine soil, and a large amount of limestone nearby. "A town is being built beside the river," wrote a physician who had traveled to the New World on the sovereigns' orders. "It stands immediately above the water at the top of a steep ravine, so that no defensive works are needed on this side. On the other side it is bounded by a forest so thick that a rabbit could hardly get through. The forest is so green that it would be impossible to burn it at any time of the year. They have begun to divert an arm of the river which the workmen say they will bring through the center of the town, and they intend to place mills and waterwheels on this channel and anything else that can be driven with water."

The pale gray rock was quickly quarried, and a house overlooking the ocean was built for Columbus. It was made of limestone and was the first stone house built in the New World. Similar houses for the settlers, as well as a church and an elaborate waterfront plaza, were also constructed. The colonists planted crops using seeds brought from Spain, which much to the their delight, sprouted from the fertile soil in half the time it took back home. Pigs, horses, and cows — also from Spain — allowed the colonists to enjoy some staples of the traditional Spanish diet, although beef was sorely missed. The colonists elected a town council and a mayor. By all appearances, La Isabela was thriving. But it was a facade. The settlers never took to the New World. Disease, mutiny, death, and disenchantment were soon the norm.

Worst of all was the weather. The north wind blew without ceasing. A fierce combination of gale force wind and horizontal rain devastated the settlement in June 1495, sinking three ships in La Isabela's unprotected harbor. It was a type of storm none of the sailors or colonists had ever seen before, more powerful than the raging Euraquilo of the western Mediterranean and more violent by far than the Hegoa, that blistering southern wind of the Basque Country. To the colonists, life in the New World seemed to be one unique terror after another.

When Columbus sailed back to Spain in March of 1496, the decks of his fleet were choked with settlers who were giving up and returning home. Of the original fifteen hundred colonists, fewer than a third remained. The quitters blamed Columbus for their inability to make a new life, and many traveled to the royal court once they got home to shout their anger at all who would listen.

The sovereigns, who already knew of the problems from emissaries who had visited La Isabela, responded by ordering the colonial capital shifted to a more hospitable locale. A new site had been located on the rocky southern shores of Hispaniola, at the mouth of the Ozama River. Nuggets of gold had been found in the Ozama's tributary streams, and a group of squatters had settled close by to search for more. It was Columbus's aim to expand the squatters' village into a bustling waterfront metropolis — a Genoa.

To supervise construction, and rule as governor in his absence, Columbus chose his now thirty-five-year-old brother Bartolomé. His brother Diego, who was a cleric, would be in charge if something happened to Bartolomé. Their top priority would be to build the new city.

It was Bartolomé who named the site Santo Domingo, after their father, Domenico. Until then the New World's cities had taken their names from royalty and religion. In a manipulative nod to this tradition, Bartolomé gathered the city's residents together for the naming on a specially selected Sunday, the Feast of St. Dominic. The Spanish crowd — and Crown — had no idea they were naming their town for a poor Italian patriarch.

Deception aside, the new city was ideally suited to aquatic commerce. Future Spanish king Philip II would one day describe it as "key to all the Indies." The mouth of the Ozama formed a natural protected harbor, with ample anchorage for dozens of ships. As Columbus sailed up that broad river for the first time aboard *la nao* in the summer of 1498, the city lay to his right, atop a hill that provided a natural defensive position (as well as an enormous population of biting ants). Though very much under construction, Santo Domingo already bore a distinctive Spanish look. Homes and ramparts made of pale yellow stones and red-orange bricks were slowly replacing the temporary wood-and-thatch structures thrown up in the city's early days. Plans included cobbling the streets. In the years to come, a grand plaza would be constructed. In the center would be a grand cathedral, and Santo Domingo's founders would be interred beneath that sacred roof. But that was in the future. Now it was enough that Santo Domingo and the colony of Hispaniola were flourishing.

Columbus, however, had been gone for two years and five months — half the life span of the Hispaniola colony. The disenchanted settlers had come to consider Bartolomé a ruthless, distant martinet. Led by Francisco Roldán, a longtime friend of Christopher Columbus's who had formerly been La Isabela's chief justice, a group of seventy colonists had struck off into the jungles to form a new society. Their fledgling civilization was based on the premises of friendship with the Indians, free love, no taxes, and gold for all — not that Roldán planned to remain in the jungles forever. He aimed to petition that Ferdinand and Isabella recognize his government and strip the Columbus brothers of all titles and authority; they were, Roldán firmly believed, Marranos.

Columbus was deeply dismayed by Roldán's betrayal and just as disappointed with the colonists remaining in Santo Domingo. Nothing made them happy. If they weren't grousing about the hard work or sweltering humidity, they were ranting about the paltry levels of beef in their diet. One hundred and sixty of them had contracted syphilis from the Taino. Only seventy or so of all the colonists were loyal to Columbus.

If ever a scenario demonstrated to Columbus the difference between life at sea and life on land, it was the goings-on in Hispaniola. At sea the men would keep such petty gripes among themselves. The inescapable daily routine of life at sea would distract them from their woes. But the land-bound colonists wallowed in their misery, holding Columbus personally responsible for the myopia and sloth that defined their days.

The weary explorer was in no mood to deal with them. He wrote to Ferdinand and Isabella in October 1498 demanding help. He described the insurrection as if expecting sympathy, not realizing that the sovereigns would be most concerned about upheaval in such a pivotal colony. Columbus was exhausted when he wrote the letter and suffering from arthritis that contracted his writing hand into a claw. In a tone both rambling and self-indulgent, he all but ordered the sovereigns to find a solution. "I may be mistaken, but it appears to me princes ought to protect their governors as long as they keep them, for without protection all is lost," he wrote, unable to veil his sarcasm. What he wanted, Columbus told them specifically, was an arbitrator who would be responsible for overseeing the rebel situation.

On October 18, 1498, Columbus sent the *Santa María de Guía* and the *Correo* back to Spain. On board were the implements that would lead to his downfall: his letter requesting a new administrator, his letter detailing his discovery of the fourth continent, his hand-drawn charts of the coastline he had explored, and a chest of Paria pearls for the royal treasury. A month later the ships arrived safely in Spain. As the sovereigns puzzled over Columbus's request, word of the new continent quickly spread through the nautical community. Though intended for Isabella and Ferdinand's eyes only, Columbus's charts and letter were surreptitiously copied and circulated. Because pearls were as prized a commodity as gold, those documents were, quite literally, a treasure map.

Back in Hispaniola, Columbus waited with growing

exasperation for his administrator. He came to the prag-
matic realization that he could not quash Roldán's new republic. Instead he brokered a harsh peace. The terms were
feudal in tone, allotting land to Roldán and each of his followers. The Indians living on the land would serve as vas-
sals, supplying the colonists with slave labor for whatever
farming or mining they undertook. The policy, known as
repartimiento, set a tone for relationships between Indians
and Spanish colonists that would endure in the Americas
for centuries.

Roldán was appeased, but peace did not come to Hispaniola. Soon others in Santo Domingo were emboldened
by Columbus's passive diplomacy. Citizens defied his authority, striking off to form their own communes. This
time Columbus reacted brutally. He and Bartolomé rode
out across the island to bring the insubordinates back to
Santo Domingo. Columbus ordered more than a dozen of
the returned rebels hanged. The bodies swayed in the ocean
breeze for days afterward, bloating and infested by flies, a
reminder to one and all that Columbus was viceroy and
governor of Hispaniola.

Columbus felt vindicated by this ruthlessness, believing
it the only way to protect his financial interests and hard-
won power. But he was not a warrior at heart. The strain of
waging war and executing men weighed heavily on him.
He was impatient for Ferdinand and Isabella to send him his
administrator. Then he was certain all his problems would
be over. Columbus would finally be able to relax and enjoy
his island domain.

Little did Columbus know, but relaxation was not in his
future. The sovereigns had indeed selected an administrator.
This man, a close friend of Bishop Fonseca's, would soon
become Columbus's worst nightmare.

CHAPTER NINE

Bishop and Pawns

May 1499–September 1500
Hispaniola

Flamboyant, temperamental, and very short in stature, Alonso de Ojeda was an ambitious young adventurer eager to curry favor with Isabella. Once, when she was inside the three-hundred-foot-tall Giralda, that stately tower looming over the cathedral in Seville, he made sure she was looking and then strolled out onto an exposed beam jutting from the side of the tower. As the queen gaped in surprise, and as the crowd in the square below craned their necks to watch, Ojeda sauntered to the end of the narrow beam. Then he lifted one leg and spun in a neat pirouette before strolling back toward the tower. Plucking an orange from his pocket, Ojeda balanced on one leg again and threw the orange up onto the Giralda's roof. Only then did he duck back inside. It was a performance the bemused Isabella did not soon forget.

Fifteen years Columbus's junior, Ojeda represented the budding breed of Spanish explorer. Some were sailors, but many, like Ojeda, were better labeled as merely adventurers. All viewed the New World with an eye toward exploitation, not exploration.

Ojeda had sailed as a gentleman volunteer under Columbus on the second voyage, and he leveraged that experience — relentlessly. Taking a cue from Columbus's own career, Ojeda shamelessly followed the royal court from city to city, his edgy, arrogant presence a daily reminder to Isabella that the Genovese was not the only adventurer in Spain. For a short time Ojeda worked as Bishop Fonseca's secretary, commencing a connection that both men would one day exploit to great personal advantage.

Columbus's voyages had some measure of curiosity and purity, but Ojeda was driven by greed. His father had sent him off at a young age to be raised as a page in the court of Don Luis de Cerda. As Duke of Medina Celi, de Cerda was one of Spain's most powerful and well-connected men. Descended from Castilian kings, he had set aside family allegiance and become staunchly loyal to Ferdinand and Isabella. During the prolonged wars that unified Spain in the latter half of the fifteenth century, the dynamic de Cerda was Ferdinand's most valued ally, eagerly leading his knights into battle against the Moors, Spanish nobles, and anyone else who opposed his sovereigns. Men like de Cerda represented the last days of Spanish chivalry, when a knight's loyalty was his most prized asset, and for this he was granted an access to the court enjoyed by few other men in Spain.

Alonso de Ojeda wasn't the first man to recognize the duke's immense power. Back in 1485 Columbus had approached the duke in Puerto Santa Maria, where he ran a shipping business. Columbus had told the duke of his theory that a man could sail west around the globe to the Orient. The duke, intrigued, momentarily considered backing Columbus, but the monies required were too great, and the international scope intruded upon Ferdinand and Isabella's power. Instead of funding Columbus, the duke had written to the queen and recommended she listen to what the would-be explorer had to say.

Columbus's first audience with the sovereigns had taken place in Córdoba, in May 1486. The setting was the royal residence. No one was in attendance but Columbus and the sovereigns, which lent the proceedings a sense of intimacy that would have been lacking before the crowds that often thronged the throne room. Columbus had brought maps and used them as proof of his radical theories, which he pitched with as much poise as he could muster. Ferdinand, who had brought a copy of *Geography* with him, quickly grew bored and left the room. The sea was the domain of Isabella's Castile, not of Ferdinand's kingdoms, leaving little reason for him to stay.

But Isabella was deeply curious about what Columbus had to say. She not only remained alone with him, she was in no hurry for him to leave. The enchanted queen and the bold Italian discussed his theories for hours. Columbus spoke softly, but emphatically, answering her probing questions in a direct and confident manner. "The Lord blessed Columbus with a certain grace," his friend Bartolomé de Las Casas once wrote, "which always induced others to look on him with love." Whether Isabella felt that deeply toward Columbus would become a matter of historical conjecture. But it is clear by the fondness and emotion she would display toward him for the rest of their lives that the explorer earned a place in her heart during their unusually long conversation. And although Ferdinand strayed often from the marital bed despite his Catholic faith, Isabella was far more devout. Any flirtation between the queen and Columbus would remain just that.

Soon after Columbus wandered back out into the warm night air, no doubt high on adrenaline and the sublime titillation of an evening alone with a beautiful and powerful woman, Isabella arranged for him to stay at the home of her financial comptroller, Alonso de Quintanilla. Then she put him on the royal payroll and ordered her advisers to fully investigate Columbus's grand scheme. As the king busied himself with other affairs of state, she took charge of the inquiry.

This went on for six long years. Isabella's interest in the voyage was secondary to the ongoing wars against the Moorish invaders. Her interest in Columbus's grand plans was waning in 1489, when Columbus left her court and hustled over to Portugal to meet with João, only to be stunned into silence by Bartolomeu Dias's Africa success. He had also sent Bartolomé off to England to sell the expedition to Henry VII, only to have his adventurous brother taken prisoner by pirates on the way. Bartolomé was released after several months and doggedly pursued his original mission, but the Tudor king laughed at Christopher's foolish designs. Bartolomé then traveled to France to beseech Charles VIII for financing.

Isabella, though, was Columbus's great hope. He seemed to have no shame, waiting impatiently year after year for her answer. The ordeal made him the butt of jokes among court followers. They had learned of his plan and thought him an imbecile. "People of no understanding," wrote Las Casas, "presumed to know all about it." They delivered "insulting speeches which afflicted his soul." The doubts and mocking thickened Columbus's skin. He was getting older — almost too old for such an undertaking. In January 1492 the sovereigns finally made up their minds about Columbus. But rather than give him the good news he longed to hear, they informed him that they would not fund his voyage. Downhearted, Columbus packed his bags for France, determined to join Bartolomé in selling his idea to Charles VIII.

By great coincidence, the very day that Columbus began his journey the royal accountant appeared before the queen. Quintanilla, who considered Columbus a "wise and prudent man and of excellent intelligence," had studied Columbus's plan with a skeptic's eye. His conclusion was profound: if the sovereigns didn't finance the voyage, then

Quintanilla would personally underwrite Columbus's adventure for them. There was no downside. If Columbus succeeded, Spain would be rich. If Columbus failed, he would likely die. Spain would be undiminished. Over Ferdinand's objections, Isabella agreed. The royal constable was sent to find Columbus and give him the news.

Columbus was four miles outside of Santa Fe, crossing an ancient bridge in the city of Pinos-Puente, when the constable caught up. His horse panting after a hard gallop, the constable delivered the news that would change Columbus's life forever: the voyage was on.

In 1493, in the euphoric wake of Columbus's discovery, Ferdinand and Isabella had shown their appreciation to the Duke of Medina Celi for his farsighted letter of introduction by granting him the right to send caravels to the New World each year. This was not a breach of the Capitulations of Santa Fe. They were granting the duke a percentage of their profits, not Columbus's.

Alonso de Ojeda lacked de Cerda's regal charisma but strove to emulate his mentor in every other way. The page was an exceptional horseback rider and swordsman. He was athletic and brave, exceptional in battle, and imbued with a boisterous optimism. But Ojeda was also a man of modest means who was both blessed and cursed to travel in a circle of wealthy men. He could never stand alongside them as an equal until he made his fortune. The duke understood this, so although Ojeda was entirely lacking in nautical knowledge and ability, the duke allowed him to command one of his caravels bound for the New World. It was thus that Ojeda had joined Columbus's swollen second expedition.

While on Hispaniola Ojeda had been ordered by Columbus to find the legendary gold mines of Cibao, which were supposed to be hidden somewhere in the island's interior. Ojeda's initial foray had been successful. The smattering of flakes encouraged Columbus to write the sovereigns that Hispaniola would soon give up "as much gold as the iron mines of Biscay." He had ordered Ojeda to return to the interior and find more gold.

The tempestuous little Spaniard's second march to Cibao was remarkable not for finding gold but for his acts of violence against an Indian chief. "This was the first injustice, with vain and erroneous pretension of doing justice, that was committed in these Indies against these Indians," wrote Bartolomé de Las Casas, whose father and three uncles were among the new colonists, "and the beginning of shedding the blood which has since flowed so copiously on this island." Although he would make a great name for himself over the course of his lifetime, Ojeda's enduring legacy would be those acts of violence. His brutal precedent set a tone for relationships between Europeans and Indians that would linger for more than four centuries.

In the wake of his violent mission, Ojeda was emboldened. He didn't sail with Columbus on the third voyage, thinking it was the ideal to lead an expedition all his own. He shared this hope with Bishop Fonseca.

In the waning months of 1498, when Columbus's request for an administrator for Hispaniola reached the sovereigns along with his maps of Paria and the chest of pearls, Fonseca showed them to Ojeda. The ambitious adventurer pored over Columbus's glowing letters and detailed charts. Just as Fonseca hoped, the descriptions of a tropical Eden brimming with pearls, spices, and gold were too tempting for Ojeda to ignore. Both men also foresaw that the instability in Hispaniola might mark the end of Columbus's reign over the New World, thus creating a power vacuum they could exploit. In a carefully worded dispensation, Fonseca authorized Ojeda to undertake the first voyage of exploration to the New World that was not led by Christopher Columbus. To avoid open conflict between Ojeda and the Admiral, the bishop publicly prohibited Spain's newest explorer from traveling to Hispaniola while privately encouraging him to do just that. The bishop then signed Ojeda's orders with a flourish. It was the document's lone signature.

The winter of 1498–99 found Ojeda making the rounds of Seville's bankers, seeking funding to procure ships and men. The winning combination of Bishop Fonseca's power, Ojeda's reputation for daring, and the obvious wealth of Paria impressed potential investors. They were, however, worried about Ojeda's lack of nautical ability. To allay any concerns, Ojeda hired Juan de la Cosa, yet another Columbus disciple, as chief pilot of the four-ship fleet. Cosa was a widely known and highly respected member of Spain's seafaring community. He had been the owner and master of the *Santa Maria,* Columbus's ill-fated flagship on the first voyage. Columbus had hired Cosa again for the second voyage, placing him in charge of chart making, and Cosa drew history's first maps of Hispaniola, Cuba, and Jamaica. He considered himself Columbus's equal as a mariner — if not his better.

Finally, to tabulate the heaps of riches the voyage was sure to accrue, the investors stipulated that a Florentine merchant named Amerigo Vespucci make the journey on their behalf.

Ojeda and Cosa sailed from the Duke de Medina Celi's home port of Puerto de Santa María on May 20, 1499. For good luck Ojeda brought a Flemish painting of the Virgin Mary that Fonseca had given him. It was small enough for Ojeda to carry on his person, and he planned to wear it into battle, should the occasion arise.

The Atlantic crossing took just twenty-four days. Following Columbus's charts a little too precisely, Cosa steered the fleet along Columbus's intended, not actual, route of the *rumbo austral*. They reached land six hundred miles southeast of Trinidad and were forced to parallel the coast of the continent ("coasting," in sailor's parlance) to find Paria.

Those six hundred miles set the tone for the rest of the voyage. Ojeda's vessels spent the summer exploring the northern coast of the new continent. Cosa charted the environs brilliantly; Vespucci took careful note of the tall, muscular local Indians; and Ojeda, once again emulating his mentor the duke, led his men into battle against the Carib Indians. Although their armor was hot to the touch and made them sweat profusely in the equatorial sun, it protected the Spanish from the spears and arrows tipped with sharpened tortoiseshells that were fired in their direction. Ojeda suffered only one casualty that summer.

The Caribs were infamous, even to the Spanish, who knew of them from Columbus's voyages. As one Spanish observer wrote: "They travel 150 leagues to make war in their canoes, which are small *fustas* hewn out of a single tree. These people raid the other islands and carry off all the women they can take, especially the young and beautiful, whom they keep as servants and concubines. They had carried off so many that in fifty houses we found no males and more than twenty of the captives were girls. These women say they are treated with a cruelty that seems incredible. The Caribs eat the male children they have by them, and only bring up the children of their own women. And as for the men they are able to capture, they bring those who are alive home to be slaughtered and eat those who are dead on the spot. They say that human flesh is so good there is nothing like it in the world."

By defeating the Caribs in battle, the Spaniards temporarily ended that threat. The other local tribes showed their overwhelming gratitude with an outpouring of warmth and generosity, and Ojeda took advantage of this appreciation by sending twenty-seven of his men into the jungle to search for gold. It was a journey they would never forget. For nine days those men lived an elaborate tropical fantasy. They encountered nothing but friendly tribes, all beside themselves with joy that the Caribs had been vanquished. Each evening these tribes assembled elaborate feasts, complete with games and tribal dancing. At the end of the night, a wife or daughter was sent to sleep with each man. It was with deep regret — and no gold — that they returned to the boredom and austerity of shipboard life.

By August the warm tropical waters were proving amenable to shipworms. Ojeda's caravels began leaking like sieves. Ojeda fled the coast of the new continent before the boats could sink altogether, but he did not order Cosa to set a course for Spain. Instead he disobeyed the bishop's strict orders and sailed for Hispaniola.

It was September 5, 1499, when Ojeda's fleet anchored off a place the Taino called Yaquimo, on the southwest coast of Hispaniola. He planned to fill his holds with an exotic lumber called logwood, also known as dyewood because oxidation of the cut lumber produced a beautiful black dye for coloring wool and silk. The longer the period of oxidation, the greater the color enhancement. (To accelerate that sometimes-lengthy process, the Spaniards simply urinated on the wood for a few months. Despite the residual aroma of this act, the wood would fetch a fair price in the markets of Seville.) Ojeda had found little wealth so far and needed the wood badly. He was determined that his backers see a return on their investment.

Ojeda hadn't been to Hispaniola in almost five years. From Columbus's letters he knew of the Admiral's difficulties with the colonists but was unaware that Columbus had ceded portions of the island to Roldán in order to make peace. Yaquimo, with its palm tree–lined sands, fell under Roldán's jurisdiction.

It was not long before he got his bearings. Anti-Columbus sentiment was high, and Ojeda wasted no time fomenting further rebellion, telling the colonists that Columbus should be deposed. Fresh off his running battles with the Indians of Paria, Ojeda was poised to take on the Admiral. The young adventurer rightly believed that a successful overthrow of Columbus's regime would be supported by Bishop Fonseca — and by proxy, the sovereigns. Acting quickly, Ojeda rallied a large number of rebels to his cause.

It took three weeks for word of Ojeda's arrival to reach Columbus in Santo Domingo. Having finally made his peace with Roldán, the Admiral was in no mood to travel down the coast and confront the interloper. A furious Columbus ordered Roldán to handle the matter. Ojeda was to be expelled immediately.

Roldán sailed for Yaquimo on September 29, leading a two-caravel fleet and a large number of men loyal to his cause. Ojeda's fleet lay at anchor in the harbor, but at the time Ojeda himself was miles inland, searching for wood. Roldán sent his men ashore and set up a rear guard to prevent Ojeda from returning to the sea and then struck off to find him.

The two played a game of cat and mouse for five long months. Roldán finally succeeded in ousting Ojeda, but not before making major concessions to those rebels who had supported him. Ojeda's journey next took him to the Bahamas, where he added to the paltry supply of wood he had cut in Hispaniola by kidnapping a group of local residents to sell as slaves. In late spring 1500 his fleet set sail for Cádiz.

Meanwhile Bishop Fonseca had granted permission for yet another explorer to harvest the wealth of Paria. Once again the mission was to be helmed by a Columbus protégé. Peralonso Niño was from Moguer, a seafaring town in southwest Spain's Niebla region. He was of modest birth and means, but Niño came from a family of sailors and was greatly respected by his peers. Prior to Columbus's first voyage, it was Niño who convinced the mariners from his region that the foreigner's plan to cross the Dark Sea to find India wasn't a suicide mission. Based on this vote of confidence, Columbus was able to find ample men to crew his vessels. Among them was Peralonso's brother Juan, who owned the vessel *Santa Clara*. (Per sailing custom, her nickname was the feminine form of her owner's surname. Thus the *Santa Clara* became the *Niña*.) The speedy caravel was the smallest of Columbus's three ships from that voyage and his personal favorite. Such was Columbus's fondness for the *Niña* that he later bought a half ownership in her.

Columbus had named Peralonso Niño chief pilot of the *Santa Maria*. Niño crewed on the second voyage, too, serving as master on a vessel ferrying colonists to La Isabela. Five brothers and cousins had also served Columbus on that voyage, and Columbus had honored the Niño family by selecting the *Niña* as his flagship to lead the grand fleet.

Unlike his brother, Peralonso Niño did not own a ship, nor did he have the means to lead a large fleet to Paria. For that he turned to the bankers of Seville, but just one backer answered his request for financing — and he offered enough money for just one ship. Adding insult to injury, banker Luis Guerra stipulated that his brother Christoval be the caravel's commander instead of Niño. Despite the ludicrous notion of being second in command on his own expedition, Niño agreed.

During the first week of June 1499, just as Ojeda was arriving on the coast of Paria, Niño, Christoval Guerra, and a crew of thirty-three set sail in a small caravel. They carried a copy of Columbus's charts and closely followed the Admiral's path. To his credit Guerra quickly stepped down as commander, deferring to the more knowledgeable Niño. The veteran pilot did not disappoint. The lone caravel reached Paria in almost the exact same spot near Trinidad as Columbus had. They sailed immediately to the island of Margarita, the place where Columbus had found his pearl-adorned natives, and began searching for treasure.

It was July by then. Ojeda and his fleet blundered along the coast of Paria to the west, making war on the Caribs and having a grand adventure but discovering little in the way of wealth. For Niño it was a different story. He and his men spent the next three months sailing along the coast, trading glass beads and other trinkets for pearls. Both parties felt they were taking advantage of each other (indeed the Indians were amazed that anyone could place such value on pearls). Those Indians who had waged war with Ojeda just a few months before were understandably suspicious of Spanish travelers, despite Niño's good intentions. But Niño's emphasis on maintaining friendly relations with the Indians succeeded, and the caravel's fifty-ton hold was soon brimming with pearls great and small.

Coasting westward, Niño came to an area called Cauchieto, where a large Indian settlement could be seen on the banks of a river. Anticipating yet another profitable day of trading, Niño was about to send his men ashore when he noticed a thousand defiant Indian warriors lined up on the sand, armed with clubs and bows. He quickly ordered the ship to steer out to sea, far beyond the reach of arrows or hostile warriors in canoes.

In that instant Niño unknowingly began his trip back to Spain. The hostile Indians terrified him, and he stopped pushing westward, turning back to where he knew the tribes to be friendly. Soon after the new year, Christoval Guerra, exercising his right as representative of the expedition's chief financial backer, suggested their holds contained enough pearls. Peralonso Niño turned the caravel toward home.

Even as Ojeda and Niño explored Paria, Bishop Fonseca conspired to make more mischief, authorizing a third voyage to Columbus's new discovery in December 1499. Yet again the commander was a protégé of Columbus's, but Vicente Yanez Pinzón was different from Ojeda and Niño. Neither of those men harbored animosity toward the Admiral. Not so with the forty-year-old Pinzón. His family, like Niño's, was a prominent seafaring clan. The Pinzóns reigned over Palos, a whitewashed city at the mouth of the Rio Tinto that served as one of Spain's major Atlantic ports. The patriarch of the family was Martín Alonzo Pinzón, who was fifty-one when he commanded the *Pinta* on Columbus's first voyage. Like many Spanish mariners Martín Alonzo Pinzón chafed that a foreigner had received royal permission and funds to command such an epic voyage. But the slight ran much deeper. Martín Alonzo Pinzón claimed that the voyage was his idea, not Columbus's. The riches and glory, he insisted, belonged to him.

He certainly deserved some credit for Columbus's success, although not as much as he believed. On the initial voyage Pinzón was the first man to quell talk of mutiny when the *Niña,* the *Pinta,* and the *Santa Maria* hadn't seen land in two weeks — a record for the Palos sailing community.

But three weeks into that first voyage, Martín Alonzo Pinzón's support dissolved. When the sailors shifted their eyes now and again to the horizon, alternately grumbling and praying for the sight of land, he no longer encouraged hope, nor did he discourage the revived muttered talks of mutiny. Pinzón was enough of a mariner to know that Columbus would soon lead them to land. He had seen the dolphins and terns flittering about the ship, ensuring the fleet's imminent safety, but he was content to let his men wallow in their fear, hoping they would snap. When the mutiny came, as it surely would, he would take control. "I know Martín Alonzo cannot be trusted," Columbus wrote during one of those darkest moments on that first journey. "He wants the rewards and enterprises of this journey to himself."

Within days Pinzón was publicly begging Columbus to alter his course, hoping his bold opposition to the obvious folly of Columbus's mission would spark rebellion. Columbus bravely refused. The whispers of mutiny grew stronger with each passing sunrise. Columbus heard them all. "The men continue to murmur and complain," he noted on October 4, 1492.

Mutiny was forgotten when land was discovered, but Martín Alonzo Pinzón was not through tormenting Columbus. He slipped away from Columbus and the fleet's other two ships off the coast of Cuba, guiding the *Pinta* on a furtive exploration of the new lands. Six weeks later Pinzón joined up with the fleet as abruptly as he had left. On the journey home Pinzón sailed off once again, this time taking advantage of a storm near the Azores to race home and be the first to tell the sovereigns about the discovery of the New World. A fierce storm drove him toward the northwest coast of Spain, into the port of Baiona, where he quickly sent word to King Ferdinand in Barcelona, requesting an audience. The sovereigns refused; it was Columbus they wanted. Pinzón immediately sailed home to Palos, following the contour of the Iberian Peninsula. But Columbus, fresh off his stop in Lisbon to meet with King João II, got there first. On March 15, 1493, Columbus sailed the *Niña* up the Tinto to a hero's welcome just hours before Martín Alonzo Pinzón and the *Pinta* arrived. For a third time Pinzón rushed away from Columbus. He struck off on the long overland journey to Madrid, trying yet again to meet with the sovereigns and claim he had discovered the New World, but once more he was defeated. A royal messenger met him along the way. By order of the king, the Palos patriarch was forbidden from seeking a royal audience. Martín Alonzo Pinzón returned to Palos in shame and went into seclusion, and the enraged Columbus immediately severed all ties with the old captain. Pinzón died later that summer, many claiming the cause of death was disgrace.

Vicente Yanez Pinzón, the second of three Pinzón brothers, had captained the *Niña* on that first voyage. He did not blame Columbus for his older brother's death but was upset that Columbus had received all the credit for the success. Like Peralonso Niño, Vicente Yanez Pinzón now considered the New World the province of Spain's sailing community, not of one man. He had spent his life at sea but always in the employ of other men. Pinzón longed to explore Paria and make his fortune.

Vicente Yanez Pinzón scraped together a fleet of four ships with the limited funds at his disposal, sailing, as always, from Palos. After outfitting his ships little money had been left for stores, so Pinzón purchased what he could on credit. The merchants of Palos, ruthless in their zeal to make a profit, charged Pinzón twice the going rate for every last barrel of salted beef and wine. He had no choice but to pay.

Pinzón's plan was to sail far below the equator, and he followed the course with such resolution that he bypassed the Canary Islands and Cape Verde Islands stopovers that were becoming a tradition on transatlantic voyages. No sooner did he cross into the southern latitudes than a gale savaged the fleet, almost sinking it. The troubles didn't end with the weather. Pinzón's men were disoriented by the sight of a heaven filled with unknown stars. Pinzón didn't panic, forgoing celestial navigation to sail by dead reckoning toward the continent's known location, nor did he panic when the seas continued to be storm tossed throughout much of the voyage. Even as his course took him farther and farther below the equator, he pushed westward, certain that landfall was imminent. On January 28, 1500, two long months after leaving Europe, Pinzón rejoiced as the lookout finally spotted green shores in the distance.

That joy lasted just a night. When Pinzón rowed ashore

the next morning to claim this new country in the name of Castile, he was greeted by the sight of giant footprints in the sand. Terrified, he rowed quickly back to his ship. That night, while pondering his plan of attack, Pinzón spotted campfires from a settlement on the beach. He was unsure whether the natives were friendly, so when Pinzón sent a second landing party ashore just after sunrise, it was not a small detail, but forty men armed with swords and knives.

As their boat reached the sandy shore, the forty Spaniards were startled to see an equal number of very tall Indians marching toward them. The Indians were armed with bows and arrows and sauntered with an air of fearlessness. The Spanish could see more members of the tribe in the distance, rushing to reinforce their fellow warriors.

The Spanish didn't attack. Neither did the Indians. They squared off on the beach, each waiting for the other to make the first move. When the Indians continued to scowl but made no other attempt to attack, the Spanish offered them beads and bells as welcoming gifts. The Indians simply sneered and held their ground, then walked away. The Spanish did not follow.

That brief encounter was enough to convince Pinzón to move on. He sailed northwest along the coast, still south of the equator and hundreds of miles from Paria. At the mouth of a shallow river, he sent another armed contingent ashore. The men rowed inland in two boats, following the course of the languid river and looking for an open stretch of bank on which to land. The equatorial heat was oppressive, and thick vegetation spilled over into the water on either side. Wary from their previous encounter, the Spanish fearfully studied the shore for signs of hostile Indians.

Finally they spotted a safe-looking spot. A tribe of nude Indians watched their every move from a rise overlooking the water. When the Indians didn't immediately attack or appear outwardly hostile, the Spanish sent a lone man ashore to initiate contact. He was short, barefoot, and slender, and he marched uphill with a wobbly gait because he had not yet found his land legs. Several paces from the Indians, the Spaniard stopped. He stared at the naked locals, who appeared to be unarmed, trying his best to look simultaneously fearless and friendly. In a gesture of goodwill, he threw them a small bell — a standard token for pacifying Indians. It seemed to work: the Indians made a show of being thankful, and the Spaniard relaxed.

Much to his surprise, the Indians then threw a gift of their own back toward him. The elaborately decorated stick landed at the Spaniard's feet. He shifted his sword to an opposite hand and bent down to pick up the stick. As his mates watched helplessly from the riverbank, the Indians sprung their trap. They sprinted to the lone Spaniard and grabbed him, trying to drag him away. Amazingly, he held them off, deftly slashing at his captors with his sword until they let go. But the Indians didn't flee, even as the other Spaniards began racing up the hill. They circled and taunted the man, waiting for him to drop his guard.

By the time the Spaniards came to their shipmate's defense, a reinforcement of Indians had appeared, armed with bows, arrows, and blow darts. The Spanish fought with swords and lances, ideal weapons for hand-to-hand combat but useless in retreat. At least eight of Pinzón's men were killed before they could crab back downhill, frantically swinging their useless weapons the whole way. When the sailors finally leaped into their boats and shoved off, the Indians plunged into the water and surrounded them, grabbing the thick wooden paddles at the same time. The desperate Spanish hacked at the Indians with their swords and impaled them with their lances, the water turning red with the blood gushing from the maimed and dying.

But the Spanish were greatly outnumbered. Even as one boat crew fought its way free from the bank and desperately rowed toward the faraway safety of their ships, Indians surrounded the other boat. They wrenched the oars from the Spaniards and used them as bludgeons. The entire crew was slain. The Indians danced back up the hill and left the Spanish bodies for the flies.

Pinzón was so distraught by the tragedy that he temporarily forgot the primary purpose of his voyage. Setting aside all thoughts of wealth, he sailed a hundred miles out to sea, then turned northwest again. In this way he paralleled the coast of the fourth continent. He could not see it, let alone explore it or trade with its inhabitants, but at least he and his men were safe.

Then a peculiar thing happened. The smell of salt air, normally so all-encompassing while at sea, subsided. The ocean water miraculously turned fresh. A mystified Pinzón ordered the ships' water casks refilled. In a lifetime at sea, Pinzón had never replenished his water supply beyond sight of land. He was so enchanted by the miraculous occurrence that he set aside his fears of Indian attack and made course for land. Soon he was sailing into the most massive estuary he had ever seen, one so broad he couldn't make out one side from the other. The water turned from the dark blues of the deep ocean to a muddy brown. Islands, lush and vivid green, dotted the center of the estuary. Pinzón named this newfound geographic wonder the Marañón, though it would soon become a historical asterisk. A later Spanish explorer would change the bulk of the waterway's name to Amazon, for a tribe of female warriors encountered far upstream.

Meanwhile, back in Spain, the expeditions of Peralonso Niño and Alonso de Ojeda were coming to an end. First into port was the veteran mariner from Moguer, who arrived in Baiona in April 1500. His lone bark made for a pitiful fleet compared with the other two voyages sanctioned by Bishop Fonseca, but Niño returned to Spain with more wealth in his holds than any expedition to the New World thus far — including all three of Columbus's. It was an extraordinary achievement and irrefutable proof that the New World was truly as rich as Columbus had long claimed. Even after accounting for the percentage due the royal coffers and monies owed financial backer Luis Guerra, Peralonso Niño was now a very wealthy man. It was a fine reward for a lifetime of hard work and the undertaking of a bold journey.

But Bishop Fonseca was not satisfied. As the overseer of all New World incomes, he was convinced Niño was withholding treasure. He ordered Niño and Christoval Guerra thrown into prison on grounds of defrauding the crown.

In June 1500 Alonso de Ojeda's bedraggled fleet sailed into Cádiz. His holds were filled with captured slaves and logwood, but very little gold. The voyage's profit after expenses was a mere fifteen thousand maravedis, which was split among the fifty-five men who had survived the voyage. Considering that forty maravedis a day was considered a good wage for a skilled laborer, the men could have made more money staying home. Ojeda's grand voyage, begun in deceit, had ended as a humiliating second best to Niño's humble journey.

As Niño languished in prison and Ojeda's descent into disgrace began, Vicente Yanez Pinzón sailed into the harbor at Santo Domingo. He had left the Amazon and worked his way slowly northward along the coast. The natives were friendlier, though still poor. Because they could not give him gold or pearls, Pinzón captured three dozen Indians and chained them in the sweltering holds of his vessels, destined to be sold as slaves back in Spain. Like Ojeda and Niño, Pinzón was soon following Columbus's path through the Gulf of Paria. Unable to find much in the way of gold or pearls there either, he decided to quit the voyage, setting a course for Santo Domingo, which he reached on June 23, 1500. As his ships were refitted for the voyage home, Pinzón met with Columbus, the only one of Bishop Fonseca's three Andalusian explorers to do so.

Despite Columbus's anger that other explorers were encroaching on his domain, he still extended all kindnesses to Pinzón, who stayed for two weeks before setting sail for Palos. The two men parted on good terms.

Pinzón's disasters recommenced shortly thereafter. A tremendous gale struck his fleet off the Bahamas. Two vessels sank. The other two returned to Santo Domingo for repairs. It was late September 1500 by the time Vicente Yanez Pinzón returned to Palos, a broken man. His ships were immediately seized by his creditors. His actions on land and sea had resulted in the deaths of dozens of Palos residents and were soon being scrutinized by the dead men's widows.

It seemed that everyone but Bishop Fonseca had been cursed by the three voyages of 1499–1500. Ojeda had found no wealth, Niño had found fortune but wound up in jail, Pinzón was on the verge of being sent to a debtors' prison. A fourth explorer, Diego Lepe, had sailed even farther south than Pinzón and presented Bishop Fonseca with a map of his travels on his return. A fifth explorer, Rodrigo de Bastides, a wealthy notary from the Seville suburb of Triana, was due to set sail from Seville within days of Pinzón's return to Palos. Voyage by voyage, discovery by discovery, Bishop Fonseca was wresting the New World from Columbus. The continuing troubles on Hispaniola had further chipped away at Columbus's domain.

Columbus, however, still had total control over Santo Domingo, and that was enough. It was the crown jewel of the New World, the port through which all trade flowed. He could not have guessed that his grip on this power was in its final weeks.

PARADISE LOST

CHAPTER TEN

The Administrator

October 1500
Hispaniola

The two caravels scudded back and forth across the indigo sea, four miles off Hispaniola's jagged coast. It was Sunday, an hour after sunrise. The morning air was pleasant, not yet thick with the humidity and heat that would make midday torturous. As with all coastal regions, Hispaniola's winds blew from the land toward the sea during the night and early morning hours, when the land is cooler than the water. Once the sun rose and heated the earth, the wind direction reversed itself. Waiting for the wind to switch directions and fill the square sails so they could then thrust their overcrowded vessels into troubled Santo Domingo, the masters of *La Gorda* and *La Antigua* bided their time offshore.

Commanding the small fleet was a non-sailor and friend of Bishop Fonseca's, the eminent Francisco de Bobadilla, a knight of Calatrava, Spain's oldest chivalric order. He was patient and wise, with snow white hair that contrasted sharply with his coal black battle armor. Bobadilla carried letters from the sovereigns, instructing Columbus's colonial administration to submit to the knight's authority in administrative matters. One such letter stated: "We command you to go to the islands and the said mainland of the Indies, and you will find out who the people were who rose against the Admiral and our magistrates, and you should seize them and confiscate their goods, and when they have been made prisoners, you should proceed against them."

Should the process become rocky a contingent of soldiers had also made the journey. As Bobadilla passed the morning in his cabin aboard *La Gorda,* those warriors lined the rails, gazing across at the vast green sprawl of Hispaniola, so flat near the water's edge that it seemed a green continuation of the ocean, which then rose to jungle-covered peaks nudging up into the clouds.

Shortly before noon the wind shifted. Within an hour *La Gorda* and *La Antigua* concluded the last miles of their transatlantic passage. Sailing into the harbor and up the broad mouth of the Ozama River, they dropped anchor. Bobadilla's eyes were immediately drawn to a pair of gallows, one on either side of the river. Spaniards hung by the neck, both of their bloated, decomposing carcasses fouling an otherwise sensuous tropical breeze. One of them — rebel leader Adrian de Mujica — was still recognizable. The other man had already rotted beyond recognition.

An enraged Bobadilla stormed ashore and ordered the bodies cut down. As the special attaché of Ferdinand and Isabella, the command was well within his rights. Suddenly his plan of attack was clear: arrest the men responsible for Hispaniola's problems. And those men appeared to be none other than Christopher Columbus and his younger brothers.

Santo Domingo was a small settlement. The arrival of caravels was greeted with all the joy of a public holiday. Within an hour of Bobadilla's arrival, every citizen knew why he had come — and most were thrilled, hoping Bobadilla would be their salvation from the reign of the fiercely clannish Columbus brothers. In their eyes the Columbus brothers were nothing but foreigners, "cruel enemies and shedders of Spanish blood . . . the king's enemies." Bobadilla didn't disappoint them. He seized Columbus's residence and personal property within moments of setting foot on land, making it very clear that Hispaniola was about to have a new governor.

But a showdown with Columbus would have to wait. He was on the plains just inland, making war on yet another uprising. Bartolomé was doing the same, but in the jungles. Only their milquetoast younger brother, Diego, remained in town, and he was taking great pains to hide from Bobadilla.

Sunday became Monday. Bobadilla had spent the night in Christopher Columbus's bed, his soldiers gamboled about the streets of Santo Domingo, and his very presence had electrified a citizenry that despised the Columbus brothers, but he had neither heard from nor seen Diego. It was time for a confrontation. Bobadilla assembled his men and went looking in the one place he was sure to find Diego: at Mass.

The move was carefully calculated. Even in far-flung Hispaniola, fear of the Inquisition made religious devotion a daily fact of life. Ambushing Diego at Mass provided Bobadilla a dramatic, symbolic backdrop for stating the reasons he had come. As expected, Diego came out of hiding and took a seat on a hard wooden pew in the front row. Bobadilla, as befitting his noble birth, did the same.

Nothing happened until the priest concluded the service. As the parishioners filed out into the bright summer sunlight, Bobadilla greeted Diego and then ordered his notary to stand outside the church and read aloud several of the king and queen's proclamations, introducing Bobadilla as the administrator sought by Columbus. When the reading was concluded, Bobadilla turned to Diego and demanded that all the rebel prisoners be set free.

Diego was not cowed. Scoffing at the suggestion, he

informed Bobadilla that his oldest brother's powers were "better and more guaranteed." No business would be conducted, Diego informed Bobadilla, in the Admiral's absence.

Tuesday brought another trip to Mass. Once again Diego and Bobadilla attended, and once again Bobadilla waited until Mass was over before ordering his notary to read aloud the sovereigns' proclamation. This time it was the order removing Christopher Columbus from power and proclaiming Bobadilla governor. With great solemnity, and in view of the residents of Santo Domingo, Bobadilla took the oath of office. Then, turning to the defiant Diego Columbus, he once again demanded the release of the prisoners.

And once again Diego refused.

Bobadilla ordered yet more proclamations read aloud. They were the most potent of all. By order of the Crown, Bobadilla was granted power over all fortresses and arms on Hispaniola. Furthermore, all of Christopher Columbus's money was to be seized and dispersed among the citizens of Santo Domingo.

With the cheering crowd now firmly on his side, Francisco de Bobadilla turned to Diego Columbus one last time and demanded the release of all prisoners. Diego, ever loyal to his brother, refused.

Bobadilla didn't care. He ordered his troops to storm the jail. Eager local citizens rushed to join them, and the prisons were soon emptied. A fearful Diego Columbus went into seclusion and awaited the return of his oldest brother.

When two weeks passed and Columbus wasn't back, Bobadilla dispatched a messenger bearing a note from Ferdinand and Isabella. "Don Christopher Columbus, our Admiral of the Ocean Sea," it began, making no mention of his titles of viceroy and governor, "we have sent this Knight Commander Francisco de Bobadilla, the bearer of this letter, to say certain things to you in our behalf. We desire you to give him full faith and credit to act accordingly." Columbus raced back to Santo Domingo, where he encountered Bobadilla. "He lodged himself at my house and took everything he found there for himself," Columbus wrote bitterly, adding a sarcastic retort. "He was welcome. Perhaps he had need of it."

The two had met before. Columbus had been nothing more than a wide-eyed dreamer living off Isabella's patronage back when Bobadilla was captain of the Royal Guards in 1488. And from 1495 to 1497, when Bobadilla was chief magistrate of Córdoba, Columbus was one of the city's most famous residents. To the well-heeled Bobadilla, Columbus was a reminder of Spain's place in the world before Ferdinand and Isabella's reign — divided, poor, and weak, its power and resources leached away by Genovese, Jews, and Moors. The sovereigns were intent on making Spain the greatest power in Europe. To Bobadilla it was an abomination that a foreigner controlled Spain's Caribbean crown.

For all his failings as an administrator, Columbus was a dynamic individual, capable of great charisma and warmth. He practiced moderation in drink and temper and rarely swore. So despite his outrage that Bobadilla had confiscated his home, papers, and possessions, and despite the military might at Bobadilla's disposal, Columbus maintained his poise while scheming a way to get the upper hand.

A week passed. Bobadilla, so calculating and smug since his arrival, had underestimated the Admiral, and it was beginning to show. He was becoming deeply threatened by Columbus's presence. It was also becoming clear that not all the citizens of Santo Domingo disdained the Admiral. In fact, a growing number were expressing their outrage at his treatment. Sensing that he was losing control of the situation, Bobadilla impulsively ordered Columbus's arrest. The sovereigns had never suggested such a drastic act. For a loyalist like Bobadilla to risk offending Ferdinand and Isabella was a marker of Columbus's powerful personality.

To a man, no member of Columbus's household staff would obey Bobadilla's order. But the Admiral patiently waited for a Judas to step forward and clap the chains about his ankles and wrists, and finally, Columbus's personal cook, a man named Espinosa, finding inspiration in some long-buried disdain or slight, grabbed the heavy fetters and manacles. They were made of cast iron, with thick anklets and bracelets connected by weighty links of chain. The look on Espinosa's face, eyewitnesses said, was the same eager expression he wore when serving a sumptuous feast.

Columbus was marched to the town citadel and locked away. Diego Columbus was also arrested and then imprisoned in the fetid, sweltering hold of a caravel. Bartolomé Columbus was thrown in irons upon his return to Santo Domingo and locked in the citadel. Meanwhile, Bobadilla severed all contact with Columbus. "My greatest complaint is about my papers, which he took from me," Columbus fumed. "I have not been able to get a single one from him, and those that most firmly prove my innocence he has kept most carefully hidden. What a just and honest inquisitor!"

Now it was Columbus's turn to feel threatened. His agonizing month in jail passed slowly. He slept little, spending his days and nights in prayer and rumination. The impulsive nature of his arrest and the sweeping powers granted Bobadilla meant anything was possible, and Bobadilla's silence left Columbus unsure of what might be next. He had personally led men into battle against the rebels, risking his own life so that the colony of Hispaniola would be united again. "In Spain they judge me as if I had been sent to govern Sicily or some province or city under settled government, and where the laws can be strictly applied without fear of a complete upheaval," he noted bitterly. "Here by God's will I have brought under the dominion of our sovereigns a new world, whereby Spain, which was called poor, has now become rich. I should be judged as a captain who has borne arms for a long time and bears them still, not laying them aside for a single hour, and I should be judged by knights of conquest and experience, not by men of letters." But for now the man who had crossed the ocean so many times could travel no farther than his chains and cell allowed.

On the day Columbus was arrested, the citizens of Santo Domingo had erupted in cheers. His faction of supporters could only look on in dismay as crowds had gathered to mock him and swear at him while soldiers marched the Admiral of the Ocean Sea to jail. Soon after, the town's walls and street corners were plastered with handbills denouncing Columbus and his brothers. Back in Spain, foreigners — and specifically men of Genovese extraction like Columbus — were seen as a destabilizing influence. An ethnic cleansing of the Spanish population had been under way for a decade. Foreigners had been forced from positions of power or denied jobs. Many were banished altogether. A sign of this contempt was yet another Columbus rumor swirling about Santo Domingo's narrow, open-sewered streets: the explorer was a Genovese secret agent. He planned to steal Hispaniola from Spain and give it over to his native republic.

The notion wasn't farfetched. Columbus was more comfortable around Italians than Spaniards, and Italians sailed with him on every voyage. Giacomo the Rich of Genoa had sailed as a ship's boy on the first voyage. Childhood friend Michele de Cuneo sailed on the second. Giovanni Antonio Colombo, the Admiral's Genovese cousin, was captain of *La Rábida* on the third. And Columbus was adamant that a regular portion of his income be deposited into Genoa's Bank of St. George, to be used to ease the tax burdens of Genovese and to maintain his family's house.

Most damning, the Genovese trading houses of Centurione and Pantaleon Italian channeled monies into

Columbus's third voyage, giving them a financial claim in the New World profits. Spain was a poor nation in comparison to the Italian city-states. To uninformed observers Columbus appeared to be working against Ferdinand and Isabella's best interests.

The penalty for such treason, if it were true, was death. And if Columbus were a Jew, as the revived rumors that now swept through Santo Domingo stated, the punishment was far more terrifying. The Inquisition was in full force, and the penalty for faking conversion to Catholicism was torture to the point of death — on the rack, usually, or having flesh ripped off with white-hot pincers. Only then would the individual be burned at the stake. If the inquisitor were feeling generous, the converso would be strangled before the flames were lit, thus sparing the person the horror of immolation.

Murder passing for benevolence; oppression passing for justice. Small wonder that Columbus was depressed and anxious as he languished in prison. He had been there a month when Alonso de Vallejo unlocked the door and ordered Columbus to pick up his chains.

Vallejo was an employee of Bishop Fonseca's, but he was known as a man of integrity. Columbus trusted him. "Where are you taking me?" a frightened Columbus asked. Those who witnessed the moment spoke of the Admiral's "aggrieved countenance and deep sadness, which plainly showed the vehemence of his fear."

Vallejo spoke to Columbus with respect. "Sir, Your Lordship is now going to the ship, to embark."

"To embark? Vallejo, do you speak the truth?"

"By your Lordship's life, it is true, that you are going to embark."

Columbus had got his wish. He was being sent back to Spain. Surrounded by soldiers, his gait distorted by chains, arthritis, and rheumatism, Columbus waddled down the hill to the Ozama River, where the caravel *La Gorda* was one of the ships at anchor. Bartolomé was led to the harbor as well. Diego was already aboard a ship.

As the Columbus brothers clanked past, colonists screamed insults, including *Faraones,* another nasty slang term for Jews. All this was, of course, done with the implicit blessing of Bobadilla. "He even permitted the malcontents and rabble to shout innumerable insults at them in the public squares," Columbus's son Fernando would write of the walk later, "to blow horns in the harbor when they were being taken aboard, and to post scandalous handbills about them on the street corners. Although he knew that one Diego Ortiz, the governor of the hospital, had publicly read a handbill in the town square, he not only did not punish him, but showed much glee over it, which made all the others seek to outdo each other in devising taunts and insults."

On Bobadilla's orders Columbus remained chained as he climbed aboard *La Gorda.* Even then the white-haired knight was fearful Columbus might escape, overcome the weight of his manacles, swim to shore, and then somehow clamber up onto the riverbank, shed his chains, and reclaim the government.

Once on board Columbus settled into his quarters — the same cramped cabin occupied by Bobadilla on *La Gorda*'s outbound journey — under heavy guard. He seethed with self-righteousness and self-pity but was already planning ahead to his arrival in Spain. Bobadilla had ordered the ship's master, Andreas Martin, to keep Columbus in chains all the way to Spain and deliver him directly to Bishop Fonseca. But when Martin, in a sign of respect, discreetly offered to disobey Bobadilla and unlock the chains, Columbus refused. The fetters had been clamped on by order of the sovereigns, he told Martin; they would not be removed without their direct command.

Columbus was bitter, but alive. Behind him lay the gallows of Hispaniola. Before him, if they would grant him the audience Columbus so desperately craved, lay the day of reckoning with Ferdinand and Isabella.

Best of all, Columbus was at sea.

As *La Gorda* sailed east, a two-caravel expedition approached from the opposite direction. They had sailed from Cádiz, under the command of Rodrigo de Bastides. Bastides had sailed on Columbus's second voyage and on Ojeda's voyage, so he was no stranger to the New World. His navigator was the esteemed Juan de la Cosa — Columbus's erstwhile mapmaker and Ojeda's pathfinder — who was making a record fifth voyage to the New World. They charted a course for Paria, arriving just as Columbus reached Spain.

Of all the men Fonseca had sent, these two had the most potential to usurp Columbus's mantle as the New World's supreme explorer — and to find the elusive passage.

CHAPTER ELEVEN

Tears of Rage

November 1500–October 1501
Granada

Columbus's voyage to Spain was uneventful and brisk. It was November 20, 1500, when *La Gorda* docked in Cádiz. Columbus went ashore determined to make a theatrical statement about his incarceration. He shuffled through the narrow waterfront streets, chains clanking loudly over the cobblestones, celebrating the indignity of it all. His audience was sailors, dockhands, and their wives — people predisposed to sympathize with a great mariner — and for the first time since Espinosa the cook had slid the iron bracelets around his ankles, Columbus was enjoying a modicum of power. His intent was to play the martyr, and he succeeded. The uproar throughout Spain over his arrest was almost as great as the fanfare he had received after discovering the New World. Those who had previously opposed him cried out in his defense.

If his intent was to get the attention of Isabella and Ferdinand, he succeeded on that count also. He had written down his side of the story during the voyage home. "I swear on oath that I cannot imagine why I have been made prisoner," Columbus recorded, chains clattering lightly as his quill scrawled across the parchment. "I am conscious that my errors have not been committed for the sake of doing ill and I believe their Highnesses will accept my word for this." Andreas Martin, *La Gorda*'s captain and Columbus's friend, had the letter delivered to the royal court by a swift courier and relegated Bobadilla's version of events to a slower messenger. Isabella was indignant when she read Columbus's report. Even the hardheaded Ferdinand was convinced that Bobadilla had exceeded his bounds. The sovereigns were at the Alcazar, their garden palace in sun-baked Córdoba, just a hundred miles east of Seville. They ordered Columbus freed and summoned him to appear in court and explain himself.

To cover the cost of his travel and ensure that "he could appear in court in a state befitting a person of his rank," the sovereigns also sent along a purse containing two thousand ducats. Before Columbus had even departed for Córdoba, the sovereigns and their entire royal court had moved southeast, to their palace in Granada. Christopher, Bartolomé, and Diego set out for Granada by horse (mules were a more comfortable means of travel, but Isabella and Ferdinand had issued a royal decree in 1494 stating that only priests and pregnant women could travel by mule; this was done to encourage the breeding of horses, for use by the army), traveling across the dry plains and low mountains, bound for the splendor of Granada's magnificent Moorish palace, the Alhambra.

The journey from Seville was just a few hundred miles but in many ways was more treacherous than sailing the Atlantic. The Spanish had a reputation as Europe's foremost tourists — fond of pilgrimages to the Holy Land and visits to far-flung merchant centers like Bordeaux and London — but medieval travel was never completely safe. Villages were fifteen to twenty miles apart, the land in between considered the domain of the highwaymen and degenerates. In famine years travelers were even waylaid by hungry farmers and their families — people who enjoyed a diet of bread, sausage, wine, poultry, and ham in bountiful years but were forced to survive on bark, white clay, grass, and unsuspecting travelers when their crops failed. A victim's flesh was eaten raw.

Moving by day, sleeping at night in roadside inns for security, the Columbus brothers arrived in Granada without incident. It was mid-December, a few short weeks after their arrival in Cádiz. They trotted their steeds through the cobbled streets of the ancient town and then left the city behind, riding up the long, steep hill to the Alhambra.

Isabella and Ferdinand had palaces throughout Spain — Madrid, Valladolid, Seville, and Córdoba among them. They traveled from castle to castle by horseback throughout the year, administering to different parts of their kingdom. These constant court relocations not only allowed a broad number of their subjects to glimpse them, but it also enforced a cohesiveness on Spain, which had been sorely divided before their reign. Just as practically the movements prevented any one local populace from being stretched to the point of starvation by their presence; Spain's subsistence economy meant that no single community had enough food or livestock to continually provide year-round provisions for the courtiers, courtesans, soldiers, hangers-on, and official guests who constantly hovered about the royal court.

The sovereigns spent as much time as possible, however, at the Alhambra. Nothing matched the splendor of this strategic and aesthetic marvel. Narrow at its western and eastern tips, a half mile thick in the middle, the Alhambra perched atop a forested Sierra Nevada foothill named the Sabika like the prow of some great ship in dry dock, poised to set sail over the Spanish plains. Its walls were ten feet thick and hundreds of feet high in places. They were once ruby red — indeed Alhambra is a translation of *al-hamra,* "the red," in Arabic — but had faded over the centuries to the pale orange of a winter sunset.

The soothing patter of running water permeated the fabric of daily life within those magnificent walls. A multitude of gardens, cisterns, aqueducts, fountains, and streams flowed through and around the fortress, watering its gardens, orchards, laundries, lavatories, aviaries, zoos, and livestock. Those sounds were overlaid by hustle-bustle, for the Alhambra was a palatine city with its own military precinct and merchant district. Soldiers, shopkeepers, functionaries, members of the royal court, and dignitaries seeking an audience with the sovereigns jammed its cobbled streets, sun-drenched courtyards, and narrow alleys.

The sovereigns lived and ruled from a castle within the castle known as the Comares Palace. An architectural grace note to the centuries-old fortress, it was built at the decree of Muhammed V in 1370, in celebration of his conquest of the pivotal port at Algeciras. The Comares Palace was lavish, intricate, and reverential, an aesthetic homage to God and state. The throne room was to the rear, forcing visitors to navigate a series of ornate rooms and gardens before approaching the sovereigns. It was Arabic in design, festooned with intricate Islamic wood carvings offering praise to Allah. "Eternity is an attribute of Allah"; "Delight in good for surely it is Allah who insists"; "To Allah alone belongs grandeur, glory, eternity, empire and power" were repeated over and over, left in place despite the current staunch Catholic residents.

The throne room's mesmerizing beauty was undeniable. It was a square, with nine alcoves along the walls to allow light to filter in. The ceiling, meant to inspire thoughts of heaven, soared 140 feet above the maroon marble floor, with its tile mosaic inlay in the middle. From their thrones Isabella and Ferdinand could view a courtyard known as the Court of the Myrtles just beyond the white marble entryway and the calming visage of a long, rectangular reflecting pool. Here the sovereigns awaited the Columbus brothers.

Through the years of intrigue and power jostling, Isabella and Ferdinand had grown to love each other a great deal, despite their being total opposites. Where Isabella was generous, Ferdinand was tightfisted. Where she was direct, he was cunning. They complemented each other perfectly.

The Columbus situation troubled the sovereigns, but there had been so many serious crises during their reign that the Hispaniola problem was almost a nonissue. Indeed, one reason they didn't receive the explorer until December 17 was that another delicate matter took precedence. In mid-November they had signed a treaty with Louis XII of France (who had assumed the throne in 1498, when Charles VIII died after smacking his head on a door frame) that divided the kingdom of Naples between the two nations (the fact that war would be waged to capture Naples was itself a niggling detail). What mattered was that Naples was a bustling Mediterranean trading hub, a place of spices and silks and grand palaces. Santo Domingo was a backwater pauper's port by comparison. "The King of France complains that I have twice deceived him," Ferdinand said of the ever-paranoid Louis XII. "He lies, the fool; I have deceived him ten times, and more."

Louis XII had a right to be suspicious. By 1503 Ferdinand would break their Treaty of Granada (not to be confused with the 1492 Treaty of Granada between Spain and the Moors) and place Naples entirely under Spanish control. Such duplicitous behavior, however, wasn't reserved for Spain's enemies or even for matters of state. Isabella was vibrant and even flirtatious, especially with Columbus. It was obvious to anyone who looked closely that the two were deeply taken with each other. But Isabella's deep religious convictions precluded her from taking a lover. Ferdinand's did not.

Ferdinand and Isabella had appointed Bobadilla as their special messenger a full year before actually sending him on his way, hoping that Columbus could sort out his colonial woes on his own. But once da Gama returned from India and the news was trumpeted throughout Europe, their patience evaporated. Making matters worse, the Portuguese explorer Pedro Alvares Cabral landed on the fourth continent on April 22, 1500, in what would later be termed Brazil. Because Brazil lay within Portugal's sphere of influence, per the Treaty of Tordesillas, Spain's neighbor now controlled the expected passage to India and had a significant toehold in the New World. As all that was going on, the Admiral of the Ocean Sea was chasing Roldán's rebels through the jungles of Hispaniola, a waste of Columbus's considerable talents. He had ceased to be an explorer. Da Gama had surpassed him. Getting thrown in jail was a sharp reminder of how far he had strayed from his calling.

On December 17, 1500, at the Alhambra, Columbus marched past the Court of the Myrtles reflecting pool, through the marble entryway into the Salon des Barcas, and through the portal into the throne room. The strapping Bartolomé and bookish Diego walked one step behind. All three were clean shaven and wore resplendent new clothes of many bright colors, showing their lofty status in society (drab fabrics were for peasants). They were not the only Columbus men in attendance. Back in 1494, after Columbus had already made two voyages to the New World, he had had enough political clout to arrange for his six-year-old son, Fernando, to work alongside his fourteen-year-old brother, Diego, as pages for Juan, crown prince of

Spain. It was an auspicious assignment, the first of many that would make Fernando an eyewitness to some of his era's most pivotal events.

Prince Juan was sixteen, a young man beloved by his father and doted on by his mother. But Isabella was afraid her only male offspring had lived a life of "little sacrifice and little glory." She said he was too educated in "freedom and luxury" instead of timeless academic knowledge. She appointed the Italian classicist Pietro Martire as Juan's personal tutor. In addition to the chivalric arts of horseback riding and swordplay, the young prince was soon devoting himself to Latin, literature, the Flemish school of Renaissance painting, grammar, and mathematics. These were not mere liberal arts to Isabella. This was a pointed acknowledgment that Spain was on the verge of becoming the most powerful nation in Europe. It was important that Prince Juan rule with a comprehensive worldview. And it was just as vital that his royal court be on the same intellectual level. As pages Columbus's sons received the most well-rounded education a Spaniard could enjoy. Fernando became a voracious reader, a habit he carried with him throughout his life.

At just nineteen years old, Juan died (some in the Spanish court insisted it was due to nonstop lovemaking with his new bride, Princess Margaret, daughter of Maximilian, ruler of the Holy Roman Empire). Fernando was at his bedside as he slipped away. Isabella was devastated by grief. She and Ferdinand, dressed all in black, ordered forty days of mourning throughout Castile. She also summoned faithful pages Diego and Fernando Columbus to continue their service as royal pages but working directly for her. Being so close to the sovereigns, their educations took on a different tone, as they witnessed the delicate manipulation of power and politics that was a daily fact of court life. More personally, they heard the waning praise and increased scorn directed at their father. Some of that scorn was even aimed at them:

when bands of disenchanted colonists returned from Hispaniola and loitered in the Alhambra, wailing about their treatment at the hands of Columbus, Fernando and Diego were castigated as "mosquitoes of the man who found lands of vanity and deceit, which are the tomb of the Castilians."

Columbus was relieved when the sovereigns seemed happy to see him and beckoned to him warmly. Emboldened, he approached Ferdinand and kissed the king's hand. Then, head bowed, he reached for Isabella's. Some great emotion was released as he placed his lips to the back of her small hand — relief, perhaps; maybe affection.

Columbus had knelt before her so many times, petitioning, receiving orders, announcing great triumphs. She had known him a dozen years and had been the driving force behind his career. Appearing in disgrace before this embodiment of intellect, beauty, and piety was too much for Columbus. He began to cry. Tears soon became sobs, and Columbus collapsed to the floor, not caring that his brothers and the king looked on. Sons Diego and Fernando pressed silently against one wall and watched as their father cried, not pleading or begging for mercy, just overcome by all that had gone wrong.

And then a marvelous thing happened: Isabella cried too. "The Queen in particular consoled him," wrote one observer, "for in truth she more than the King ever favored and defended him, and so the Admiral trusted especially in her." Isabella reassured him that his imprisonment was not at the sovereigns' command and that it had offended them deeply. The guilty parties, Columbus was promised, would be punished.

Consoled, Columbus picked himself up off the floor. He told Ferdinand and Isabella at length of his deep loyalty. Then he petitioned for the return of his governorship of Hispaniola, all his rights and titles, and all his confiscated belongings and monies. This time the reception was mixed. It was understood that Columbus would never, under any circumstances, rule Hispaniola again. "They ordered his business promptly attended to," wrote Fernando. "They decided to send a governor to Hispaniola who should right the wrongs done to the Admiral and his brothers. Bobadilla should be commanded to make restitution to the Admiral's property; the Admiral would receive all that belonged to him according to the capitulations between him and the Sovereigns, and the rebels were to be tried and punished as their offenses demanded."

The Catholic sovereigns bade Columbus and his brothers a fond farewell. The Admiral left the throne room with a song in his heart, determined to stay near the royal court and await the next beckoning from Isabella and Ferdinand — which he hoped would come soon and send him on his way back out to sea.

In fact Columbus spent the next year waiting for the sovereigns to fire Bobadilla and restore himself as governor and viceroy of Hispaniola. Throughout, he lingered in Granada, researching a book about biblical prophecies and waiting for the grand moment when Isabella and Ferdinand once again summoned him to the throne room. The sovereigns, meanwhile, grew exasperated by Columbus's persistence. Through emissaries they suggested the explorer retire, promising him a castle in Andalusia and a pension. But Columbus brushed the entreaties aside, determined to return to Hispaniola in triumph to live out his days there as governor.

On September 3, 1501, Ferdinand and Isabella dealt Columbus's fantasy a crushing setback. Ferdinand had become alarmed by the Portuguese and English voyagers making their way to the New World. Anxious to consolidate Spanish holdings and annex more lands, his plan was to make Santo Domingo the hub of his colonial outpost and then build new cities on other islands. Clearly Columbus was not Ferdinand's ideal leader for such an enterprise.

Instead the sovereigns appointed a red-bearded monastic warrior named Don Nicolas de Ovando, knight commander de Lares, as governor and supreme justice of the islands and mainlands of the Indies. Through both his mother and father, the fifty-two-year-old Ovando had enjoyed a long connection with Isabella. He had also been one of the ten knights constantly at the side of the late Prince Juan, protecting him from harm.

With this assignment Bobadilla was finally being recalled. He had made the bad situation in Hispaniola even worse, enslaving the island's Indians, who were put to work in the gold mines or on farms. Women and young girls became concubines. Many of the colonists delighted in having their personal slaves carry them to and fro on a litter and fan them with palm leaves and feathers. Despite the fact that Bobadilla's reign yielded more gold for the sovereigns and that the settlers lived a pampered life due to slavery, Isabella was furious when she heard about the Indians' mistreatment. She ordered Ovando to proceed with all haste to the New World and send Bobadilla home to account for his behavior.

Two days after the sovereigns definitively stripped Hispaniola from Columbus, they took away the fourth continent, too. Royal permission was granted to Vicente Yanez Pinzón to colonize and govern the areas he had explored south of the Amazon. The sovereigns charged Pinzón with establishing an outpost to stop Portuguese incursion — truthfully, an incursion onto lands the Portuguese rightfully owned.

Feeling wary and betrayed, Columbus appeared before the sovereigns one last time, in October 1501. He begged them to promise to defend and protect his rights and privileges. When they agreed to take it under consideration, Columbus left Granada for Seville. He would never see his beloved Isabella again.

As Columbus languished in Granada, Rodrigo de Bastides, the most promising of the explorers out to unseat Columbus, was fast approaching the westward passage to the Orient. His original charter from the Crown had been to secure any treasures he could find, paying special attention to gold, silver, copper, lead, tin, quicksilver (mercury), pearls, and precious gems. He was also to keep a sharp lookout for serpents, monsters, spices, and drugs.

But previous explorers had picked the land clean and frightened the Indians into a state of perpetual hostility. Consequently, throughout late 1500 and 1501, Bastides sailed farther and farther west in search of riches. Finally shipworms began destroying the hulls of his ships. Taking on water at an alarming rate, Bastides left his search for wealth behind. He raced for Santo Domingo.

Bastides survived the Caribbean crossing but landed on Jamaica instead of Hispaniola. Recognizing his error, he refilled his water casks and firewood stores and set sail once more for Santo Domingo. Battered by storms and slowed to a crawl by opposing currents, Bastides barely made it. His ships sank almost as soon as he made land at the Indian village of Jaragua, on the island's western coast. Unfortunately Bastides had taken Indians as slaves during his explorations; chained in the hull, they went down with the ships.

Bastides split his surviving crew members into three groups before beginning the overland march to Santo Domingo. Each group was given a supply of the gold and pearls they had accumulated thus far, to use as barter for food and drink. This simple act would be his downfall. As soon as Bastides arrived safely in Santo Domingo, Governor

Bobadilla arrested him for illegal trade with the natives. Bastides and all his men were thrown in prison, destined to return to Spain for trial on the next available caravel.

In the midst of it all, the significance of Bastides's voyage was lost. He had sailed farther west than any explorer in history, leaving Paria behind and coasting along the narrow isthmus separating the Caribbean and the great sea Columbus had sought for so long. Voyage by voyage Spain was coming closer and closer to finding the westward passage.

CHAPTER TWELVE

Shipping Out

January–May 1502
Cádiz, Spain

The first two months of 1502 were heady times for the port of Cádiz. In January Alonso de Ojeda once again sailed for the New World, leading a fleet of four vessels out of the harbor. Despite the failure and discord of Ojeda's earlier voyage, Bishop Fonseca had praised him extensively to the sovereigns as the future of Spanish exploration. That endorsement, coupled with his penchant for boasting about his adventures, made Ojeda a new favorite of the court. He was in Granada at the same time as Columbus, which made for a study in contrasting career paths — the inscrutable and bumbling Ojeda on his way up, the brilliant but conflicted Columbus down and out. At a time when the Admiral of the Ocean Sea was having difficulty gaining an audience with the sovereigns, let alone being allowed to sail the very sea over which he reigned, Ojeda had become so popular that he was granted a twenty-square-mile estate on Hispaniola and named governor over the northern coast of Paria. On top of that, and just to remind Columbus who truly reigned over the New World, Bishop Fonseca saw to it that

Ojeda was also allowed to outfit a fleet and continue the westward exploration of Paria.

Columbus passed the time in Seville making detailed lists of stores and other equipment the new governor Nicolas de Ovando would need for the journey to the New World. The advice was ignored. When Ovando sailed from Cádiz on February 13, 1502, his fleet was the largest ever to embark on a journey across the Atlantic. It numbered thirty-five vessels in all, carrying twenty-five hundred soldiers, colonists, and sailors. Ovando had strict orders to build towns and forts, monopolize trade, and treat the Indians with the utmost courtesy and respect. Moors and Jews were forbidden to make the voyage, but twelve Franciscan friars sailed with Ovando. This trip also marked the first time African slaves, accompanying their Spanish owners, went to the New World.

A new age had dawned in the New World, an age firmly under the rule of men loyal to Spain. Columbus had been eclipsed.

But he would not let go so easily. Seven long years after the start of the second voyage, when Columbus had begun putting wealth before exploration, the heart of a discoverer beat inside him once again. He longed to lead one final expedition and undertook a meticulous study of each New World exploration, trying to pinpoint the exact location of the passage. After drawing a detailed map of his findings in order to get a better visual take on what had been accomplished, Columbus made an astounding discovery: the push westward had stopped (the lone expedition he didn't study was that of Bastides, who had continued the push westward but was still rotting in a Santo Domingo prison, unable to share his exploits). The new wave of explorers had been so intent on sailing south and north that nobody had sailed west of islands Columbus had discovered almost a decade earlier. The oceans between Cuba and Paria were still unknown. And there, Columbus was convinced, lay the passage to India.

Ever the dreamer, Columbus conceived the most outrageous plan of his career: a voyage around the world. He would discover the passage to India and then sail to Arabia Felix (the Arabian Peninsula), returning to Spain via the southern tip of Africa. Not only had such a voyage never been undertaken, no one had even dared imagine such a thing. Further, he considered a stopover in the Muslim-held city of Jerusalem to wage a holy war that would return it to Christian hands.

On February 26, writing the sovereigns from the Las Cuevas monastery in Seville, Columbus requested the men, ships, and permission to lead a fourth voyage of discovery. Ferdinand and Isabella, worn down by his constant pleas for recognition, immediately consented. Columbus had become a tiresome pest, a well-intentioned gadfly with too much time on his hands. His constant battles to regain the monies and property confiscated by Bobadilla and his letters offering advice on administering Hispaniola and on New World navigation all combined to make Columbus persona non grata in the royal court. "I am not now much sought after," Columbus had admitted in a letter to a friend in May 1501.

The sovereigns' letter authorizing a fourth voyage was written on March 14. In it they reiterated their displeasure about Columbus's imprisonment, assured him that his claims in the New World would be passed on to his heirs, and told him to sail as quickly as possible. "We therefore pray you not to delay your departure," they implored. The sovereigns granted Columbus ten thousand pesos to cover all costs and as many cannons and guns as he might need. In return Columbus was to search for spices, pearls, silver, and gems. Capturing slaves was forbidden. It was common knowledge that Columbus had been ill frequently since his return from Hispaniola. The fatalistic tone of the sovereigns' farewell letter makes it clear they didn't expect the Admiral to return. Just in case he had any ideas about making trouble on this finale, they expressly forbade him from going to Hispaniola.

The sovereigns no longer believed Columbus was capable of finding a path to the Indies and mentioned nothing of it in their orders. However, just in case, they presented him with a letter addressed to the Portuguese explorer Vasco da Gama, should the two meet in India. "If you meet," the sovereigns instructed Columbus of da Gama, "you are to treat each other as friends."

In actuality Columbus was far more likely to link up with Alonso de Ojeda. If both explorers followed the courses they had proposed, their paths would converge.

Columbus channeled all his energies into preparation, becoming a fixture on the bustling riverside docks of Seville, while he quickly assembled a fleet of four ships. Since the second voyage he had wanted to design and build a new sort of vessel specially engineered for exploration. But time did not allow for that now. Instead he handpicked ships that previous experience told him were best for discovery. He favored vessels small enough for quick maneuverability and a light draft but big enough to hold the stores he would need for sailing around the world. In Columbus's mind this meant a vessel very much like the *Niña,* which he sailed on his first and second voyages and which served as a supply vessel on the third. "If she had not been very staunch and well found," Columbus reflected after she rode out a horrific storm in February 1492, "I should have been afraid of being lost." The *Niña* had three masts (a square-rigged mainmast and foremast and a lateen-rigged mizzenmast; for the third voyage a lateen-rigged countermizzen was stepped just aft the mizzen), and she drew just six feet of water. Her armament consisted of carriage-mounted lombard cannons roped to the decks and breech-loading swivel guns known as falconets for repelling boarders. She was seventy feet long and twenty-three feet wide, with a tonnage of sixty and a hold nine feet deep amidships.

The *Niña,* however, was too old to make the fourth voyage. Columbus would have to make do with ships constructed in her image.

The seventy-ton *La Capitana,* largest of the four ships Columbus selected for the fourth voyage, was one such vessel. It would serve as his flagship. In addition to Columbus and his illegitimate son Fernando, who had forsaken the comforts of the royal court to make his first voyage alongside his father, she carried a crew of forty-four. Half of that complement were boys between the ages of twelve and eighteen. The rest were veteran hands charged with teaching the "grommets," as the younger men were called, the ropes.

The *Santiago* was smaller than *La Capitana* and was a divisive force even before the fleet left Spain. Her captain was Francisco de Porras, a middling mariner who owed his position to his sister's love affair with the treasurer of Castile, the man controlling the royal purse strings. Since every sailor on the fourth voyage except those in the Columbus family was technically on the sovereigns' payroll, the treasurer — and by proxy, the treasurer's mistress — wielded considerable clout. Not only was Francisco de Porras given charge of a ship he was unfit to command, but his brother Diego sailed at his side as chief auditor of the fleet.

Columbus was not one to be trumped. He installed his beloved brother Bartolomé on board the *Santiago* as a way of quietly asserting his authority. Tall and rugged, with broad shoulders, a narrow waist, and a dry wit that was often misconstrued as antagonistic, Bartolomé was almost his big brother's equal as a sailor. He was a brave man, a daring and demanding leader of men, and a natural linguist. And there was no questioning his perseverance, that one trait most vital to an explorer: when seeking funding for Columbus's first voyage, Bartolomé had pursued French financing for so long that he was still in Paris when he received the astounding news that his brother had sailed across the ocean and found a new world. King Charles VIII personally passed along word of the New World's discovery and bestowed a congratulatory purse of one hundred crowns in traveling expenses. Bartolomé then raced for Spain, but the news had traveled so slowly that when Bartolomé boarded the *Niña* at the voyage's conclusion to congratulate his brother, it was at the end of the second voyage, not the first.

Columbus was quite certain the Porras brothers were unhappy about sharing a vessel with Bartolomé, who was sure to repeat their words of intrigue and criticism, but having had the Porrases foisted upon him, Columbus had little interest in their happiness. What mattered was the integrity of the fleet, especially when sailing through storms or uncharted waters. Ironically it was a personnel decision that would save the Porrases' lives, though they would display their thanks in a most unchivalrous fashion.

The four-masted *El Gallego* measured sixty tons (tonnage was not a matter of weight but of the number of wine casks — *tuns,* measuring one meter by a meter and a half — a ship could carry). Her master and owner was Juan Quintero, boatswain of the *Pinta* on Columbus's first voyage.

La Vizcaino rounded out the small armada. At fifty tons she was the smallest and was commanded by a young Genovese named Bartolomeo Fieschi, whose family had known the Columbuses long before Christopher had been born.

If the seamen of Seville had any issues with two of the four vessels being helmed by Genovese, particularly in light of all the bad blood directed at foreigners, it had no effect on recruitment, nor did Columbus's problems with Fonseca and Bobadilla. The explorer was still revered along the waterfront as being the consummate navigator of his age, and the call for hands was quickly answered. Sea chests, the sailors' personal slices of Spain (containing everything from a change of clothes to weapons and prayer books), were brought on board and stowed in the hold.

All told, the fourth voyage's crew list numbered 140, among them coopers, caulkers, a chaplain, trumpeters, gunners, ship's boys, able seamen, boatswains, pilots, and 14 "gentleman volunteers" on a joyride to the New World. Many of the men had sailed with Columbus before, and it was clear they were putting to sea in the best-equipped vessels of exploration Columbus had ever commanded.

The fleet bobbed at anchor in the Guadalquivir River, waiting for the signal to embark. On April 3, 1502, just three short weeks after the sovereigns approved his expedition, Columbus ordered the fleet to sail downriver to Puebla Vieja for final work on the hulls. Each vessel was careened on the beach, cleaned of barnacles and algae, caulked, and then slathered with black pitch. Thus watertight, they were refloated and pushed south down the river to Sanlúcar de Barrameda and finally to Cádiz, where the river emptied into the Atlantic. It was there, from the same docks onto which he had hobbled ashore in chains, that Columbus ordered the fleet to set sail "in the name of the Holy Trinity" on May 9, 1502.

CHAPTER THIRTEEN

The Crossing

Summer 1502
The Atlantic

The unlikely series of adventures that would define the fourth voyage began the instant Columbus set sail. He had received word that a Portuguese citadel on the Moroccan coast was under siege by the Moors. Columbus ordered that his ships alter course and rescue the beleaguered Portuguese. "We sailed," wrote thirteen-year-old Fernando, "to succor the Portuguese; they were said to be in dire straits." Despite the rivalry between Portugal and Spain, the relationship between the two neighbors was often sympathetic and sometimes even symbiotic. In a deft diplomatic move, King Ferdinand had brought the two nations closer by arranging for Doña Maria, youngest daughter of the Spanish sovereigns, to marry Manuel I, king of Portugal. Columbus, thanks to his late wife and his many years residing in Lisbon, had a strong emotional connection to Portugal. To sail for the Indies without coming to the aid of the Portuguese would have been unthinkable.

Columbus's personal rescue plan, however, was ludicrous. The puny, breech-loading lombards measured fewer than nine feet in length and shot a ball just three inches wide — hardly large enough to wipe out an army. And the swivel guns — the *versos normales* — mounted on the ships' rails were even less impressive. At just six feet long, with a bore diameter of less than two inches, the *versos* guns shot scraps of metal instead of bullets, making accurate marksmanship impossible. They had neither the range nor the heft to drive away a conquering army. And if Columbus were to send his men ashore armed with only the sailor's ubiquitous knife, it would be a slaughter. The Moors were armed not just with cannons but also with longbows, crossbows, handguns, and darts. They had been trying to drive the Portuguese out of Arzila, a small town just south of Tangiers, since 1471 and were battle hardened. Columbus's crew carried personal weapons ranging from knives to crossbows, but more than half of his men were under the age of thirteen and had never drawn blood. Those the Moors didn't slaughter and disembowel would be enslaved.

Still, disregarding the possibility that Moorish cannons could sink one or all of his ships, Columbus sped to Arzila. Sailing into a powerful, southwesterly headwind, the fleet pushed south past the Pillars of Hercules, from Gibraltar, on the European side, to Mt. Acha, in Africa. "Against it, I sailed to rescue," he wrote of the stiff blow. But by the time Columbus arrived in Arzila, the battle was over. "When we arrived," wrote Fernando, who had begun keeping a journal of the voyage, "the Moors had already raised the siege. The Admiral sent ashore his brother the Adelantado Don Bartolomé Columbus and myself, together with the ship captains, to call on the captain of Arzila, who had been wounded by the Moors in an assault."

The wounded Portuguese commander repaid Columbus's kindness with one of his own. Several cousins of Columbus's late wife happened to be visiting the castle. Two of them had even sailed with Columbus previously, although they had become something of a thorn in Columbus's side.

They came aboard *La Capitana* for a brief and unlikely family reunion.

Once his visitors rowed back to shore, Columbus ordered the fleet to set sail for the Canary Islands, some sixty miles off the northwest African coast. There he hoped to take on fresh water and firewood for the journey across the Atlantic. Named for wild dogs that once roamed the islands (from the Latin *canis*) and destined to give a small yellow native bird a name of that derivation, the Canaries also offered Columbus and his men a slice of paradise before the deprivation of a long voyage. The jumble of physical features made for stunning beauty: vast beaches, sand dunes, snow-covered peaks, deserts, and wondrous craters. Papayas, bananas, mangos, and avocados grew wild in the tropical climate.

The fleet anchored near Las Palmas on May 20, but water and wood were scarce. Columbus pushed along the coast to the long, sandy beach of Maspalomas, where his men cut wood and filled their water casks in a small, freshwater lake. All hands were ordered to bathe and to wash their clothing — long-sleeved shirts, the baggy *zaraguelles* pants, and the *sayuelo* pullover, almost all made of wool. It would be their last chance for personal hygiene until the New World.

On the night of May 25, 1502, Columbus was gripped by the impulse to set sail. He ordered anchors weighed and set a southwest course. The seas were rough. *La Capitana, La Vizcaino, El Gallego,* and *Santiago* squared their sails. Lit by starlight, they were thrust toward the New World by a cool blast of wind.

It was a euphoric moment, for the meat of the ocean crossing was finally under way. That euphoria might have been tempered if the 140 on board had known that all of the ships and a fourth of the men would never return to Spain.

Three weeks later the fleet reached the New World. It was Columbus's fastest crossing ever and came thanks to powerful trade winds blowing from astern. Arriving on the island of Matininio, a name changed to Martinique by the French two centuries later (Empress Josephine, Napoléon's first wife, would be born there), Columbus immediately sent the men ashore to wash their bodies and clothes — the stench of a shipload of wool-clad men who had gone three weeks without a bath being colossal. The lush, volcanic island was just ten miles wide and forty miles long, but its abundance of protected natural harbors and food made it an ideal stopover. Firewood was chopped and water casks filled. For three lazy days the crew reveled in dry land and the abundance of personal space after the caravels' claustrophobic confines. Then it was back to sea.

The crossing had Columbus feeling like his old defiant self again. And being back in the Indies, with its familiar sights and smells, was a homecoming of sorts. Once again he was thousands of miles away from the sovereigns' rule, in a place where he felt very much like the king — so much so that Columbus ignored their specific order and set a course for the one place he was forbidden to land: Hispaniola. His excuse was that he had letters to mail home to Spain and that he hoped to find a replacement vessel for the useless *Santiago,* which was not only slow but had almost sunk several times. "Thence we went away to Santo Domingo," Fernando wrote. "The Admiral's intention had been to reconnoiter the coast of Paria and cruise down it until he came to the strait. . . . But because of that poor ship he had to go to Santo Domingo to trade her for a better."

The fleet coasted north through the Leeward Islands, a chain of mostly dry specks of land extending from Puerto Rico down to the verdant Windward Islands. Columbus had discovered the Leewards on his second voyage and knew to follow the chain as it curled northwest, ultimately ending up at Santo Domingo. The sailing was uneventful, even idyllic. The men gaped at the dolphins and seals frolicking alongside the ships. In the hot, humid summer weather, the Caribbean's vibrant, blue waters were smooth to the point of appearing slick. Each day the only clouds in the sky were the wispy, fragile cirrus ones floating high in the stratosphere. Each night the sunset was blood red, like the core of a raging fire. The men felt as if they were sailing through Paradise.

But Columbus was deeply troubled. To his trained eye the oily seas, cirrus clouds, and preponderance of marine life were signs of an approaching storm. He didn't have the benefit of a barometer (an invention still a century away), but his rheumatic joints ached, which told him the air pressure was doing odd things. The air felt funny, almost heavy, as if it weighed him down. And the tides weren't following their usual, predictable patterns. In his forty years at sea, he had felt weather like this just twice. The first time was in August 1494. The second was a year later. Both times it preceded storms greater and more destructive than any others he had witnessed in his lifetime at sea. Not even Columbus realized that he had discovered — or been discovered by, as the case may have been — the phenomenon that would later be known as the hurricane.

Columbus sped for Hispaniola. He needed shelter from the storm for his ships and men and to warn all other ships to stay in port. With the massive fleet that had carried Ovando and the new colonists to Hispaniola due to return soon to Spain, such a warning could save hundreds of lives. Columbus was all too aware that he would be unwelcome. Sailing up the Ozama and making outlandish claims about the great tragedy lurking over the horizon wasn't going to change that. If anything, it would make him only more unpopular. Weather forecasting was the domain of soothsayers and witches, and those colonists who had expressed doubts about the sincerity of Columbus's faith would have all the more reason to label him a heretic. But Columbus didn't care. Hispaniola was rightfully his. Although cast out in chains, mocked in public, and shipped home to Spain in disgrace, Columbus was nevertheless bent on saving the very people who had cheered at his shame.

The temperatures were stifling as Columbus approached Santo Domingo on June 29. He had arrived just in time: there, still in harbor, was the homebound fleet. Numbering twenty-eight ships in all, it choked the mouth of the Ozama. The ships' thick masts swayed side to side, and so many vessels were crowded into such a narrow space that their yards nearly touched. A month's supply of fresh water, wine, and food was being stowed in the holds. None of the seamen seemed to have any inkling that a storm was approaching as they worked diligently to prepare the fleet so it might sail for Spain the following morning.

Because the sovereigns had forbidden Columbus to land on Hispaniola, he ordered his vessels to come to just outside the mouth of the Ozama, within an easy row of the harbor's mouth and plainly visible to the hundreds of sailors scurrying about the docks. He waited patiently for officials to paddle out and greet him or at least to ask his business. Yet it was as if Columbus's vessels were invisible. "The Knight Commander," Fernando recorded, "took no notice of our unexpected arrival."

The knight commander in question was not Bobadilla, but Nicolas de Ovando. Columbus's mirror image in age, hair color, headstrong personality, and devotion to the queen, Ovando was a forceful man of vision who let nothing stand between him and his ambitions. The Admiral was the last man Ovando wanted to see prowling the streets of Santo Domingo.

The Admiral sent Captain Pedro de Terreros of *El Gallego,* a loyal confidant who had sailed on all four voyages, ashore with a written explanation of his fleet's presence. The letter was addressed directly to Ovando and expressed Columbus's desire to replace one of his ships and also told of his expectations of a great storm. "The Admiral also advised [the governor] not to permit the homebound fleet to set sail for eight days because of the great danger," Fernando wrote.

On board *La Capitana,* Columbus waited with growing impatience. He was being squeezed by Ovando on one side and the storm on the other, and his safe-departure window was narrowing with each passing minute. The escalating winds and high tides told him the storm's center was approaching quickly. It was imperative that he find safe anchorage immediately. The best place, obviously, was Santo Domingo. If Ovando forbade that, then Columbus would have to act quickly, sailing far and fast from the storm if he were to save his ships.

But the disgusted Ovando considered Columbus's presence an act of grave impertinence. Just two months into the job when Columbus sailed over the horizon, Ovando was in no mood to receive Terreros, despite the skipper's pleadings that the contents of Columbus's letter were a matter of life and death. Ovando made Terreros wait an entire night ashore before summoning him to deliver the letter. The morning air was sticky and blustery. The wind blew in from the ocean, which was unusual for so early in the day. In the harbor, despite growing indications of a storm, the fleet was weighing anchor.

Ovando was of noble birth and treated the gruff Terreros like a second-class citizen. He accepted Columbus's letter with disdain. A huddle of preening sycophants gathered around as Ovando read Columbus's request and warning aloud. Taking their cue from Ovando, the listeners laughed derisively, scorning Columbus as nothing but a "prophet and soothsayer." As Columbus's emissary, a brooding Terreros endured the abuse but struggled to keep his growing rage in check.

After Ovando delivered his verdict, a furious Terreros rushed down to the waterfront and rowed quickly back to *El Gallego*. There he signaled the news to Columbus: the answer was no; the warnings had fallen on deaf ears. Columbus was denied permission to enter the harbor, and the fleet would not delay its departure. It was a knee-jerk decision based on the irrational fear that Columbus had come to reclaim Hispaniola, and the Admiral knew it. But that was now irrelevant. There was no time, or point, in arguing it further.

As the Spanish fleet set sail for home, pouring out of the harbor under a bright orange sky and tacking east into the wind, Columbus fled in the opposite direction. There was no time to waste. He left so quickly that *El Gallego*'s crew didn't even have time to bring the small boat Terreros had rowed ashore back on board and were forced to tow it behind the ship as they chased after Columbus.

Luckily the wind and Caribbean current were in Columbus's favor. He stayed close to shore, searching for a natural port or protected cove where he might shelter from the storm. If he failed to find refuge, the odds were high that he and his men would die. Ovando's apathy toward the fate of Columbus and his men, which Columbus perceived as a passive act of betrayal, grieved him more than any other. "In a time of mortal danger he was being denied refuge in the land that he had given to Spain for its honor and exaltation," observed Fernando, who knew Ovando's petulant manner well from their time in the royal court.

The mood aboard all four vessels was unmitigated gloom — not because of the impending danger, which many of Columbus's young sailors still didn't believe was real, but because the crews were unable to enjoy the fruits of the city after a month at sea. Most had never been to the New World before. Santo Domingo would have been their first taste of what life was like in this mysterious corner of the globe. They could look out from the decks and see the city on the hill, with its women and warm beds, as it receded into the distance. The sailors were simple men, uneducated and poor. Their lives were defined by periods of extreme hardship punctuated ever so briefly by revelry. They were superstitious and simple and had no interest in the politics of Hispaniola. The only thing in the world they wanted was to go ashore and enjoy life for a brief interval.

Until Santo Domingo the men had no cause to dislike Columbus. Indeed they were awestruck at being a part of the great man's crew. But being denied even the simplest of creature comforts after the deprivation of life at sea gnawed at them. As the storm gathered, the seeds of mutiny were sown. "This caused much grief and chagrin to the ships' crews, who on account of being with the Admiral were denied the hospitality that should be accorded foreigners, and all the more to men of the same nation," recorded Fernando.

Columbus studied the shoreline with a keen eye. Based on the hurricanes he had witnessed before, Columbus knew the combined force of wind and water would be capable of reducing a wooden caravel to splinters within moments. What he needed was an anchorage where the coast was not rocky or exposed to waves and gale.

He sailed past the broad mouth of a muddy jungle river known as the Rio Jaina. Under normal circumstances its delta would have been a fine sanctuary, but if the storm proved too strong, his ships would easily be run aground — perhaps never to be floated loose. Finally, forty-five miles west of Santo Domingo, Columbus rounded the cape at Las Calderas and entered broad, horseshoe-shaped Ocoa Bay.

The wind was blowing down from the north. He ordered the ships close to land for protection. His vessels each had seven anchors: four in the bow, a spare storm anchor stored in the hold, and two grapnels used while moving about a harbor. The anchors were all made of wood and metal, and the largest of them — the bowers — weighed a thousand pounds each. Knowing that he needed as much purchase as the sandy ocean bottom would allow, Columbus ordered each vessel to drop all its anchors.

Sails were struck. Fires were snuffed. As the rain and wind increased, the crews found it impossible to remain on deck. They went below through one of the two centerline hatches into the smelly confines of the hold, sharing space with stores and wine casks and rats. The next twenty-four hours would be unforgettable for the forty-man groups down there, bucking and swaying along with the storm-tossed ship. Both hatches had covers, but it was inevitable that waves washing over the decks would slosh through the cracks and drizzle onto the men. The more senior men made themselves comfortable atop the spare sails, while the rest of the crew made do on the hard, wooden casks. Either way, sleep and peace of mind would be only fantasies. Personal space would be nonexistent. Food would be limited to a slice of cheese or a sip of wine, as there was no way to cook or to open a cask of dry food such as hardtack without spilling or drenching the contents. And with every odd-sounding hull creak, they would glance at the ship's caulker or carpenter for signs of concern.

Columbus, meanwhile, was on deck, focusing his attention on keeping his fleet together. The daytime sky became a bleeding red that faded into total blackness with the onset of night. Counterclockwise winds in excess of one hundred miles per hour blew spume and mist at his face like a thousand bee stings when he stepped outside. Rain fell in fat drops that sounded like hail as it struck the decks.

Columbus hunkered in his cabin with Fernando. It was the smallest of rooms, crammed with a table, washstand, bunk, desk, and seaman's chest full of personal belongings. In addition, Columbus crowded in his crucifix and statues of the Virgin Mary, as well as shield, sword, armor, and the flags of Castile and León (which he brandished when going ashore to claim a new land for Ferdinand and Isabella). Nautical charts decorated the walls. Father and son, after a lifetime apart, were getting to know each other very, very well.

Meanwhile *La Capitana* rode up and down with the swells, her anchors keeping her safe and somewhat stable. It was only the illusion of safety, to be sure, but it was better than floating wherever the current and winds might take them.

In the dead of night that came to pass, *El Gallego, La Vizcaino,* and the *Santiago* were ripped from their anchorages and thrust out to sea by the monstrous wind, now blowing from the north. "The storm was terrible," Columbus wrote, "and on that night my fleet was broken up. Everyone lost hope and was quite certain that all the rest were drowned."

Braced in his cabin aboard *La Capitana,* Columbus prayed for deliverance, fearing the worst about Bartolomé. He raged against Ovando with the ferocity he had once saved for Bobadilla, questioning the moral fiber of a man who would damn 140 others to spend a night at sea in a hurricane. "We were forbidden the land and the harbors that I, by God's will and sweating blood, had won for Spain," Columbus railed, comparing himself to Job. The comparison was dramatic, but apt; Columbus's litany of woes was taking on a distinctly biblical feel. But his horrendous night in Ocoa Bay was pampered luxury compared to what the Spanish fleet was enduring.

The storm, as Caribbean hurricanes are wont to do, was born off Africa near the Cape Verde Islands and had tracked west for thousands of miles across the Atlantic. After making landfall on the Leeward Islands, it had begun the lazy northward turn that would take it over the North American landmass. But first it would have to cross the Mona Passage and once again make landfall on Hispaniola.

The Spanish fleet was under the command of Antonio de Torres, yet another captain who had sailed under Columbus. In Torres's case, he had served as master on Columbus's flagship the *Mariagalante* during the second voyage. He had made one other voyage to the Indies when he delivered supplies to La Isabela in 1494. But he had made a disastrous mistake on that return voyage, opting to lead his four-caravel fleet south instead of northeast toward the westerly winds. In the holds of those ships were five hundred Taino Indians being sent back to Spain to be sold as slaves. Almost all of them died in that sweltering hellhole when Torres's southerly course saw the fleet becalmed. Torres had learned well the importance of turning northeast after reaching the tip of Hispaniola; it was the way home.

Now, when Torres and the fleet raced away from Santo Domingo, they encountered winds swirling from the north, west, and southwest. The fleet was not sailing together, and soon the ships were strung out in a line almost twenty miles long, the fastest and most prominent vessels out front, racing for Spain with their cargo of dignitaries and treasure; the slower, less important tubs dawdled in their wake. At the tip of Hispaniola, the faster ships duly made the crucial northeast turn into the Mona Passage. But experience in this case offered terrible lessons: turning northeast sent the boats directly into the approaching hurricane's path.

The faster vessels were in the heart of the Mona Passage when the full measure of the nameless hurricane struck. The roiling seas no longer ebbed and flowed in long, greasy swells but lifted straight from the depths into jagged, whitecapped peaks and troughs. The wind screamed like an armada of banshees. The rain made a staccato drumbeat on the ship's planks, the thick drops falling at a speed of twenty miles per hour, bruising any man fool enough to venture on deck.

The sea swallowed some vessels outright. Others made for shore, only to be driven into coastal rocks by the swirling cyclonic wind. More than five hundred sailors and passengers drowned, among them Torres, Bobadilla, Roldán, an Indian chief captured in battle, and many of the rebels whose uprising led to Columbus's ouster. A king's ransom of gold from Hispaniola's mines also settled to the bottom, never to be seen again — including one legendary nugget purportedly weighing thirty-five pounds.

Only four of the twenty-eight ships survived. They were the fleet's slowest — and luckiest — vessels. Lagging far behind, they hadn't made the Mona Passage when the storm hit. Instead this handful of caravels was navigating the shallow channel between Hispaniola's coast and a small island twenty miles offshore named Saona. They wisely chose to hunker down in the sandy lagoons and mangrove swamps on the lee side of Saona rather than search for a harbor on Hispaniola, whose eastern shoreline is lined with steep cliffs in places. Throughout the terrifying night, their compatriots either dead or dying, the sailors aboard these four wretched ships rode out the storm.

Luckily for Columbus, one of these was the caravel *Aguja*.

As part of Columbus's postarrest settlement, Ferdinand and Isabella had allowed him to appoint an accountant who would travel to Santo Domingo. There he would tally Columbus's share of the gold due him from Hispaniola's mines. Columbus chose Alonso Sanchez de Carvajal, a trusted friend from Baeza who had sailed on the second voyage and was a former employee of Isabella's. It was a savvy choice. Carvajal had professional experience as both a judge and a sea captain and possessed an analytical mind and strong backbone. Traveling to Santo Domingo late in 1501, he defied the anti-Columbus fervor of the Bobadilla administration to ensure the explorer received every peso that was owed. The final tally came to a healthy 240,000 maravedis, promising that Columbus would be wealthy for the rest of his days — providing he managed to return safely from the fourth voyage.

Ovando had personally designated the *Aguja* as the vessel to carry Carvajal and Columbus's wealth, thinking it the most pitiful ship in the fleet. Of the four vessels surviving the hurricane, three limped back to Santo Domingo "in a tattered and pitiful state" for repairs. Among those was a ship carrying explorer Rodrigo de Bastides and his navigator, Juan de la Cosa, just released from a Santo Domingo prison. Only one caravel was seaworthy enough to continue the passage home to Spain. That vessel was the *Aguja*.

The coincidence did not go unnoticed. Columbus's enemies swore he used mystical powers to cause the storm and extract revenge on Bobadilla and then used those same powers to ensure that his gold remained safe. Fernando chose to cast the tragedy in a spiritual light: "The fleet carried the Knight Commander Bobadilla, who had made prisoner the Admiral and his brothers, Francisco Roldán, and all the other rebels who had done the Admiral so much hurt. God was pleased to close the eyes and minds of all those men so that they did not heed the Admiral's good advice. I am certain this was Divine Providence, for had they arrived in Castile, they would never have been punished as their crimes deserved."

Not all the dead were Columbus's enemies. Paria explorer Peralonso Niño of Moguer, recently released from prison and whose family staunchly supported Columbus, had sailed to the New World once again as chief pilot of the vessel carrying Ovando to Hispaniola. For the return

Niño had signed on with his old friend Torres, also serving him as chief pilot. He too was lost to the waters.

Before the storm, as his ships dropped anchor and steeled for whatever lay ahead, Columbus had anticipated that his group might get separated. If that should happen, he told the other three captains, the fleet would regroup in Ocoa Bay, at a harbor called Azua he had seen on the third voyage. When the storm had ended, he sailed there and waited. Three days passed before he saw the first square, white patch of sail bobbing on the horizon. By the end of Sunday, July 3, all four vessels were together again. Most of their provisions had been destroyed, but no lives were lost. "The ships, which the Lord had taken from me, leaving me alone," Columbus wrote after the storm, "the Lord sent them back when it pleased Him."

Columbus reveled in the stories of bravery that sprung from that epic night, especially how Bartolomé, headstrong as ever, had taken control of the *Santiago*. Its captain, Francisco de Porras, had panicked when the *Santiago* was ripped from its anchor and was swept toward a reef. Bartolomé took the helm and steered her out to sea — a risky plan, but one that had worked. "The unseaworthy vessel had put out to sea for safety," Columbus wrote. "My brother was in the unseaworthy vessel and he (after God) was her salvation."

There were other stories, too. One was about how Captain Terreros, aboard *El Gallego,* was so consumed with the safety of his men that he forgot all about the ship's boat he'd towed since Santo Domingo. The boat was ripped away, never to be seen again. Another told about the shredding wind and the waves that stretched up like foam-flecked mountains and into canyon-like troughs so deep a ship could be swallowed whole.

Columbus's undamaged fleet was ready to set sail immediately — even the *Santiago,* which Columbus had once been so eager to jettison. But Columbus knew the men needed a break. The journey from Spain had been long. The disappointment of being denied Santo Domingo was still a bitter memory, even as surviving the hurricane left the crew awash in giddy euphoria. Whatever their thoughts about him beforehand, the crew all knew it was Columbus's great seamanship that had saved them. Knowing that — and knowing that once he set sail again it was into the unknown, where it might be a very long time between landfalls — Columbus set aside several days for rest and relaxation. "The Admiral permitted his men to rest from the ordeal of the storm," Fernando remembered with wonder. "And since fishing is one of the pleasures offered by the sea in such times of idleness, I shall describe two remarkable kinds of fish among the many they caught. The first was a ray as large as a medium-sized bed, which the men on the *Vizcaino* stabbed with a harping iron while it slept on the surface, and held fast so it could not escape. And being tied to the boat by a long thick rope, it drew the boat through the harbor as swiftly as an arrow. The men aboard the ship, not knowing what went on, were astounded to see the boat running about without oars. Eventually the fish died and was hauled aboard by tackling gear used for raising heavy objects. The second fish was caught by another means: the Indians call it a manatee, and it is not known in Europe. It is as big as a calf and resembles one in taste and color, but it is better tasting and fatter; and those who believe that all matters of land animals live in the sea argue the manatee is not a fish but a calf, since it does not look like a fish and feeds only on the grass it finds along the shore."

As Columbus and his men enjoyed their idyll, relaxing under the tropical sun and keeping a wary eye out for the approach of another storm, a somber mood prevailed in Santo Domingo. Ovando had no way of knowing the fleet's fate, but if descriptions of the storm brought by the three vessels returning to port were any indication, things looked bleak.

The fate of those ships and men, however, was not the most immediate of Ovando's worries. The hurricane had completely leveled Santo Domingo. Every last wood and thatch house had been literally blown away, as were Columbus's jail cell and the waterfront gallows. Ovando, who had survived the carnage unscathed, was faced with the daunting task of rebuilding a city from scratch.

The new Santo Domingo would be a city of Ovando's design. To escape the colonies of biting ants that had long infuriated the city's residents, he moved the new Santo Domingo across to the hillier left bank of the Ozama, laid out around a cathedral and town plaza, in a regimented quadrilateral pattern that would become the archetype of Spanish colonies throughout the Americas for centuries to come. Although the city's name remained the same, Columbus's thumbprint was no longer anywhere to be found. Just like his La Navidad and La Isabela, the Santo Domingo he had conceived and built was gone, swept away by the same Atlantic winds that had brought him to the New World in the first place.

It didn't take the storm to end Columbus's emotional connection to Santo Domingo. Ovando's dismissal was proof that Hispaniola would never again be his. An idea took root soon after: Columbus decided he would start a new colony in some new, undiscovered land. It would be an even better place than Santo Domingo, abundant in gold and self-sustaining natural resources. All he had to do was find this magical place. Although, as the pessimistic members of his crew were fond of snidely noting, what good was looking for new lands if Ovando would be given control of them anyway?

Adventures of a Perilous and Swashbuckling Nature

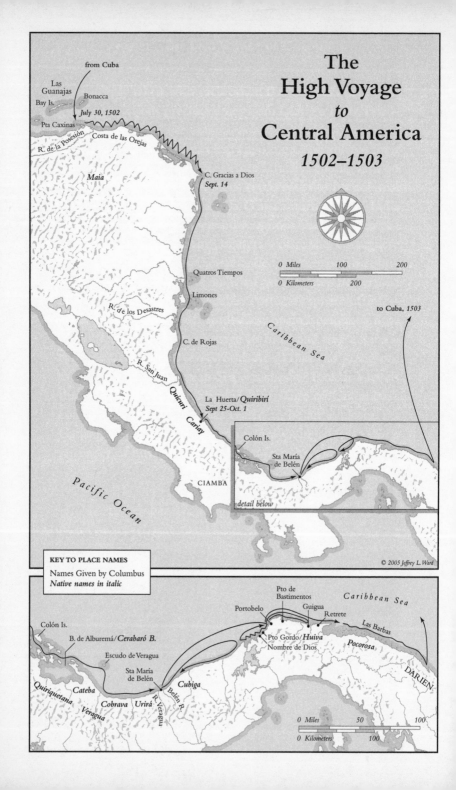

The
High Voyage
to
Central America
1502–1503

from Cuba

Las
Guanajas
Bay Is.

Bonacca

July 30, 1502

Pta Caxinas

R. de la Posesión

Costa de las Orejas

Maia

C. Gracias a Dios
Sept. 14

Quatros Tiempos

Limones

R. de los Desastres

C. de Rojas

R. San Juan

Quicuri

Cariay

La Huerta / *Quiribirí*
Sept 25–Oct. 1

Colón Is.

Sta María
de Belén

Caribbean Sea

to Cuba, *1503*

Pacific Ocean

CIAMBA

detail below

0 Miles 100 200

0 Kilometers 200

© 2005 Jeffrey L. Ward

KEY TO PLACE NAMES

Names Given by Columbus
Native names in italic

Colón Is.

B. de Alburemá / *Cerabaró B.*

Escudo de Veragua

Sta María
de Belén

Cubiga

Quiriquetana

Cateba

Cobrava

Urirá

R. Belén

Belén R.

Pto de
Bastimentos

Portobelo

Guigua

Retrete

Pto Gordo / *Huiva*

Nombre de Dios

Las Barbas

Pocorosa

DARIEN

Caribbean Sea

Veragua

R. Veragua

0 Miles 50 100

0 Kilometers 100

CHAPTER FOURTEEN

The Unknown

Summer 1502
The Caribbean

There is a point in every exploration when a portal into the unknown is breached. The familiar is left behind, and the novel becomes the reality of daily life. In July 1502 Columbus entered that realm once again.

His refreshed fleet hugged the coast as it sailed from Ocoa Bay. The days were hot, and the sea still rough. Rain doused the ships constantly. Columbus spent his time during storms studying maps and writing in his logbook. When the weather cleared he stood on deck, peering at the horizon and sniffing the wind for signs of another storm. "Till I reached there I had as good weather as I could have wished for," Columbus lamented of "Dominica," as he now called Hispaniola. "I have been dogged by bad weather ever since." When another hurricane threatened after just a few days under sail, he made for the river mouth at Yaquimo, on Hispaniola's southwest side. The storm passed over without inflicting damage, and the fleet left Hispaniola's shores for good on July 14. In all they had spent just two weeks there, but those two weeks had changed the tone of the voyage. For the crew that meant an evolution from novice, teenage sailors to storm-tested seamen, brusquely introduced to the ocean's awesome capabilities and aware that similar experiences might lie ahead. For Columbus it meant the end of his ten-year investment in Hispaniola's development. His journey into the unknown involved not just the physical realities of sailing into a dark spot on the map but the emotional challenge of forgetting the insults and rejection of the past two years. He needed to refocus his energies on finding the path to the Orient.

The fleet was becalmed as they began their westward push. The current drove them due west toward Jamaica. Columbus knew the area well, having discovered and circumnavigated the lush, mountainous island on his second voyage. Before leaving Spain he had even intended to stop there first instead of at Hispaniola. "My intention was to hasten my voyage while I had good ships, crews and provisions, and that my course was for the island of Jamaica," he acknowledged in a letter to Isabella and Ferdinand. But the interlude on Hispaniola had sated Columbus's desire for a landfall; he longed to bypass Jamaica entirely and push on toward the Orient. Once again the weather conspired against him. For a week he waited for wind to fill his sails, but the fleet could only drift on the current. Particularly daunting was that this current acted like a mighty river, fed by smaller tributaries. Although Columbus did not know it at the time, currents from the equator and South America enter the Caribbean at the Lesser Antilles and then merge into one mighty current due south of Hispaniola. That Caribbean current moves in just one direction: west. Without wind his caravels were nothing more than large rafts bobbing wherever the ocean decided to take them, and they were shoved inexorably toward Jamaica.

During those long, listless hours, the sailors busied themselves with the routine of shipboard life. The crew was divided into two shifts, with each shift alternating a four-hour watch. These began at 3, 7, or 11, depending upon a man's assignment. Every dawn was greeted by a grommet singing a ditty on deck: "Blessed be the light of the day," he would sing in Spanish, "and the Holy Cross we say; and the Lord of Veritie, and the Holy Trinity; Blessed be the immortal soul, and the Lord who keeps it whole. Blessed be the light of day, and He who keeps the night away."

And each night, a grommet would greet the darkness with prayers for safety and then would sing the "Salve Regina."

Even without wind in the sails, the men had plenty to keep them occupied on watch. Water had to be pumped from the hold, and every ship leaked just enough to make this chore a constant. The decks were scrubbed with salt water. Inspections of the rigging were carried out on a regular basis, with any frayed ropes being repaired or replaced. Lookouts at the bow and atop the mainmast scanned the surface for signs of reef, whale, turtles, waterspouts, or the surprising amounts of detritus — logs and branches, in particular — borne along by the current.

Columbus was brilliant at telling time by the sun and stars on clear days, as were most of his sailors. But a more exact method of timekeeping was the *ampolleta,* a half hourglass near the ship's pilot. A grommet turned the glass the instant the sand ran out, chanting a series of lengthy ditties as he did so. Although Columbus sometimes fretted that the young seamen forgot this vital chore, it didn't happen very often. Eight turns of the glass marked a full watch, so the grommet was keen to turn the glass quickly, knowing all eyes were on him. "On deck, on deck, Mr. Mariners on the right side," the grommet called out when the watch was done, summoning the next watch. "On deck in good time, you of Mr. Pilot's watch, for it's already time. Shake a leg."

Nowhere was the watch change more important than on the helm. The ship's course was barked out and repeated by the ship's master and helmsman, so there could be no error. This exchange took place on the elevated aft deck known as the poop, which also served as the roof of Columbus's personal cabin. The name is an abbreviation of *pupa,* which is Latin for "doll." It was common for the ship's helmsman and master to place religious icons near them on the ship's rail as they steered the ship, taking solace from having these small statues or doll-like representations of the saints near them, sure the *pupae* would guide them and keep them safe. Over centuries of sailing, this high rear deck became synonymous with those icons.

Similarly, the boards with the single, large, round hole that were hung over the fore and aft edges of the ship were known as *jardines* to Columbus's men. It was a humorously nostalgic reminder that back home in Spain the family outhouse was generally in a fragrant garden rather than a plank hovering above a sea that sometimes rose up and drenched sailors' backsides (in England, to which Columbus had sailed in his youth, the ships' lavatories were known as beakheads because they were situated at the pointed forward end of the ship; in time this was shortened to "head").

No matter the nationality, sailors used a length of pitch-covered rope to wipe themselves. And it was always the youngest and most inexperienced sailor who was later dangled over the side by rope to scrub the side of the ship. For the sake of appearances, this task was especially vital before making port.

As for off-duty life aboard ship, it was marked by a singular absence of personal space. There were no beds. If a sailor wanted to sleep on deck at night, he would curl up on his vermin-infested straw mat under the stars. Only Columbus and the ship's captain had enclosed cabins. The master, pilot, and boatswain slept in wooden bunks beneath the raised quarterdeck. The rest of the men slept wherever they could find space. Many chose the protective awning of the forecastle or afterdeck. A coil of rope often served as a pillow. Night was a cacophony of snoring underscored by under-the-blankets masturbation and surreptitious acts of homosexual love — little of which occurred in stout seas, when rain and drenching waves forced all hands into the hold for protection from the elements.

When the weather was at its most raw, the entire crew took their bedding into the cramped hold. Such a move was not taken lightly. The front of the hold — the curved section near the bow — was reserved for piling firewood, dry goods, sails and sailcloth, and spare cannons. The rear section, just below the hatch through which the men lowered themselves into the cramped darkness, was reserved for stores and wine casks. In the midst of it all, the mainmast (middle of the ship), mizzenmast (aft), and foremast (bow) jutted at right angles. Rats, lice, and cockroaches skittered over and around the exhausted and increasingly demoralized men, who were aching for sleep because they would be back on watch in a matter of four hours or less. No flat spot existed to get what could be called restful sleep; it was just a continuum of casks and ballast stones. Indeed the hold was a disgusting, odiferous place in which to attempt catching forty winks. It reeked of salted fish, spoiling stores, and stagnant bilge water. This revolting perfume grew more wretched during bad weather, when the men — unable to go above — were forced to creep over the barrels and stores to the bucket that served as an impromptu lavatory, where they would brace themselves in any way possible to do their business. A grommet would be sent up top to dump the bucket when it was full.

As for food, fresh meat was a rare but welcome addition to the daily menu. Most of the food was dried, salted, pickled, or preserved because the ships had no refrigeration. Salted beef and pork were packed in brine and then stored in barrels. When the barrels were poorly made, or the ship's cooper failed to keep the casks tightly bound, the brine leaked out, and the meat would spoil.

"Victualling them should be done in this manner," Columbus once wrote to the sovereigns of feeding his crew. "The third part to be good biscuit, well seasoned and not old, or the major portion will be wasted; a third part of salted flour, salted at the time of milling; and a third part of wheat. Further, there will be wine, salt meat, oil, vinegar, cheese, chickpeas, lentils, beans, salt fish and fishing tackle, honey, rice, almonds and raisins." Other popular foods were garlic and molasses. The wine, after a cask was opened, was poured into earthen wine jars shaped like ancient Greek amphorae. They hung from nets in the hold to prevent breakage. The same was true of olive oil.

When it came time to prepare a meal, the food was cooked in a small, three-sided metal firebox called a fogón. It was lashed to the deck, and a layer of sand in the bottom allowed a fire to be built without its spreading to the deck below. A cooking pot hung by a rod over the flames. None of the ships, however, carried an individual specially designated as "cook." That specific duty was shifted from sailor to sailor on a regular basis, with those demonstrating cooking skill getting it more often than others.

The crew used their personal wooden bowls or the communal ladle to scoop broth and meat from the cooking pot, taking care not to spill as the ship rolled and heaved. Hardtack was handed out so each man could sop up the broth or gravy from his bowl. They sipped cups of wine or water as they ate. Their utensils were their hands or omnipresent belt knife. (Along with the woolen overcoats that kept them warm during the chill of a midnight watch and the red wool Catalonia stocking caps or Toledo bonnets pressed down tightly on their heads, no sailor was ever without his knife.)

Columbus, in the manner of a nobleman, sometimes

wore stockings like tights with his woolen garments. On cold days at sea, he preferred an ankle-length, brown coat with a hood, but otherwise he dressed very much like the men. Columbus was, however, the lone member of the crew who ate alone, preferring to dine in the solitude of his cabin. His food was served on pewter plates and brought by a ship's boy.

The watches, the meals, and the daily recitation of religious services helped pass the time while the crew was becalmed. Constant activity kept the crew from lapsing into boredom, grumbling, and homesickness, especially among the teenage sailors. Those on board without a nautical role to play — trumpeters Juan de Cuellar and Gonzalo de Salazar, for instance — were left to entertain themselves and stay out of the way unless their help was needed for some larger chore.

Columbus was not responsible for the day-to-day running of his ship. Choosing to focus on the broader ramifications of the voyage, he had abdicated the role of *La Capitana*'s captain to Diego Tristan. The Seville native was a longtime personal servant who had first sailed with Columbus as a volunteer on his second voyage. Tristan's promotion was reward for years of loyal service. It also freed Columbus to focus on the entire fleet. He busied himself keeping track of wind and weather, plotting the fleet's relative location compared to his planned course. In an era without an accurate way of measuring longitude, which made dead reckoning the truest way of determining location, careful observation of those elements pushing a ship off course could be all consuming.

After less than a week of drifting, Jamaica's inland mountains loomed on the horizon. Thirty miles off the coast, Columbus landed on a sandy cay and sent the men ashore to refill the water casks. They found no running water but, rather ingeniously, dug deep into the sand and found pools of murky brown water fit for drinking. It wasn't ideal, but with a voyage of unknown duration ahead and much of the fleet's food spoiled, a full water supply was vital. Columbus named the land Isla de Pozas, after the water pools.

Then he immediately put to sea again, content to let the wind and current mark his course for the time being. But his haste was for naught. Another long week of drifting passed before the wind turned. By then his fleet, its white sails hanging slack and growing yellowed by the sun, had watched the southern coast of Jamaica glide by off the port bow, then the southern coast of Cuba (also discovered by Columbus on his second voyage) glide by off the starboard. Like Columbus, those members of the crew who had also sailed on the second voyage remembered well the differences between the two islands. Back then the Indians of Cuba had been friendly, while the Indians of Jamaica had attacked the explorer and his men with wooden spears and stones the instant they went ashore. On Jamaica the fleet had anchored in a gorgeous broad cove Columbus named Santa Gloria. For all its beauty, though, Santa Gloria did not compare to a Cuban archipelago that enchanted the explorer so much he lingered for twenty days. The Cuban air had been filled with the aroma of wildflowers and the skies full of primary-colored flocks of tropical birds. Riven by shallow channels dividing a scattering of keys, it was a place he named El Jardin de la Reina — "The queen's garden." To Columbus it was an unforgettable reminder of the New World's natural opulence.

As his father busied himself with navigation and logistics, young Fernando Columbus was continuing a personal evolution that had begun with Columbus's return to Spain in chains. The thirteen-year-old had been born out of wedlock on August 15, 1488, in the city of Córdoba. His mother was the remarkable Beatriz de Arana. Orphaned at six, she was raised by a grandmother and maternal aunt who took pains to ensure that Beatriz was well educated. In an era when most women of noble birth couldn't even sign their name, this commoner could read and write and was schooled well into her teenage years. She was twenty-two and never married when she met Columbus through mutual friends in 1487. He was fourteen years older and had followed the Spanish court to Córdoba in March of that year. By October their affair was sexual. Soon she was pregnant.

Fortunately for Columbus and Beatriz, the Spanish Inquisition wasn't imprisoning adulterers. Still, having a child out of wedlock carried a significant social stigma in Roman Catholic Spain. Beatriz, bravely, chose not to marry Columbus. At the time he was recently widowed, on the run from Portuguese creditors, and trying to interest the sovereigns of both Spain and Portugal in the far-fetched notion that he could find the aquatic route to the Indies by sailing west. She bore Fernando and raised him to the age of six, all the while remaining the explorer's mistress. Despite the couple's never marrying, the bond between Beatriz's family and Columbus would remain strong. Her cousins Diego and Pedro played pivotal roles in Columbus's first and third voyages, respectively. She and the explorer, however, had a falling out that would haunt Columbus for the rest of his life. "She weighs heavily on my conscience, though I am at present unable to tell you why," Columbus once told his son Diego. In 1492, after the sovereigns awarded him monies for being the first to sight land in the New World, he had accepted it with gratitude — and then gave it to Beatriz.

Now the offspring of their tempestuous relationship would see the New World for himself. While Diego pragmatically remained in Spain to continue his service to Isabella, Fernando had opted to give up the privilege of the royal court to sail with the father he barely knew. The Admiral had been a fleeting presence in Fernando's life, appearing for a few weeks or months between voyages and then leaving on another adventure just as abruptly as he had arrived. With Columbus getting on in years, the fourth voyage might be their last chance to explore the New World side by side. Columbus indoctrinated his son to the rigors of life at sea by putting him to work as a grommet.

It was a harsh adjustment. Not only was life at sea a sharp contrast to the court's luxuries, but Fernando had no peers. The young men his age were from impoverished backgrounds. Their brief childhoods had been spent in the slums of cities like Seville and Córdoba, not dressed in bright-colored clothing, educated by the finest minds in Europe, and attending to royalty's every need. The older crew members, with their perpetually tanned, weather-toughened skin and gruff professionalism, had no use for a passenger who might overhear gossip not intended for the Admiral's ears. Fernando's was not a pleasure cruise. Day by day the young man was evolving from royal page to explorer. He closely observed the rhythm and flow of the voyage, chronicling it in minute detail on parchment. And when the journey ended (should he survive), Fernando had no idea where his life would lead, but already he had an inkling he would not return to the royal court.

On July 24 the fleet was fast approaching the western tip of Cuba. Up to that point in the journey, Columbus knew the waters and currents through which he was sailing. He had been there before. But Cuba's end was also the end of Columbus's known world. Had he let the current continue to carry him westward, his fleet would have been shot through the Yucatán Channel into the Gulf of Mexico and then driven in the opposite direction as the current changed its course. This Gulf Stream, as a portion of it would later be named, would then drive him along the coast of modern-day

Florida and Georgia before disgorging him into the North Atlantic for the journey back to Spain. No explorer had ever followed this path; indeed, Columbus was unaware of the great continent due north of Cuba. Even if he had known about a great landmass to the north, Columbus wouldn't have continued in that direction, no matter how alluring. He was fixated on finding the Orient, once and for all.

But first, the passage. The Admiral was convinced it lay southwest of Cuba. The passage, in Columbus's mind, was bracketed by Paria to the south and Cuba to the north. The time for letting the current and contrary wind dictate his course was past. He ordered the fleet to set its sails for the Island of Pines, near the western tip of Cuba. There Columbus dropped anchor off a small cay he named Anegada and waited for the wind to change direction. It had the potential to be a long wait; air currents are the main thrust behind surface currents, their patterns mimicking one another. What he needed was a rogue wind whipping down from the same direction as the hurricanes of Hispaniola.

Water casks were filled. The ships were made ready. A day passed. Then another. On the third morning Columbus got his wind. On July 27, 1502, the breeze clocked around to blow from the northeast. He barked the order to weigh anchor. "*Oeste, quarta del sudoeste,*" west by southwest, he called out to the captain of the watch, setting the course. The history-making command sent shivers of fear and excitement down the spine of all who heard. Pedro de Ledesma, an able seaman aboard *La Vizcaino,* later commented that it was common knowledge among the crews that their next landfall would be Asia.

Like powerful thoroughbreds that have spent too long in the barn, Columbus's fleet galloped across the deep blue water of the Caribbean. Steering by dead reckoning, Columbus altered the course to coincide with the wind's changing direction, so that by the time his lookout called out land just three days later, they had traveled 360 miles. "I sailed as soon as I could to the mainland," Columbus wrote with understatement.

His next landfall wasn't the mainland, however, but an island the Indians called Bonacca. Twelve miles long and four miles wide, the island had a presence belying its size. Columbus approached carefully, taking note of a well-formed barrier reef a half mile offshore that would have torn the bottom off his ships. The island was entirely green from a thick canopy of Caribbean pine trees. Most striking of all was the mountainous terrain, with peaks sprouting a quarter mile up out of the ocean. Columbus's small fleet dropped anchor outside the reef. Columbus was suffering from an attack of gout. Despite the horrible pain and tender, inflamed joints, his mood was buoyant. He had reached his target. Columbus ordered his brother to paddle to shore and set foot upon the newfound Asian island. Bartolomé, up to the task as always, did as his big brother commanded.

CHAPTER FIFTEEN

Mosquito

July–September 1502
The Caribbean

Columbus's certainty that he was in Asia was grounded in the maps of Ptolemy, the writings of Marco Polo, his own experiences at sea, the Bible, and a slew of other sources. Having worked as a chart maker in his younger days, he was abreast of the most modern theories on the shape of the world. No doubt about it: this must be China. Columbus would have been a madman to believe otherwise. On the second voyage Columbus had cruised the southern coast of Cuba, searching for proof that he was correct or for signs that he was mistaken. Although the daily sight of land comforted the men, Columbus was concerned with finding that elusive passage to India. The gold and population of a major continent were nowhere to be seen, but Columbus was so convinced Cuba was part of the Chinese mainland that he insisted the crew swear an oath stating they had seen a Chinese province.

The fourth voyage was meant to be so conclusive that something as subjective as swearing an oath would be unnecessary. He meant to bring back tangible physical proof — pepper stalks, silk, and people. After cutting the tangent from

Mangi to Cathay — in reality, Cuba to Honduras — he would coast south and west past Indonesia. Along the way Columbus expected to pass the islands of Java Major, Pentan, Seilam. Then he would squeeze through the Strait of Malacca, cross the Indian Ocean, and kiss the coast of India.

However, if that theory was true, it also meant that Alonso de Ojeda, currently exploring the coastline of Paria, might find the passage first. Columbus did not have the luxury of lingering too long in any single place.

It was July 31, 1502, when the gout-stricken Columbus ordered Bartolomé ashore to explore his latest discovery. "Having come to the island of Guanaja," Fernando wrote, "the Admiral sent ashore his Bartholomew with two boats. They encountered people who resembled those of the other islands, but had narrower foreheads. They also saw many pine trees and piece of earth which the Indians called *calcide* to cast copper."

Bartolomé was dumbstruck to see a massive canoe paddle over the horizon. Hollowed from a tree trunk, the boat was eight feet wide and long enough that it was paddled by twenty-five men and carried fifteen women and children as passengers. To protect the women and children from the intense tropical sun, a green awning made of palm leaves was arched from one side of the hull to the other.

Bartolomé was a nonchalant man, not easily dazzled. But he was so taken with the canoe that he wanted the Admiral to see it immediately. He stepped aboard the canoe and gestured for the Indians to paddle it out beyond the reef to Columbus's flagship. The Indians outnumbered the Spanish but did as they were told. Much to Bartolomé's delight, Columbus was stunned by the canoe and its inhabitants. The jaded world traveler wasn't just taken with the fact that people of Guanaja were clothed — a decided change of pace from the barely clothed tribes of Paria and Hispaniola — but that they obviously had knowledge of navigation and metallurgy. To Columbus it was clear that a cultural progression was taking place as he neared the Orient. Just one look at the canoe told him that the closer he got, the more advanced the people were becoming. The contents of the canoe and the fine way in which the people were dressed confirmed that. It was an anthropological time capsule: food, drink, intellect, morality, attitudes on war. "The Admiral gave thanks to God for revealing to him in a single moment, without any toil or danger to our people, all the products of that country," Fernando wrote.

Or so Columbus thought. It was common for explorers to gaze upon other civilizations with a mixture of fear and pity — on the one hand frightened of war, on the other as if gazing upon a lesser people. It was true that the Mayans of whom Columbus and his men were getting Europe's first glimpse were a society in decline. Their heyday had been a period between AD 250 and 900. But Mayan civilization still had a vibrancy and intellectualism that paralleled European cultures. Just as in Spain, the Mayans had a ruling class, who relied on priests and an administrative bureaucracy to refine their power. There were artisans and divisions of labor. Historians tracked the epic and the minute; astrologers sought divination from the stars. The Mayans, whose empire stretched south from the Yucatán Peninsula, were militaristic and dynastic. They built elaborate castles, with moats and gardens. Population was centered around these castles and then dispersed throughout the countryside in small villages.

The Mayans Columbus encountered were an offshoot known as the Chontals. Much like the sailors aboard Columbus's ships, grown up in coastal towns and raised to become mariners, so too the Chontals were born to the sea. They made their home on the coast of the Yucatán Peninsula, guiding their canoes inland via rivers and out to coastal islands in order to barter with other Mayans and with their neighbors to the north, the Aztecs. The Chontals purveyed jaguar skins, tortoiseshells, cacao beans, and brightly colored feathers in exchange for corn, lumber, salt, and copper. So great was their paddling prowess that the Yucatán was also known as Acallan — "Land of the canoes."

Rather than try to learn more about the Chontal Mayans, or show respect for fellow mariners, Columbus gave in to his more base impulses. Aware that his voyage would be compared with those of Ojeda and Bastides in terms of accumulated wealth, he ordered his men to seize the boat's possessions. The women were pawed in the process, and the ornately colored breechcloths ripped off the men. Fernando shared his father's enthusiasm for impressing Ferdinand and Isabella, and when he wrote of the degradation of the Chontal Mayas, it was with pride: "He took aboard the costliest and handsomest things in that cargo: cotton mantles and sleeveless shirts embroidered and painted in different designs and colors; breechclouts of the same design and cloth as the shawls worn by the women in the canoe, being like the shawls worn by the Moorish women in Granada; long wooden swords with a groove on each side where the edge should be, in which were fastened with cord and pitch, flint knives that cut like steel; hatchets resembling the stone hatchets used by other Indians, but made of good copper." The thieving continued: "And hawk's bells of copper, and crucibles to melt it. For provisions they had such roots and grains as the Indians of Espanola eat, also a wine made of maize that tasted like English beer."

The Chontals endured the seizure without fighting back. One treasure they frantically scooped up when the Spanish tossed it aside as worthless, however. The Spanish had mistaken handfuls of purple and off-white beans for almonds. In fact they were cacao beans, valuable in producing everything from chocolate to medications, and in the Mayan empire, only gold and salt were as valuable. "I noticed that when they were brought aboard with the other goods," Fernando wrote with curiosity of the Mayans' penchant for cacao, "and some fell to the floor, all the Indians squatted down to pick them up as if they had lost something of great value — their greed driving out their feelings of terror and danger at finding themselves in the hands of such strange and ferocious men as we must have seemed to be."

In exchange for robbing the Chontals of their belongings and dignity, Columbus gave them the usual cheap beads and curios used in trading with indigenous cultures. He refrained from taking slaves, realizing that few actions would infuriate Isabella more. Instead he took an older man named Yombé as a prisoner, whom he intended on using as his translator with other tribes he might encounter.

Columbus spent two weeks exploring Guanaja, and then, with the uncowed Yombé along for the ride, the fleet set sail for the mainland. The temperature hovered in the high eighties. Sudden, intense storms doused his fleet, ending as quickly as they came, the rainwater causing steam as it evaporated from the fleet's decks. The dark blue ocean waters led Columbus to name the new land off his starboard bow Honduras, Spanish for "depths."

The fleet completed the thirty-mile sail from Guanaja by the middle of August, making landfall at a spit of land Columbus named Caxinas Point, for the trees growing onshore. Based on the canoe's riches and conversations with Yombé, Columbus had briefly considered sailing north to the Yucatán instead of continuing his southwest push toward Asia. But whatever wealth lay to the north could be discovered on the return voyage, so he pushed east and south in leisurely fashion. The coast was a mosaic of green: banana trees, palm trees, pine trees, marshy swamps, and grasslands. Black clouds of mosquitoes marauded through the air. The wind was not as strong as on the open sea, making the humidity and ninety-degree heat feel all the more oppressive.

More Chontals were encountered, as was a naked, non-Mayan tribe known as the Lencas. They had very dark skin, and Yombé spoke disparagingly of them, telling Columbus through sign language of their fondness for the raw flesh of men and fish and a propensity to pierce their ears until the hole is large enough "to insert hen's eggs," as Fernando wrote. Columbus promptly named the site La Costa de las Orejas — "The coast of the ears."

Columbus didn't think the passage to the Orient existed this far north, and the poor cannibals obviously weren't as wealthy as the Chontal Mayans, so he was uninterested in what he saw of the mainland. He couldn't be bothered to go ashore, and it was almost an afterthought when he claimed the region for Spain on August 17, 1502. Columbus was feeling ill again, so Bartolomé, dressed in ceremonial red (to impress local chiefs) and bearing the standards of Castile and León, rowed ashore to claim the new country for the sovereigns. At his side were ship's captains Fieschi, Porras, Terreros, and Tristan; Yombé; and a small contingent of sailors that included young Fernando.

As the boats nestled up against the sand, and sailors leapt out to drag them from the water, Bartolomé was stunned to see a hundred Indians approaching. Men and women alike were naked except for a small cloth over their loins. Tattoos of lions, deer, and castles covered their bodies. Some had red stripes painted on their faces, while others had blackened the area around their eyes. Suddenly, Bartolomé was very overdressed.

Young Fernando was spooked by the Indians' face paint, even though the tribe appeared friendly. "They do this to look beautiful," he wrote of the makeup, "but they really look like devils."

The Indians were a tribe known as the Payas. Without speaking, they approached the Spaniards and bestowed platters of food. It was the first time the sailors had smelled fresh-cooked food in almost three months. Since leaving Spain in May, the fleet had lived on salted and dried ship's rations. They had drunk stale wine and muddy water. But arrayed before them were heaping mounds of roasted chicken, goose, fish, and vegetables. The Spaniards' excitement was so intense, it was frightening. The Indians — who still had not uttered a word — retreated. Bartolomé called them back and hastily ordered that the gift be repaid with bells and beads.

The following day Bartolomé went ashore once again. This time he was greeted by twice as many Indians carrying twice as much food. "These Indians," Fernando wrote, "being pleased with what had been given them, next day more than two hundred others came to the same spot bringing foods of various kinds." In addition, the Spanish learned that deer lived in the pine and oak forests of the nearby mountains. It seemed a natural place to lay over. Stores and morale could be renewed before the vagaries of exploration once again took their toll. But Columbus was driven to push on.

The rainy season in Honduras typically begins in May and ends by December. But as Columbus hugged the coast in the days that followed, the landscape changed from hilly to flat as he entered an area that would one day be known as the Mosquito Coast. Named for the Indian tribe making it home instead of the Spanish word for the insect ("little fly"), the Mosquito Coast was carpeted by thick, tropical rain forest. It was a place with no beginning or end to the rainy season. It was the wettest part of Honduras, drenched by a hundred inches of rainwater each year.

Columbus was aware that he was entering a new system of air and water currents. The winds had begun to blow from the east, against his ships, meaning he would have to zigzag back and forth across the clear blue waters to curry favor with the breeze. This tacking would make for slow going. But if all was well, his course would be steady and the weather clement, giving him plenty of time to ponder the coastline, pray, and study the stars — all the while seeking his path through the seas.

That turned out not to be the case. For the next month the prevailing easterly winds gusted so powerfully that the fleet was actually shoved backward at times. Waves washed over the decks. Nonstop rain drenched the men as they worked on deck and sought refuge in the hold. No place was dry — the hold was partially flooded, the covered quarterdeck's cannon ports let in the elements, and the forecastle not only rose and bucked like a wild horse as it plowed into wave after wave, but the water washing over was sure to douse anyone foolish enough to attempt sleeping there. When off duty the terrified men huddled wherever they could find shelter, shivering despite the tropical heat, chilled to the bone and unable to sleep from being wet for days on end. Adding insult to injury, as soon as the rain ended, mosquitoes swarmed out to the ships from the coastal mangrove swamps. "Rain, thunder, and lightning was so continuous that it seemed the end of the world," Columbus wrote. "I had never seen the sun or the stars on account of the high seas. My ships were stripped, the sails torn, anchors, rigging and cable were lost, and also the boats and many stores. The crew were very sick and all repented their sins, in turning to God. Everyone made vows and promised pilgrimages, and very often men went so far as to confess to one another. Other storms have been seen, but none have ever lasted so long or been so terrifying. Many of whom we thought were brave were reduced to terror on more than one occasion." Columbus worried about his boy, forgetting that Fernando turned fourteen just days before the storms. "The distress of my son, who was with me, racked my soul, for he was only thirteen, and he was not only exhausted, but he remained so for a long time.

But the Lord gave him such courage that he cheered the others and he worked as hard in the ship as if he had been a sailor for eighty years. He comforted me."

Forward progress was further hindered by staying so close to shore. If Columbus had gone farther out to sea, he could sail around the clock, but his desire to find the passage to the Orient meant keeping the coast under continuous observation. It also meant the possibility of running aground on a reef or low-lying island or missing the passage in the dark. To prevent such a disaster, Columbus ordered the ships to sail by day and then drop anchor close to land each night.

In the midst of it all, Columbus became deathly ill. His usual ailments were gout that swelled his joints with ureic acid and rheumatoid arthritis that sent him to bed with painfully deformed, inflamed joints in his hands and feet. These were now joined by a severe cold brought on by ignoring his pain and standing out in the elements to scan the coastline for the passage. Despite having the only enclosed cabin on *La Capitana,* he insisted on giving orders on deck, his aging body buffeted by rain and wind. Day and night he grasped the rungs of the wooden ladder outside his door with crippled hands and then slowly climbed up onto the roof of his cabin to stand atop the poop deck. Even after catching cold, he continued this practice. The crew became fearful of losing Columbus. They constructed a small cabin atop the poop — a doghouse, in sailing parlance — to protect the aging mariner from the elements. "I was sick and at many times lay at death's door, but gave orders from a dog house the men clapped together for me on the poop deck," wrote a thankful Columbus.

On September 14, after twenty-eight agonizing days and nights, the tattered ships finally rounded a headland and were able to turn in a more southerly direction. For the first time in a month, the men weren't into the wind. As the fleet continued its relentless push along the coast, the look-outs sighted sandbars submerged just below the surface. These shoals ran perpendicular to the coast, angling several miles out to sea. With the water casks nearly empty and fire-wood either soaked or gone, Columbus couldn't sail around the shoals without first replenishing these simple, vital stores.

Each ship lowered its boats and a crew. Gathering water and wood was hard manual labor — the search for trees that might burn long and without smoking, the hauling of casks weighing hundreds of pounds. Under normal circumstances going ashore was a break from the tedium and routine of shipboard life. After the hurricane of Hispaniola, the calm of Jamaica, the downwind sprint to Guanaja, and the everlast-ing easterly, going ashore was a privilege.

The boats approached the swampy, flat coastline. The pungent smell of a tidal marsh — equal parts salt and decay — became stronger with every oar stroke. Whether a fifteen-man launch or a nine-man yawl, each boat balanced men and barrels. It made for a precarious paddle, but the sailors had done it many times and paddled successfully through the small breakers and up the wide mouth of a river. Its banks rioted with tall grasses and reeds growing "as thick as a man's thigh," as Fernando described it. Eventually the men found an opening and beached their boats. Trees were chopped down and cut into smaller pieces for kindling. The river water that filled the casks was muddy but fresh. Mis-sion accomplished, the grimy, sweating sailors loaded their boats, shoved off, and moved away from the dank, green river, back toward the refreshing air of the blue Caribbean. The boats sat low, top heavy from hundreds of additional pounds of water and wood. The sailors cursed the weight and strained hard against the oars.

The wind had been slack when they left the ships early that Saturday morning, but it had begun blowing in hard from the sea while the men were ashore. As a result the ocean went from calm to choppy, whitecaps dancing across the surface. The surf break, that confluence of ocean and mainland, began booming with the heave and thunder of crashing waves.

The sailors had no choice but to paddle straight through the breakers and struggle with all their might to hold their line. Getting turned sideways for even an instant meant the possibility of broaching. The boat would be flipped, its contents tumbling from the boat as the wave rolled over it.

As the wind picked up, one of the boats lost its bearings. Boatswain Martin de Fuenterrabia and ship's boy Miguel de Lariaga had been sent ashore from *La Vizcaino*'s twenty-four-man crew. The ship had already lost one man, able seaman Gonzalo Gallego, who jumped ship in Hispaniola. Now Fuenterrabia and Lariaga's boat flipped, and their bodies were tossed into the curl of waves so harsh they seemed to have teeth. Their corpses washed up on shore, along with their boat, casks, and firewood. The supplies were retrieved, and the dead sailors buried along the banks of the river Columbus named for their demise — Rio de Desastres. Yombé was returned to shore because he no longer spoke the local language and walked back home alone.

Columbus continued his inexorable push toward Asia, sailing by day and anchoring by night. The coastal jungles grew mountainous once more. He named the promontory Cabo de Rojas for its red cliffs. On September 25 the fleet came upon an island so pretty that the Admiral gave it the name La Huerta — loosely translated, "the Special Garden." "Here we found the best country and people that we had yet seen, because the land was high and abounded in rivers and great trees, and the island itself was verdant, full of groves of lofty trees, palms, myrobalans, and many other species," wrote Fernando. Spider monkeys, pumas, and wild boars inhabited the jungle.

In this land brimming with beauty and life, even Columbus, who had recuperated from his illnesses, relaxed. The men had gone almost three months without a break. He ordered the vessels to drop anchor and take a much-needed ten days to rest.

CHAPTER SIXTEEN

Ojeda, Again

As Columbus basked in La Huerta's sublime wonders, it was Alonso de Ojeda's turn to be thrown in chains. He had made such a fiasco of his nine-month second voyage of exploration that he had been sent to Santo Domingo and bound over for trial.

Ojeda had a nose for trouble, and he had proved it again and again over the course of his latest journey. After sailing from Cádiz in January, his fleet had hastened across the Atlantic. The lone stipulation the sovereigns had placed on Ojeda was that he must not seek to enrich himself by trading for pearls in Paria. For once Ojeda did as he was told: he led his fleet through the Gulf of Paria and then west to a village along the shore known as Cumaná. There he dropped anchor and sent the crews ashore to forage for supplies.

The beach at Cumaná had a singular beauty — white sands, lush rows of palm trees, clear blue waters — and the natives were friendly. But then Ojeda was seized by a powerful, curious notion: if he was going to establish a colony and fortress in this exciting new land that he ruled as governor, then he needed furniture. Not just tables and chairs —

Ojeda needed plates and eating utensils and cups and bowls. Instead of manufacturing these items himself, or even using the implements already available aboard the ships, Ojeda decided to steal the furniture from the natives at Cumaná. That way there would be no need for theft from the Indians surrounding his colony. Friendly relations could be maintained.

Two of Ojeda's financial backers, Juan de Vergara and Garcia de Campos (who also went by Ocampo) had made the voyage with him. As a good partner Ojeda considered it his duty to share his furniture-stealing plan. Vergara and Ocampo didn't find the idea particularly just but agreed with its underlying brilliance.

Soon after, the Indians of Cumaná were ambushed by the Spanish, who had been exceptionally polite until then. The Spaniards stole hammocks, cotton, and eating utensils as they ransacked hut after hut. Impassioned by their raid, the Europeans also began killing the people of Cumaná, cutting down any man, woman, or child who fought back. At least seven died, and many were wounded, but none of Ojeda's force was hurt. The Spanish imprisoned Indian women of all ages for their personal pleasure — Vergara and Ocampo, based on their role as primary investors, demanded the first pick. The rest were given to the crew or ransomed back to their tribe for gold.

Ojeda was more comfortable in the company of men and had no interest in the women. As his ships overflowed with plunder, he took only a hammock for himself. Then, leaving the distraught Indians of Cumaná to rebuild their lives and pine for their mothers and daughters, the four ships sailed west.

Despite the wonderful hammocks and cotton, Cumaná had been poor, its pathetic food stores insufficient to feed the Spanish. As a result Ojeda and his partners became convinced that the fourth continent lacked natural resources;

consequently, Vergara sailed for Jamaica in the caravel *Santa María de la Granada* to forage for food. Plans were made to meet up again in Maracaibo, a large harbor five hundred miles due west of Paria that Ojeda had discovered on his prior trip.

Ojeda and his three remaining ships followed the coast, searching for a proper spot to found a colony. Finally, after rejecting locations that he considered unworthy, Ojeda landed in a bay he named Santa Cruz. Much to his surprise a sailor left behind by the Bastides exploration a year earlier emerged to greet them. He had become friendly with the locals and spoke their language. Ojeda took this as confirmation that he had found the right place. Soon afterward, when Ojeda quelled an Indian uprising by attacking in force, the locals apologized with lavish gifts of gold. Ojeda took this to be another sign.

But despite their gifts the Indians were not through waging war and began a series of harassments. Spaniards sent to cut down trees or work on the fort Ojeda ordered built were attacked on a regular basis. Once again Ojeda went to war, driving the Indians from their homeland entirely. The lombard cannons from his vessels were brought ashore and mounted on the finished fortress as protection.

All should have been well. But when the Indians returned, the Spanish became prisoners inside their fort, afraid to venture outside for fear of attack. Provisions dwindled, and the men became agitated, worrying that the ships would be destroyed by shipworms, forever stranding them on the coast. They also taunted Ojeda, saying he had no real jurisdiction over them. Rather than support his partner, Ocampo sniped about Ojeda behind his back.

By the time Vergara finally returned, the young colony was sharply split. Not even the new provisions could raise morale enough to breach the divide. Ocampo secretly formed an alliance with Vergara to overthrow Ojeda's tenuous government. The two men lured the explorer aboard the *Santa María de la Granada* on the pretext of inspecting the new supplies. As soon as they had Ojeda aboard, however, Vergara and Ocampo placed him under arrest. They informed him the fleet was sailing back to Santo Domingo so a judge could hear the case against him.

Alonso de Ojeda was a contentious man, fond of war and adventure, but he was also clever, and though small, the most physically imposing of the three partners. Instead of acquiescing or pleading, he struck a simple bargain: Ocampo and Vergara were free to take two ships and sail home with the gold accrued so far. In return they would leave him a caravel and whichever men chose to stay.

They agreed; but ten days later, as final preparations were being concluded, they changed their minds. Ocampo and Vergara ordered their followers to arrest Ojeda. The outnumbered explorer raced for a caravel, hoping to weigh anchor and be the first to sail to Santo Domingo, where he could plead his case before his partners had the chance. Ocampo and Vergara caught him before he could sail and clapped him in irons. By the beginning of September, as Columbus was enduring the winds off Honduras, the demoralized and homesick men of Ojeda's voyage, thinking that no good could ever come from that hostile land, abruptly abandoned Santa Cruz. The erstwhile colonists set sail for Hispaniola, which they reached two weeks later. The ships dropped anchor on the island's western coast, a few days' sail from Santo Domingo.

A less zealous man might have resigned himself to fate, but the rage and determination that drove Ojeda would not let him quit. While the ships lay at anchor, he quietly slipped over the side and into the Caribbean. He had chains on his ankles but not his wrists and was sure he had the upper body strength to swim the fifty yards to shore. But Ojeda had badly misjudged the weight of his chains and the strength he had lost after nine months of poor nutrition and lack of physical exertion. Halfway to shore he began to sink. Ojeda fought his way back to the surface and cried for help and then settled under the waters again. He continued struggling to the surface until a boat was finally lowered over the side. Soaking wet and nearly drowned, Ojeda was hauled aboard. By the end of September, he was standing in a Santo Domingo courtroom, explaining himself to the chief judge of the island. After hearing both sides the judge stripped Ojeda of all his titles and properties. The diminutive explorer sailed to Spain a free, if untitled, man, vowing to plead his case before the sovereigns.

Thus, by October 1502, a decade after the discovery of the New World, Columbus was once again the only explorer sailing the Caribbean. If the westward passage to the Orient existed, he was now in prime position to discover it.

CHAPTER SEVENTEEN

Shipworms

Fall–Winter 1502
The Caribbean

Constantly buffeted by foul weather, Columbus pushed farther and farther south. As he did so the water got warmer, and the incidence of shipworms increased. Left to their own devices, these boring clams ("shipworms" is a misnomer) carve into the hull like nautical termites. Also known as a teredo, the shipworm's diet consists of wood particles and microscopic organisms found in seawater. It has a coarse, equivalve shell covering just the front end of its body. The sharpened edges of this shell serve as a burrowing tool. As the shipworm grows to more than three feet long, the shell covers less and less of its body. Eventually its appearance is long, stringy, and serpentine, like a tapeworm. And just like a tapeworm, the shipworm is a parasite, infesting and feeding off its host until the host dies — or in the case of a ship, sinks.

The process is gradual but unstoppable. The shipworms infest the hull in a larval stage, then begin growing longer and longer as they consume its timbers. At first just a few inches of water seep into the hold from the pin-size holes. But as the shipworms bore deeper and proliferate, more and more liquid squeezes through. Left unchecked, the ship-worms would gorge themselves until the hull resembled Swiss cheese. To fight the leaks, the crews would man pumps, eventually working almost nonstop in a Sisyphean attempt to halt the inevitable. If the unlucky vessel was close to shore, she would have to be beached and abandoned, her crew stranded or assigned to a sister ship. If the ship was far out to sea, and no sister ship existed, she would sink. The only survivors would be those men senior enough to secure a spot when the ship's boats were launched.

Prevention is the watchword when it comes to ship-worms, and La Huerta afforded Columbus the perfect chance to reseal the fleet's hulls before sailing on. This process is known as careening. Ideally a ship would be careened at the start of a voyage and every few months throughout. The vessels would be guided ever so carefully onto a sandy beach, generally at low tide. Using a system of ropes and pulleys anchored to nearby trees and rocks, the ship would be leaned over — first one side, then the next. The bottom would be cleaned of any algae or barnacles. A sticky layer of pitch — generally pine resin or tar — would be slathered over the entire hull, sealing the seams. Then the newly water-tight ship would be relaunched. The specialists overseeing this labor were known as caulkers, and Columbus carried two such men on the fourth voyage. La Huerta marked a prime opportunity for Domingo de Arana and Domingo Viscaino to ply their trade, and within a week they had sealed all four ships.

Yet Columbus lingered in La Huerta after the ships were repaired and the holds restocked with fresh water. In his zeal to interact — for reasons of obtaining wealth — with each culture whose shores he touched, Columbus was beginning to flirt with the annihilation of himself and his men. In this case the problems arose when Columbus sent men ashore for water. The rowboats encountered Indians armed with clubs, bows and arrows, and spears made from palm leaves tipped with fish bones. The tribe was the Talaman. The men wore cotton cloaks and pendants around their necks. Their black hair hung in braids, while the women's hair hung straight down their backs. Instead of using their weapons to kill or maim, however, the Indians eagerly sallied forth and offered them to the surprised seamen, hoping to trade them for whatever gifts the Spaniards might have. The boat crews had come empty-handed, but the Indians were undeterred. They swam out to Columbus's ships to broker a deal. The explorer, however, seeing no gold and fearing a sudden change of heart by the Talaman, declined.

"The Admiral did not allow his people to accept any of their articles," Fernando wrote, "since he wanted to show them that we did not covet their possessions. Instead, he ordered presents to be distributed to them."

Offended but proud, the Talaman returned to shore with their gifts. They made a pile of the bells and beads on the beach and left it. "There our men found it when they went ashore on Wednesday," Fernando wrote.

The Talaman weren't finished with Columbus yet. They sent two young virgins out to his ships as sexual offerings. Fetching but nervous, the virgins were mere children. One was just eight years old, and the other fourteen. "The girls displayed much courage," wrote Fernando. "For though the Christians were completely strange to them in aspect, manners and race, they showed no fear or grief, but always looked pleasant and modest. On this account they were well treated by the Admiral, who caused them to be clothed and fed and then sent them ashore."

Fifty Indians lined the banks and received the untouched girls with joy. It was as if Columbus had passed a test. The Indians, it seemed, were even more eager to trade with Columbus. But when Bartolomé rowed to shore the next day and sat down on a patch of grass with village elders, things abruptly changed. He asked the Talaman questions and ordered his scribe to make notes of the conversation. But as the scribe, without a second thought, began writing with quill and ink on a sheet of parchment, the terrified Indians fled. They had long suspected that the Spanish, with their great ships and disdain for virgins, were powerful sorcerers. The scribe's ability to scratch a feather across a piece of paper and produce symbols was confirmation. Conversely, the Spanish had begun to think the same of the Talaman. "Yet it was they who impressed us with being great sorcerers," Fernando wrote. "For on approaching the Christians they scattered a certain powder in the air. They also burned the powder in censers and with these censers caused the smoke to go towards the Christians. The fact that they refused to take anything of ours was more evidence that they suspected us of being enchanters, confirming the adage that says a rogue sees himself in every other man."

The fleet sailed on October 5, with two Talaman on board as guides and translators. They were there against their will, but Columbus considered their tribe the most intelligent Indians he had ever seen. He promised to release them once he sailed beyond the realm of their language.

Their fellow tribesmen were devastated at the conscription. They begged Columbus to set the two men free, repeatedly trying to ransom them with gifts of wild boars and other tokens. The Admiral would not be swayed — in fact he was encouraged that he had selected the pinnacle of Talaman civilization. "This only made him more eager to learn what he could about them," Fernando noted.

As Columbus observed their habits and customs so he could report back in detail to the sovereigns, these two new interpreters were put to work the very next day. When the fleet entered a deep bay twenty miles long, the Talaman, eager to be of use, informed Columbus that the place was named Cerebaro. A quick visual inspection of the bay sent the Admiral's heart soaring; from what he could see, the labyrinthine tangle of trees and cays had all the makings of his long-sought passage. He called out the order for the fleet to make a starboard turn into its waters.

Cerebaro was "studded with islands and had three or four channels that are very convenient for getting in and out with every kind of wind. The ships sailed as if in streets between one island and another, the branches of the trees brushing the cordage of the ships," Fernando wrote. The water was not much more than ten feet deep, and the channels so narrow the ships were forced to sail single file. The air smelled of pine and greenery. The farther they squeezed inside the narrow passage, the more it seemed possible not just to sail to India but to continue on around the world. Columbus stood on deck, gazing from one side of the channel to the other and then straight ahead, searching for his new ocean.

The passage soon widened, just as every man had hoped, and a giant sea sprawled before them, the waters cobalt and salty. But in the distance lay a long, green coastline and a mountain range rising to the heavens. They had sailed into a bay, nothing more; it was a vast, beautiful, protected harbor that did not lead to India.

Columbus was deflated, but only momentarily. He had a gut feeling that the passage was getting closer and closer. The fact that his Talaman interpreters recognized the mainland as "Quiriquetana" emboldened him. Columbus took that to be their word for Marco Polo's Ciamba — China. That burst of rejuvenation was quickly followed by another, for on the shore of one of the islands lived a tribe wearing no clothing at all — nothing, that is, but huge golden necklaces from which dangled mirrors in gold. Columbus immediately sent the interpreters to find where the gold had come from. "With the aid of the Indian interpreter," noted

Fernando, "they said this gold was very abundant and that they got it on the mainland, not far from there."

That was music to Columbus's ears. The next morning he ordered boats to row ashore. The men came back with two nearly naked Indians of the Guaymi tribe, their bodies painted in red, black, and white. Patches of cotton fabric covered their genitals. They wore golden mirrors around their necks.

As Columbus sailed along the shoreline of Cerebaro for the next week and a half, his Talaman interpreters were sent ashore to meet with Indians in each village along the way. They had become expert in their task and gleaned two bits of information that confirmed everything Columbus had suspected about his planned voyage: first, that an abundant source of gold existed to the south, and second, that another ocean was nine days' march inland. Columbus wrote: "They gave me the names of many places on the sea coast where they said there was gold and goldfields, too. In all these places I had visited, I had found the information given me true, and this assured me that the same would be so of the province of Ciguare, which as they told me, lies inland nine days journey westward. They say that there is a vast quantity of gold there and that the people wear coral ornaments on their heads and stout bracelets of the same material on their wrists and ankles. They also embellish and inlay stools, chests and tables with it. I was told too that the women wore circlets on their heads that hung down to their shoulders. All the people of these parts agree about this and from all that they say I should be glad of a tenth of those riches. According to reports, they are all acquainted with red pepper." He wrote further of the land that would one day become known as Panama: "They also say that Ciguare is surrounded by water, and that ten days journey away is the River Ganges."

This stunning news was a vindication for Columbus —

the passage existed. But he was a man of the sea, as were his crews. They were not equipped to march nine days through a potentially hostile jungle to reach the other ocean. It was not enough to locate an overland passage. Finding the nautical passage was vital.

Propelled by this awareness, Columbus sailed from Cerebaro back into the Caribbean on October 17. Two days later he arrived at the mouth of the Guaiga River, where a hostile tribe tried in vain to frighten the fleet into leaving. A hundred warriors raced into the water until it reached their waists. They waved spears, blew horns, banged on drums, and even spit at the bemused Spaniards. Columbus refused to react, however, and soon a boat was sent ashore. The Indians traded sixteen golden mirrors for three hawk's bells apiece — roughly akin to trading a hefty nugget of gold for a few pennies.

For the next two weeks, Columbus's fleet sailed down the coast, trading for gold wherever possible. He even pinpointed a coastal village known as Veragua as the center of the gold trade, "where, according to the Indians," Fernando wrote, "gold was found and the mirrors were made." The rainy season was still in full swing, and the weather and seas could be daunting, but those two weeks were the high point of the journey. Everything Columbus had promised about the New World's potential for wealth was true. His critics would be forever silenced once word reached Spain.

As if crossing an imaginary boundary line, the day after passing Veragua Columbus learned from the Talaman that he had left the gold region behind. A village named Cubiga marked its southern border. As if the elements were conspiring to give the announcement greater impact, a raging storm accompanied the disheartening news. Winds blowing from the north and powerful rain strafed the fleet. "I ran before the wind wherever it took me," wrote a sullen Columbus, "without power to resist."

On November 2, 1502, Columbus discovered a harbor he named Portobello. "He gave it that name because it is very large, beautiful, thickly populated, and surrounded by cultivated country," Fernando noted. "Within the harbor vessels may lie close to shore and beat out if they wish. The country about the harbor is well tilled and full of houses only a stone's throw or crossbow shot apart, all as pretty as a picture, the fairest thing one ever saw."

The fleet spent a week in Portobello, trapped inside by a foul weather front that made sailing far less attractive than safe harbor. Each day the local Cuña Cuña paddled their dugout canoes to the ships and traded food for pieces of brass. On Wednesday, November 9, Columbus sailed from Portobello and soon found himself fighting weather and wind. He was actually pushed backward for a dozen miles on November 10. It would be like this for the next month, a continuum of battles against the elements and discovering harbors. Fourteen wearying days were spent in a place he named Bastimientos, where the storms and strong currents kept the fleet from venturing out. On the day they were finally able to continue, they made fifteen leagues before, as Columbus wrote in frustration, "I was driven back by the wind and furious current to the port I had just left."

Escaping out to sea soon after, he inched his way along the coast, battling storm after storm. Columbus's bedraggled voyage was taking on the air of an aquatic death march. The weather made each day of sailing wearying and near pointlessness. Columbus turned for land once again, anchoring his ships in yet another small cove. He named this latest sanctuary Retrete, both for its lack of size and the rescissory tack the voyage was making. Retrete, wrote Fernando, was "so small it would not hold more than four or five ships. The entrance was only seventy-five to one hundred feet wide, with rocks as sharp as diamonds sticking up on either side."

It was a desultory shelter, neither inviting nor lush. Its sandy shores were populated by hostile Indians and crocodiles reeking of a powerful musk that were "so ravenous and cruel that if they find a man asleep ashore they will drag him into the water to devour him," wrote Fernando.

The harbor was so tiny that ships were arrayed side by side, with the outer vessels almost touching the shore. The teenagers who made up such a large part of the crews and who had left Spain as mere boys in May had become grown men by November. They sneaked off the ships at night to meet up with willing Indian women on shore, which only increased local hostility toward the Spanish.

Unbeknownst to Columbus, Rodrigo de Bastides had also taken refuge in Retrete one year earlier. The harbor marked the end of his westward push along the coast of Paria. Columbus's approach had come from the opposite direction. Thus his entrance into Retrete meant the Caribbean rim had been fully explored. If there was a westward passage to be found, one of them had sailed right past it.

For fifteen long days the fleet endured the claustrophobia of Retrete, "compelled to do so by the cruel weather, and when I thought it was ending it was only beginning," Columbus lamented. During a rare moment of calm, he immediately ordered the fleet to sea. But before the ships had gone ten miles along the coast, storms struck again, pushing them backward. In the midst of it all, Columbus's chronic battles with gout and rheumatism began once again. He took to bed. "For ten days I was lost with no hope of life. Eyes never saw the sea so rough, so ugly or seething with foam. The wind did not give us a chance to go ahead or even allow us a chance of running, nor did it allow us to shelter under any headland. There I was held in those seas turned to blood, boiling like a cauldron on a mighty fire. The skies had never looked more threatening. For a day and a night they blazed like a furnace and the lightning burst in such flashes that every moment I looked to see whether my masts and sails had not been struck. They came with such terrifying fury that we believed the ships would be utterly destroyed. All this time rain fell unceasingly from the sky. One cannot say that it rained, for it was like a repetition of the deluge. The crews were now so broken that they prayed for death to replace them from their martyrdom."

With these words Columbus officially gave up the hunt for the westward passage. The dream he had nurtured for three decades was no more. Bruised in body and spirit, lacking the will to endure another horrific day of foul weather, he ordered his fleet to turn back. There would be no more hunt for the passage. The day was December 5, 1502. The time had come to return to Spain.

WAR

CHAPTER EIGHTEEN

Dark December

Winter 1502–1503
Veragua

I f only in terms of Columbus's seamanship and the courage of his crews, the fourth voyage had been a success.
But the time when merely discovering new lands guaranteed favor in the royal court was past. Back in Spain Ferdinand was contemplating a war against France and was strapped
for funding. Ferdinand also owed British king Henry VII a
dowry of 100,000 crowns for the marriage of his sixteen-
year-old daughter Catherine of Aragon to the Prince of
Wales — this, despite the prince's death of "sweating sickness" after just five months of marriage. For Columbus to return to Spain empty-handed (and passage undiscovered)
would mean humiliation.

The solution was to find more gold before sailing home.
"The Admiral, perceiving that the violence of the east and
northeast winds did not abate, and that no trade could be
carried on with these people," Fernando wrote of the
shores surrounding Retrete, "decided to turn back and ver-
ify what the Indians had said about the mines of Veragua."

Turning back did not guarantee the wind for which
Columbus longed: the endless gale changed directions

without rhyme or reason, one day pushing them toward Veragua and the next shoving them backward. "And just as we were hopeful of making port," Fernando wrote, "the wind would change again, sometimes with such terrible thunder and lightning that the men dared not open their eyes and it seemed the ships were sinking." No place was safe. If the fleet stood out to sea, it was subjected to enormous waves, nonstop rain, lightning that struck so close it made the men's hair stand on end, and gale-force winds. When they sailed for shore, the currents and waves were so unpredictable that it was impossible to take refuge in a harbor for fear of being wrecked on submerged reefs and a rocky shoreline. The foul weather made using the *jardines* a suicidal act; thus the hold reeked like a cesspool from the buckets loaded with feces and urine, which were emptied only occasionally because of the weather. Yet the men were forced to take refuge there when it came time to sleep.

Through it all, shipboard routine — the turning of the hourglass, the changing of the watch, the trimming of the sails, the chanting of ditties, the ritual of vespers each night — muted their worst fears. That routine provided distraction and the comfort of normalcy.

But no one could deny that the sea was a terrifying place during those interminable days and nights. Just when things seemed to calm down, the ocean once again found a devious way to make it worse. On Tuesday, December 13, the sky filled with ominous black clouds. They began spinning in a counterclockwise direction, racing faster and faster until they spun at almost three hundred miles per hour. The water vapor saturating the atmosphere was soon caught up in this dervish, and a tornado-like funnel cloud stretched from the sky to sea, expelling raging winds that threatened to pluck overboard any man careless enough to stand in the open. Surface water was sucked up into the cloud until the rotating mass wasn't just wind but a huge waterspout capable of decimating any ship in its path.

For Columbus's superstitious sailors the waterspout was an act of God, and as a group they prayed for deliverance. The waterspout passed between two of the ships, diffusing into just another terrifying patch of wind as they chanted the Gospel of John in unison. In a moment designed to calm his superstitious men, Columbus appeared on deck, uplifted sword in his right hand and a Bible in his left. "Fear not," he said, quoting from the famous moment where Christ calms the waters so Peter may walk across, "it is I." Whether by divine intervention or merely a weakening weather system, the wind passed and the sea grew calm, leaving men and ships safe but near the breaking point.

But again the ocean showed her terrors. This time they came from below. As if they could sense the crew's battered state, hordes of sharks suddenly gathered round the ships, their sleek fusiform bodies circling, serrated teeth bared. The dorsal fins of aptly named hammerheads, powerful makos, long-tailed threshers, tiny sharp-nosed, and aggressive tigers sliced through the sea. The sailors loathed their presence, as if it portended some greater doom. Like the calm preceding their arrival, though, the sharks were a blessing. The barrels of salted beef and fish packed in the hold at the start of the journey were long gone. The ship's biscuits were so soggy that they could be consumed only by throwing them into a stew pot and boiling them into a weevil-infested porridge. Although the sharks were capable of eating men, they were just as capable of being eaten. Nautical superstitions were set aside as the famished sailors cast hooks and chains over the side, trawling for, then clubbing, the predators as they were pulled up over the rail. The sharks were so voracious that the only fishing lure needed was a piece of red cloth. "Some viewed it as an evil omen and others thought it poor fishing," Fernando wrote, "but all did the shark the honor of eating it."

Thus fortified, the crews greeted yet another bout of raw weather. Christmas Day found Columbus's ships anchored in a protected harbor whose mouth faced north. The storms had battered *El Gallego* so badly she needed significant repairs, and the time in this secluded harbor was focused on leaning her against a rocky beach for careening, as well as replenishing wood and water on all ships. Without knowing it Columbus was anchored at the mouth of his Oriental passage, the Pacific Ocean just thirty-five miles away. But after all they had endured since leaving Spain, and with stomachs growling from dwindling food supplies, Columbus would have courted mutiny if he had ordered his men to explore the region's dense jungles, with their infestations of snakes and crocodile. New Year's Day came and went. Columbus sailed from the harbor on January 3, 1503, none the wiser about what lay across the isthmus. Four centuries later the harbor would form the opening to the Panama Canal, connecting one great sea to another — and in the exact spot Columbus had theorized before he left Spain to begin the fourth voyage.

Curiously, while Columbus was unwilling to send his sailors inland to hunt for the passage, he was more than willing to have them hunt for gold. For three long days and nights the fleet continued their endless battle against the elements as they retraced their route to Veragua's gold region. Upon discovering a pair of rivers reputed to be the site of inland gold mines — one he named the Belen (for Bethlehem), and the other which the Indians called Veragua, for the region — an exhausted Columbus immediately ordered boats to sound their depths for future investigation. "On the day of Epiphany I reached Veragua, completely broken in spirit," Columbus wrote.

The mouth of the Belen was protected by a shallow

sandbar. There was no going in or out until flood tide. But once he maneuvered his vessels inside, Columbus was pleased to find a wide, protected harbor extending a half mile inland from the sandbar. "Here Our Lord gave me a river and a safe harbor, though it was less than eight feet deep. I got in with difficulty and the next day the storm returned. If it had found me outside I should not have been able to get in because of the bar," he recorded.

Columbus's fleet was situated just outside the mouth of the river but inside the protective shoal of the sandbar, which acted like a reef to block large waves from entering the estuary. From the door of his cabin, Columbus had a clear view up the river, as well as north and south along the Caribbean coast. Low hills rose on either side of the Belen, covered by thick jungle. The river meandered inland — wide, green, and lazy.

The true splendor and mystery of the Veragua region, however, lay in the interior. Columbus could infer little by glancing at the landscape: montane forests climbing steeply upward until, at an altitude of two thousand feet, they became that ethereal wonder known as cloud forest. A vast diversity in flora was also obvious, ranging from palm trees and pines along the coast to canopy trees blocking the light far inland. Now and then a golden-headed quetzal or a saffron-headed parrot flew past. What Columbus couldn't see, but his men would discover through repeated forays into the jungle, was that Veragua was one of the most diverse eco-regions on earth. Situated on the land bridge between what would later be known as North and South America, Veragua was where the species of both continents intermingled. Exotic strains of primate such as the nocturnal western night monkey, spider monkey, brown-headed spider monkey, mantled howler monkey, and white-faced capuchin shared space in the treetops with quail, doves, screech owls, hummingbirds, salamanders, and colorful frogs. Carnivorous big cats like pumas and jaguars prowled unafraid through the moist vegetation. Smaller cats of amazing versatility and stealth hid in the brush and treetops: the swimming jaguarundi, the snake-eating ocelot, and the amazingly agile margay, with its hind feet that rotated 180 degrees. And there were snakes, of course. The most lethal was the bush-master, a twelve-foot-long viper with a dark brown diamond pattern. Before striking, the bushmaster shook its tail in warning, much like a rattlesnake. But the bushmaster had no rattle, hence its attack was sudden and silent — blindside death.

Columbus was unconcerned and uninterested in these wonders. His fear of returning to Spain empty-handed fueled a growing desperation. The only natural wonders he cared about were those interfering with his mission. "It rained without stopping until 14 February," Columbus continued. "On 24 January, when I was lying there in safety, the river suddenly became very high and violent." Like the tidal wave in Boca de la Sierpe, the flash flood in the Belen was terrifying and sudden. The endless days of rain had saturated the jungle soil from mountaintops to sea. When the land could absorb no more water and became as slick and impermeable as a sheet of glass, the rain ran off the land into the Belen. The wall of water that nearly swamped Columbus's ships and drowned his men began high in the mountains, gaining force, speed, size, and momentum as it charged toward the sea. As fate would have it, Columbus had anchored his vessels directly in the juggernaut's path. "The cables and bollards were broken and the ships were almost swept away. I had never seen them in greater danger, but Our Lord saved us as ever," wrote the Admiral. Then, showing how weary he had become, Columbus concluded: "I know of no one who has suffered greater trials."

By now Columbus's superstitious sailors were convinced the voyage was cursed. The litany of terrors was unlike that of any voyage in history: hurricane, sharks, endless rain, diminished rations, waterspouts, shipworms, and now the tranquil Belen turned furious. The men were homesick, ruing the day they had signed on. They longed for a warm bed on dry land, a hot meal at the family table, and sex — not just furtive midnight masturbation, but the comforts of a real woman or man.

Columbus was not indifferent to their misery. He was thinking of Spain, too. But a decade after discovering the New World, it was imperative that he prove his merits as an explorer all over again. Dangerous conditions were to be expected.

Redoubling his effort to find gold, Columbus sent men ashore to search for Veragua's reputed mines, even as the rains continued. The crews leaned into their oars as they paddled up the overflowing Belen, scanning the lush banks for signs of treasure, as if chunks of gold would be littered in the mud. Other crews were ordered to paddle out past the sandbar and then west along the coast before rowing inland up the Veragua River. These expeditions revealed the Belen to be a fine harbor but a poor source of gold. The Veragua River, however, was everything the region was supposed to be — and much more. On their first journey up the lazy green river, Columbus's men came back with a handful of golden quills, several golden nuggets, and twenty gold mirrors. Obviously the local Indians were as fond of gold as the Spanish. A jubilant Columbus immediately ordered another inland foray, this time led by Bartolomé.

The intrepid Bartolomé, whose worth to the expedition grew with each passing adventure, did more than just find a smattering of gold. He promptly befriended the local cacique, or chief, a man named Quibian, a Guaymi tribal leader. Noting the cacique's powerful comportment and the reverence with which his tribe treated him, Bartolomé recognized that with Quibian's help the Spanish would be able to explore the jungles without fear of Indian attack. Quibian was just as savvy, and recognizing that the Spaniards would make a fierce opponent, he was eager to placate them. The friendship was cemented the next day. Quibian took the remarkable step of paddling to *La Capitana* to meet with Columbus. The cacique and his men brought gold as a sign of goodwill. They traded with the Spanish and left.

Thus life at the mouth of the Belen took on a peaceful air. Other than the flood of January 24, which saw *La Capitana* ripped from her mooring and sent crashing into *El Gallego,* rain was the only nuisance. The nearby forests were rife with game. The rivers and ocean offered fresh fish and turtles. Mountains could be seen in the distance, rising into the clouds. Nevertheless, the weather was so severe that a return to the Veragua River was impossible. "So violent a storm raged," wrote Fernando, "that the fleet would have been shattered to pieces at the mouth of the river."

The rains were still pouring down on February 6, but the sea was finally calm enough for the ships' boats to venture beyond the sandbar. It was dawn as Bartolomé left for the Veragua River again, this time leading sixty-eight men. They immediately rowed to Quibian's village, where they spent the night and the next day. Quibian was only too happy to tell Bartolomé how to find the legendary gold mines of Veragua, providing two warriors as guides.

What Quibian didn't tell Bartolomé was that the mines in question weren't his — they belonged to his enemies, the Urira people, with whom Quibian was at war.

On Wednesday, February 8, the Spanish sailors marched fifteen miles through the jungle, following the path laid out by Quibian. It was the younger members of Columbus's corps who had been sent up the Veragua with Bartolomé; the older men remained behind. Even so, the march was a taxing slog that quickly sapped their strength. The path took them uphill, through mosquito-infested jungle, on trails slick from the rain. It was dark, because the thick jungle canopy filtered out almost all sunlight. As if intentionally worn from the earth to resemble a serpent, the root-covered trail wound back and forth across a thin, green river, requiring the men to constantly ford the waters. At the end of one day's march, they had tramped just fifteen miles and endured forty-three crossings of the meandering jungle river. The exhausted sailors slept along its banks that night, swatting mosquitoes and keeping a sharp eye for jaguars as they leaned against trees or curled up on the cool black earth.

The march resumed at first light. Within two hours the guides abruptly announced that they had arrived at the mines. Strangely, the Spaniards had brought no shovels or picks; the mission's sole purpose had been reconnaissance. But Bartolomé, not wishing to return empty-handed after such an arduous trek, ordered the men to scrounge about the jungle, plucking what gold they could from the ground. Much to his amazement, they were successful. "Within two hours of arrival each had collected some gold among the roots of the trees," wrote Fernando. "They were much pleased with their finds."

Columbus was delighted when Bartolomé returned and proudly displayed the booty. In Veragua's seemingly limitless supplies of gold, the Admiral saw the makings of a fortune. He immediately decided to build a new colony on the banks of the Belen River, one that would take the place of Hispaniola as his new seat of power in the New World. Eighty men would remain behind as the rest of the crew sailed back to Spain. Bartolomé would be their leader. El Gallego would not make the crossing home but would remain anchored just inside the sandbar, waiting to serve as the new community's transportation should they wish to journey up the coast or across the Caribbean. With its protected harbor, friendly locals, abundant food supply, and proven wealth, the region surrounding the Belen River had the makings of a dynamic new foothold in the New World. Columbus christened it Santa María de Belen and sent a group of strong men ashore to scout a site.

At the end of February, work was begun on houses along the riverbank, just inland from the mouth. The foundations were made of wood and the roofs of palm leaves. The walls were made of thatch. There were eight houses in all, along with an armory and storehouse strong enough to hold all the new colony's gold. Food supplies being low, Columbus set aside a ration of staples — wine, garlic, cheese, and vinegar — to start off the new colonists. "He also left all the fishing equipment, such as nets and hooks, because all the rivers of the great country swarm with fish. At certain times of the year various kinds of fish comes in shoals up the rivers and to the seashore," Fernando noted. "The Indians also eat much maize, which is a grain like millet that grows to a tassel or ear. From this they make white and red wine in the same way that beer is made in England, adding spice according to taste."

There was an urgency to the construction belying Fernando's anthropological notations. Shipworms were ravaging the fleet. Each vessel was taking on water, and no beach was available for resealing the hulls. Just as alarming was that water levels in the river had fallen dramatically. The fleet had arrived during the rainy season, when the swollen Belen River provided enough flow to safely float ships over the sandbar at high tide. But by March the river was so low that not even high tide could carry the ships out to sea. Ironically, Columbus's only hope for survival was rain. Without it his entire fleet would be stranded at the mouth of the Belen with no hope of rescue.

Quibian soon added a new wrinkle to Columbus's problems. He had considered the Spaniards visitors and nothing more. All along he had worked to placate them in order to avoid conflict during their stay. But the construction along the Belen worried him greatly. He sent messengers to all the tribes in the region, asking for their help in driving away the Spaniards. The tribes were eager to assist but also curious about the strange visitors of which Quibian spoke. On the way to join forces with Quibian, they often stopped by Santa María de Belen to see the new houses and the four great ships for themselves. The Indians made no attempt to conceal themselves; they simply stood on the jungle fringe, faces painted for war and armament in their hands, observing. When they had seen enough, they would leave without conflict.

Columbus became concerned when the visits, which seemed so random at first, multiplied. His prayers for rain had gone unanswered, and his leaking ships were vulnerable targets. The Indians all claimed they were merely passing through, on their way to do battle in the nearby province of Cobrava. But Columbus was doubtful they were telling the truth and increasingly anxious about their intentions. If an Indian attack was in the offing, he wanted to know in advance.

It was then that one of the voyage's hitherto minor characters stepped to the fore. His name was Diego Mendez, a thirty-year-old notary from Spain's Segura region. A former majordomo of Columbus's, Mendez had enlisted for the voyage as a "gentleman volunteer" — an *escudero* — aboard the *Santiago*. Loyalty and courage were Mendez's strengths; as a young man he had followed the Count of Penaflor into exile in France, Flanders, and England after fighting for the count's unsuccessful cause in the Spanish civil war of La Beltraneja. Mendez also had a way with languages and had quickly become so fluent in Quibian's native tongue that he served as one of the fleet's interpreters. While performing that task Mendez had become one of Columbus's most trusted assistants, displaying the sort of loyalty and bravery of which the Admiral was so fond. "My

Lord," Mendez warned Columbus of the Indians, "these men who have been going about here in battle array say they are going to join the men of Veragua to attack the people of Cobrava and Aurira, but I do not believe them. On the contrary, they are gathering to burn the ships and kill us all."

Columbus called Mendez's bluff, asking him what should be done. "I proposed to his Lordship that I should set out in a boat and go up the coast towards Veragua and see where they had pitched their camp."

The Admiral thought the idea brilliant. He ordered a boat lowered and a crew to row the brave young notary west. What Mendez discovered that March afternoon confirmed Columbus's worst fears: a thousand warriors camped on the beach just two miles away, armed for war, and well stocked with food. Mendez could see them clearly from the sea. The Indians could just as clearly see the Spanish launch feathering its oars just outside the surf break. Mendez was intoxicated by his discovery and eager to learn all he could about their intentions. To the shock of the boat crew, he ordered them to row to shore so he could speak with the Indians. The sailors had no choice but to comply. Mendez was rowed close to shore but not all the way up onto the beach. He jumped from the boat and splashed through the waist-high water up onto the sand. "I leaped ashore alone, into the midst of them, leaving my boat afloat, and spoke to them as well as I knew how," Mendez wrote, "offering to accompany them on their war in their armed boat. They stoutly refused my aid, saying that they had no need of it." The Indians made no attempt to stop the young Spaniard when he splashed back to the boat.

Columbus was relieved to see Mendez return safely but was holding out hope that the Indians' intent was not hostile. He ordered Mendez to get more definitive information. "I offered to go to them with a single companion, which I did, in greater anticipation of death than survival," wrote Mendez. "I then followed the shore to the Veragua River, where I found two canoes manned by strange Indians who informed me very clearly that these people were going to burn our ships and kill us all, but had delayed because a boat had surprised them."

Ignoring the news that his first visit had saved the lives of Columbus and all hands, Mendez pressed his investigation. He boldly offered to pay the warriors if they would paddle him upriver in their canoes. They refused and added a stern warning about traveling inland: "If I did so both I and my companion would certainly be killed," Mendez reported.

Mendez was a persuasive man, not easily deterred. Against long odds, he finally convinced the reluctant Indians to accept his money and paddle him and young Diego de Escobar, a ship's boy from *La Vizcaino,* upriver. The relative safety of the sea was left behind, replaced by thick jungle hemming the dark green river on both sides. Mendez and Escobar sat amidships, their lives dependent upon the goodwill of total strangers — warriors, their weapons at the ready — capable of killing them in an instant.

The canoes paddled farther and farther up the river, which narrowed and turned a darker shade of green. The trees hanging over the bank reached across toward one another, threatening to blot out the sun. Indian families watched their progress from shore as the canoes passed village after village, bound for Quibian's hilltop fortress. The paddlers mentioned that Quibian was sick from an arrow wound in his leg. Mendez tucked that nugget of information away for later use.

Far upriver the canoes stopped. The riverbank was lined with warriors wearing the colorful Guaymi cloak about their shoulders. They carried spears, clubs, and bows and were spoiling for a fight. It was no time to show fear, so

Mendez did not. Rather, his behavior veered toward the audacious. "They would not let me go to the principal hut of the cacique," Mendez recorded. "But I pretended that I had come to him as a surgeon to treat a wound that he had in his leg, and in return for the presents I gave them they let me go to his house, which stood on a leveled hilltop with a large space around it and was surrounded by the heads of three hundred warriors whom they had killed in battle."

As Mendez and Escobar boldly marched to the main entrance of Quibian's palatial residence, the women and children who were gathered outside ran into the house, screaming. An angry young man rushed from the house, screaming at Mendez in the Guaymi language. It was one of Quibian's sons, and he was furious that the Spaniards had come to their home. "He laid his hands on me and thrust me away in a single push. To calm him down I said I had come to cure his father's leg and showed him some ointment I had brought for this purpose." But the young man was not swayed. He forbade Mendez from entering the palace.

Mendez took stock of the situation: he and Escobar were deep in the jungle, surrounded by hundreds of men who would kill them the instant Quibian gave the order. To insist on entering the palace would be akin to issuing the death order themselves. Mendez responded by creating a third, bizarre option. "I took out a comb, scissors and a mirror and asked Escobar my companion to comb and cut my hair," wrote Mendez. Escobar quickly did as he was ordered, aware that their every move was being scrutinized by a people who had never seen a scissors before. He carefully pulled the comb through Mendez's hair, which was oily and damp from a day of hiking and the tropical humidity. Then he snipped at Mendez's black locks, letting them fall to the jungle floor.

Much to Mendez's relief, the Indians were fascinated.

"The chief's son and others who were standing around were astonished. I then made Escobar comb the young man's hair and cut it with scissors, and after that I gave him the comb and the mirror and at this he was pacified."

Seizing the moment, Mendez informed the Indians that he and Escobar were hungry from their long day. He asked that they bring food, "which they brought immediately, and we ate and drank in love and comradeship and remained friends."

Mendez and Escobar left soon after, eager to get home before dark. They were paddled back downriver and then walked to the ships. Mendez went straight to Columbus with the news. Based on Mendez's reconnaissance it was clear the Indians were planning to annihilate them. Columbus summed up the situation this way: "I knew that friendly relations would not continue for long, since they were very uncivilized and our men very peremptory, and I had taken possession of land in his [Quibian's] territory. When he saw the houses built and trade increasing, he decided to burn them down and put us all to death."

Columbus ordered a preemptive strike that would guarantee the safety of the new colony. He aimed to take Quibian and his top aides prisoner, bringing them back to Castile in chains. Once these, the most ardent advocates of killing the Spanish, were gone, a separate peace could be made with the weakened tribes.

On March 30 Columbus sent Bartolomé, Mendez, and a contingent of seventy-three men to Quibian's village. They rowed up the Veragua River as stealthily as possible, but Quibian's spies warned him of their arrival. It was late afternoon when the Spanish finally reached the embankment below Quibian's house. They were told not to approach any farther, a warning that Bartolomé pretended to heed. He marched uphill with Mendez, an Indian interpreter, and four other men, giving the appearance he had come in peace. To all who asked, Bartolomé claimed to be concerned about Quibian's arrow wound.

But Bartolomé had secretly instructed the remainder of the men to surround the palace from a distance. "He ordered the others to follow by twos, each a certain distance apart from the other. Having come within a musket shot of the house, they were to surround it and allow no one to escape," wrote Fernando.

Again Quibian sent word that Bartolomé must halt, warning them against entering the palace. "He did this to keep the Christians from seeing his wives," Fernando theorized, "for the Indians are very jealous." Columbus's sailors had routinely sneaked away from the ship to have relations with Indian girls. Quibian's outrage about that intercourse was a prime reason he wanted the Spanish dead. He had anticipated Bartolomé's arrival and had prepared a trap of his own.

Bartolomé and his small group approached the house. Quibian came to the doorway and sat down, too weak from his wound to stand for long. Bartolomé ordered Mendez and the other Spaniards to hold their position while he marched forward with the Indian interpreter.

Quibian watched them approach. He did not stand to greet them. His warriors were inside the house, prepared for battle. On Quibian's orders they were to rush out and kill the Spaniards.

Bartolomé and Quibian greeted one another. Through the interpreter Bartolomé inquired about Quibian's wound. Then Bartolomé abruptly grabbed Quibian's arm, the signal for the attack to commence. Quibian struggled to free himself, all signs of any injury abruptly disappearing. "And though Quibian was a strong man," Fernando wrote, "he managed to hold him until the other four Christians ran up and made him captive." At that instant Mendez fired a musket shot into the air. The Spanish forces surrounding the house raced forward, some carrying muskets and others armed with just clubs and knives. As Quibian's hands and feet were being bound, Bartolomé led the Spaniards inside the house. Fifty people were crowded inside: warriors, as well as women and children. In the brief skirmish that ensued, all were taken prisoner. "These offered a rich ransom for their freedom, saying that they would give a great treasure that they had hidden in a nearby wood," wrote Fernando.

Bartolomé stayed behind to claim their offering, a literal king's ransom of golden disks and gold molded into eagles. He released some, but not all, of the prisoners. The children and warriors were left behind, but Quibian, his wife, and his top lieutenants were marched down to the river and loaded into boats for the trip back to the fleet. The sun was setting, and the jungle growing dark.

The prisoners were entrusted to the command of Juan Sanchez, the chief pilot of the fleet. Sanchez hailed from Cádiz and was well respected by the men. "The Adelantado ordered him not to let Quibian escape," wrote Fernando, "and he replied he would permit the hairs on his beard to be plucked one by one if the cacique got away."

As his men rowed, their oars lapping the placid river water in unison, Sanchez sat next to Quibian, whose hands and feet were tied. Sanchez had tied a rope to Quibian's bonds and held one end as further insurance against losing the treasured captive. By the time the ocean grew near enough to smell its salty breezes, night had fallen. Quibian and Juan Sanchez sat together in silence, neither able to speak the other's language. The Indian was docile, compliant. Sanchez lowered his guard. "About half a league from the mouth Quibian complained his bonds were hurting him, and out of pity Juan Sanchez untied all the ropes but one that he held in his hand." Again Quibian settled back and feigned compliance. He chattered quietly with the other prisoners, but his tone was unthreatening. All the while he was studying Sanchez, biding his time.

As chief pilot of the fleet, Sanchez had numerous responsibilities, so as he continued clutching the rope tied to Quibian's hands, he also kept an eye on the weather, the rowboat's course toward the open sea, the other boats as they paddled in the darkness, and the possibility of an Indian counterattack from the riverbank. For an instant he turned away from Quibian. That was long enough — Quibian leaped overboard, propelling himself into the water with such force that Sanchez was almost pulled in after him. Off balance, the Spaniard let go of the rope.

Sanchez and his men anxiously scanned the water's surface for signs of Quibian, but saw none, for the chief remained underwater. The Spanish tried to listen as well, hoping to hear the sound of a man surfacing and gasping for breath or thrashing up the riverbank, but the remaining prisoners were chanting and yelling, exhorting Quibian. "He vanished," Fernando lamented, "like a stone in the water. Fearing that the others might attempt to escape, they continued their way toward the fleet, much chagrined by their carelessness."

Diego Mendez was in one of the boats as the escape took place. He remembered the moment as pivotal. "The cacique escaped through the carelessness of his captor and subsequently did us great harm."

Quibian was too smart to return home immediately. He hid out in the jungle as the Spanish searched for him the next day. They finally gave up and returned to their ships, unaware that Quibian and the other Indian tribes of Veragua were preparing for the battle that would see the rivers flow red with Spanish blood.

CHAPTER NINETEEN

Caribbean Sprint

April–May 1503
Santa María de Belen

Finally, it rained. As if pretending that the Indian uprising had been quelled once and for all, Columbus hastily populated Santa María de Belen with sailors and prepared to sail for Spain while the river would let him. His two most prized assistants, his brother Bartolomé and Diego Mendez, would lead the new colony in their search for gold and prosperity. Belen would never be a Santo Domingo, capable of harboring dozens of ships and serving as a center of commerce, thanks to the sandbar and its offbeat location. But the Veragua region was indisputably rich in gold, and until it was mined out, Columbus's new city had the potential to be the wealthiest outpost in the New World.

By April 6 *La Capitana, La Vizcaino,* and the *Santiago* had floated safely out to sea. Columbus had ordered all the ballast removed from the holds to lighten them, but each hull still scraped the sandbar and nearly stuck fast. The ballast was then replaced, and as fifty of the new colonists waved farewell from the shore, Columbus weighed anchor for the journey home. The three ships were soon three miles out to sea.

That's when Quibian attacked. His goal was to wipe out the Spanish colony once and for all. The crux of the plan was that Columbus would not only be too far out to sea to send reinforcements but that he would be so far out to sea that he would never even know an attack had taken place. The jungle would reclaim the land, and eventually, it would be as if the Spanish had never come to Veragua at all.

Quibian was a wily tactician, and surprise was on his side. When he sensed Columbus was finally far out to sea, the cacique and his men sprang boldly from hiding. "Lying concealed in the wood they gave a great shout, then another and another, and thus thanks to God gave me time to prepare for battle and organize my defense," Mendez wrote. "We remained on the shore among the huts we had built and they on the wooded mountain an arrow's flight away."

Quibian's forces — four hundred Indians armed with slings, darts, and spears — crept closer and closer, until they were just fifty feet from the huts. "They began to shoot their arrows and hurl their darts as if attacking a bull," Mendez wrote. "The arrows and darts fell thick as hail, and some warriors left the woods to come and attack us with clubs." The cries of the many Spanish wounded soon commingled with the chaotic din of battle.

Until that moment Quibian's forces had the upper hand. But once they sallied forth to fight the Spaniards hand to hand, the playing field was leveled. Bartolomé had arrived on the scene by then, and he led the counterattack, using just a spear for a weapon. Other Spaniards fought the Indians with swords, hacking off arms and legs in a frantic attempt to push the Indians back. The battle wore on; one hour, then two. The Spanish slowly pushed Quibian's forces back into the jungle, but at great cost: seven Spaniards were wounded, and one was dead. The heretofore invulnerable

Bartolomé was one of the wounded, dripping blood and gasping for breath from a dart embedded in his chest.

Meanwhile, out to sea, it was brought to Columbus's attention that *La Capitana*'s water casks were nearly empty. In the rush to set sail, no one had remembered to refill them. Impatient about the oversight, and feverish and confused by a severe attack of malaria, Columbus dropped anchor and made the unusual move of ordering ship's captain Diego Tristan to assume responsibility for the gaffe by personally leading the water party ashore to fill the casks. They were to leave immediately. Two boats were lowered, and casks were handed over the side. A mixed contingent of crew — among them caulkers Domingo Viscaino and Domingo de Arana, numerous able seaman and ship's boys, and a lone gunner named Mateo — began the long row back to Santa María de Belen. At first the sailors, rowing with their backs to land, were unaware of the scene awaiting them on shore. But as their boats drew nearer, they could hear the sounds of musket fire and the war whoops of Quibian's warriors. The sailors rowed faster, racing to their comrades' rescue.

The battle was three hours old when *La Capitana*'s boats floated over the sandbar and into the broad mouth of the Belen. Tristan could clearly see the embattled Spaniards fighting and dying. But rather than help the sailors with whom he had shared so many ordeals at sea, he ordered the boats to remain offshore, fearing that if he drew too close, the colonists would rush to the boats in panic and swamp them. When pressed about his inaction, Tristan replied that his orders were to get water, nothing more. So he waited.

"The battle had lasted for more than three hours and by a miracle the Lord gave us the victory, for we were very few and they were very many," wrote an exhausted Diego Mendez. Only then did Diego Tristan land. He offered no apologies for his lack of assistance. Instead he barked orders that his men prepare to row upriver to fill the casks, at a place where a fresh clear stream flowed into the Belen. An incredulous Mendez, now in charge of the colony and fearful of counterattack, argued against the plan, even though the captain had more authority. He had his orders, Tristan told Mendez, and he could take care of himself. His men had shields to protect them from arrows and rocks. They also carried muskets. In a pinch their oars would make fine war clubs.

As he spoke Tristan kept one eye on the weather. Puffy black clouds filled the sky. Waves were breaking over the sandbar. If conditions worsened he would be forced to spend the night ashore, putting his life in jeopardy and further angering Columbus. He also knew better than to return to *La Capitana* without water, for the fleet would never make Spain without full casks. The men from *La Capitana* quickly rowed three miles "upstream to where the river turns very narrow and dark, lined with such heavy foliage on both banks that it is almost impossible to go ashore," described Fernando.

The Guaymi were hidden in the greenery along the banks. They watched, undetected, as Tristan's boats passed. Then they quietly slipped their canoes into the water and paddled upriver a safe distance behind the Spanish. The Indians were armed with darts and with wooden spears tipped with fish bones. On a signal they accelerated their pace, preferring to attack on the water rather than make for land.

The ambush happened so fast that the men from *La Capitana* barely got a look at the men who killed them. The last thing Diego Tristan ever saw was the spear being plunged into his eye socket, on its way into his brain. The other Spaniards were quickly slaughtered as the canoes appeared all around them, the Indians so numerous and close that muskets and shields could not be wielded. Most ominously for Columbus, Viscaino and Arana, the only two caulkers in the fleet, were among the slain. The Guaymi hacked the bodies and boats and let the corpses and flotsam float downriver with the current.

Of the Spanish, just one man escaped. His name was Juan de Noya, a cooper from Seville. In the manner of Quibian, he swam underwater until he could scramble ashore safely. Then he ran, barefoot and terrified, through a jungle choked with hostile Indians to Santa María de Belen.

The colonists had no boats, no way of reaching Columbus for reinforcements. The Admiral had left the battered and leaking *El Gallego* behind, but the wind was howling, and great waves crashed over the sandbar. The fragile caravel would never make it out to sea without being destroyed by the breakers. Once Noya staggered into their midst, the frantic colonists became mutinous. Even the levelheaded Mendez was unable to maintain more than the barest modicum of order as the embattled settlement at Santa María de Belen seemed on the verge of falling, with the slaughter of Spanish survivors sure to follow. "And all the time the Indians continued to attack us," wrote Mendez, "ceaselessly sounding their trumpets and drums and shouting wildly in the belief that they had conquered us."

The malarial Columbus, by now having heard the battle, sailed back to check on his men. Lacking boats, he couldn't go ashore to investigate, but his worst fears were confirmed when the bodies of Tristan and his fellow *La Capitana* crewmen floated to the mouth of the river. Crows perched on the bloated corpses, picking at the eyes and soft flesh of the face. Inside the sandbar some of the colonists had abandoned Santa María de Belen for the relative safety of *El Gallego*. Stranded and surrounded, they had no way of putting to sea or being rescued. "My brother and the rest of the company were all aboard one ship which was left in the river and I was completely alone outside on this dangerous coast in a high fever and a state of great exhaustion," Columbus wrote. "All hope of escape was dead."

Devastated, the fifty-one-year-old admiral climbed to the top of his tallest mast and beseeched the heavens for help. "Crying in a trembling voice, with tears in my eyes, to all your Highnesses' war captains, at every point of the compass to save me," as he later described his supplications in a letter to the sovereigns. "But there was no reply."

The exhausted Columbus retired to his cabin and sobbed himself to sleep. In his dreams he heard the voice of God scolding him for his lack of faith, reminding the Admiral of His great plan and that there had been glories before, just as there was danger now. "Fear not," the dream ended. "Have trust."

Quibian's forces retreated after three days. The lack of warfare brought silence to the colonies, a silence detected by the Indian prisoners previously captured with Quibian, now on board the *Santiago*. One night, as the ship bobbed at anchor, they discovered the hatch cover unchained. The Indians quickly made a pile of ballast stones directly beneath the hatch. The stronger captives stood atop the makeshift platform and leveraged the heavy wooden opening with their shoulders. The sailors sleeping on deck awoke to the sight of the Guaymi leaping overboard and hurried to shut the hatch. A handful of the Indians escaped. Except for those men on watch, the crew soon went back to sleep. None of the sailors saw or heard anything unusual the rest of the night.

Belowdecks, however, the remaining Guaymi women and men made a suicide pact. Using coils of rope stored in the hold, they fashioned a makeshift gallows from the exposed deck beams. But as they put their full weight into the nooses, it became obvious that the hold was too shallow for them to dangle from the ropes. So they bent their knees until their bodies swung freely. All this was done without a cry or wail, and it wasn't until morning that the swaying corpses were discovered.

The news rocked Columbus. Between the bloodbath on shore and the Guaymi suicides, Santa María de Belen was becoming more and more synonymous with death, its gold a lure on a terrible barb. The Admiral began to consider cutting his losses and abandoning the lucrative colony. The fleet had just one remaining ship's boat, *La Vizcaino*'s launch. Able seaman Pedro de Ledesma, a strong swimmer and frequent critic of Columbus, was rowed to the surf break with orders to swim to shore from there and gather information about the colonists' status.

The news was gruesome. "He learned that the garrison to a man refused to stay in that hopeless situation; they begged the Admiral to take them aboard, for to leave them behind was to condemn them to death. Moreover, there were stirrings of mutiny among them, with some refusing to obey the Adelantado or the captains, and only awaiting a break in the weather to go off by themselves in a canoe," Fernando recounted. "They said if the Admiral did not take them aboard they would risk their lives in this way, rather than wait for death at the hands of those cruel butchers, the Indians."

With that Columbus gave the reluctant order to abandon Santa María de Belen. Getting the men out of there was not so easy. "When the Admiral learned of the defeat suffered by those men, and how discontented and dejected they were, he decided to wait for a turn in the weather and take them aboard. He had to do this with great danger to himself because he was lying off the coast with no possibility of saving them or himself if the weather grew worse."

The weather improved, though, and Diego Mendez once again displayed his remarkable resourcefulness. He lashed poles atop the hulls of two captured Indian canoes and tied the canoes together. Casks of wine, oil, and vinegar were roped to the canoes and ferried out to the fleet. It took seven journeys to carry all the supplies. The colonists went next. "I remained with five men to the last and entered the last boat at nightfall," Mendez recorded. "The Admiral was highly delighted with this action and repeatedly embraced me, kissing me on both cheeks, in gratitude for the service I had done him." Columbus was so thrilled by Mendez's resourcefulness and leadership that he named him captain of *La Capitana,* to take the place of Diego Tristan. "I accepted this in order to oblige him as it was a service of great responsibility," wrote Mendez.

On April 16, 1503, Columbus's fleet sailed away from Santa María de Belen. A stripped and porous *El Gallego* bobbed at anchor in the harbor, a nautical ghost that would soon settle to the bottom, never to be found. Columbus's crews were thankful to be away from the Indians and thrilled for the familiarity and relative safety of their shipboard homes. But they were just as aware that the security was fleeting. *La Capitana, La Vizcaino,* and the *Santiago* were infested with shipworms. Not only were the ships' pumps working around the clock, but the men had taken to bailing with kettles and buckets — anything to stem the ocean's advance. Still it kept coming. The fleet would be lucky to make it to Hispaniola, let alone Spain.

They had no choice but to try. Columbus sailed east along the coast once again, hugging the shore until he could make a sprint due north for Hispaniola — or perhaps, more ambitiously, farther east to Spain, should the ships miraculously increase in seaworthiness. The most important task at that point was saving his fleet. If Hispaniola were to be his course, he would deal with Governor Ovando when the time came.

CHAPTER TWENTY

Barely Afloat

May–June 1503
The Northern Caribbean

Columbus's easterly course may have made sense to him, but it was not received well by his frayed crew. Several men had overheard the ships' pilots telling Columbus that Hispaniola lay due north. Columbus, the crew feared, was trying to sail straight for Spain in his leaking ships.

The grumbling grew worse a week later, when it was necessary to abandon the rotted *Vizcaino*. The fleet was fewer than a hundred miles from Santa María de Belen, and Columbus realized there was a distinct possibility that Indian warriors had traveled along the shore from the colony, waiting for the fleet to make landfall. He sailed warily into a small protected cove and turned *La Capitana* and the *Santiago* so that their bows faced the open sea, allowing for a quick escape if attacked. Columbus's sense of urgency was so great that *La Vizcaino* never even dropped anchor — the hasty evacuation began as soon as she was run aground. Using the *Santiago*'s longboat as a ferry, the remaining twenty-three members of *La Vizcaino*'s crew were split between the other two ships. The ship had been prestripped of rigging, tackle, and sails, which were hastily rowed to the other ships and divided. Heavier items, such as lombard cannons, cannon balls, and ballast stone, were too large for the small rowboat and were left behind. *La Vizcaino*'s crew was in such a hurry to abandon the spongy planking of their sinking ship that they made the grave error of neglecting to gather all the provisions, leaving a large number of ceramic jars filled with stores dangling from their netting in the hold. In the days to come, when the sailors' bellies would quake from starvation, the oversight would haunt them.

Columbus sailed from the cove without being attacked, continuing east along the coast with his two remaining ships, passing Portobello and the narrow enclave at Retrete. Fulfilling the crews' worst fears, Columbus had begun making silent plans to attempt an ocean crossing to Spain. His rationale was that he could sail swiftly home and then return immediately to the goldfields with fresh ships and enough men to quell the Indians. But this proved to be just a passing fancy.

On May 1 Columbus abandoned any illusions about sailing to Europe. His ships were too porous, and the mood of his crews far too hostile. Just off the thick jungles that would later become infamous as the Darien Gap, the isthmus connecting Central and South America, he prudently chose the path of least resistance and turned toward Hispaniola. Within days his two remaining ships were far out in the Caribbean, fragile, waterlogged, and beyond the sight of land. After a week the easterly current joined a flow moving north. There was still no sight of land, and the men anxiously scanned the horizon, sure that Columbus was lost. The overloaded vessels soon ran low on food. All that remained were the wormy biscuits and a small amount of oil and vinegar. The ships rode low in the water because of the tremendous amount of water in the holds, and three pumps were being worked around the clock. "With all our pumps, pots and cauldrons," Diego Mendez noted, "we were still unable to draw off all the water that entered through the worm holes." Now Columbus began to believe the ships would sink before reaching even Hispaniola. Trying to ignore the stench of the hold and battling the exhaustion of too many sleepless nights manning the pumps, his crews maintained the shipboard routine of watches and catnaps, although with an overwhelming sense of anxiety.

To the Admiral's relief, and the great surprise of the pessimistic pilots, islands were sighted on May 10, south of Cuba. So many turtles populated those waters that Fernando thought the sea was full of little floating rocks. Columbus stayed to the north of the islands, which were later renamed the Caymans, hoping to reach Hispaniola before his ships went down. But it was not Hispaniola where he made landfall next, it was Cuba. He arrived at El Jardin de la Reina on May 13 and ordered the ships to follow the coast east. Having been to El Jardin de la Reina before, he knew his exact location and precisely how far it was to Hispaniola. Columbus was also well aware, however, that the winds and fierce currents of Hispaniola, Jamaica, and Cuba would be against him all the way to Santo Domingo. He had sailed seven hundred miles between May 1 and May 13. All that remained was a three-hundred-mile push to the safety of Hispaniola. He and the crews steeled for the journey. Those men not pumping the hold threw hooks over the side, hoping to catch a fish or turtle to add to the meager rations.

It was the worst possible moment for a storm. Yet two nights after making the turn toward Hispaniola, another ferocious Caribbean gale struck the fleet. "I was steering a course which would avoid the great number of islands in order to keep clear of the adjoining shoals," Columbus explained in his journal. "The stormy sea compelled me to turn back without sail. I anchored at an island where at one blow I lost three anchors and at midnight it seemed as if the world were coming to an end."

The *Santiago,* that little caravel the men had affectionately nicknamed *Bermuda,* broke its cables. Hopelessly adrift, she was tossed backward through the water. Her stern slammed into the bow of *La Capitana.* Their rigging fouled; the ships' sails and ropes and yards became more and more entangled with each gust of wind. A gaping hole appeared in the *Santiago's* aft section from the collision, threatening to pour even more water into her hold. The men managed to keep her afloat and disentangle the two ships, but the winds and rains would not cease. For nearly a week the storm went on, damaging both ships severely. The *Santiago's* boat was swept away, leaving the fleet with none at all.

His two ships were overloaded and barely afloat, but Columbus continued out to sea as soon as the weather cleared, intent on one last push east along the Cuban coast toward Hispaniola. "Six days later when good weather returned I had lost all my tackle but resumed course. The ship was as riddled with holes as a honeycomb and the crew exhausted and dispirited," Columbus lamented. And through it all his men began to die, as battle wounds, malnutrition, and malaria took their toll. Able seaman Alonso de la Calle died on May 23, able seaman Bartolomé García died May 28, and a ship's boy with the simple name of Donis died on June 1. In all, nineteen sailors had died since leaving Spain.

The ships wallowed toward Hispaniola at just one or two knots — barely walking pace. Columbus put ashore in a protected harbor on the Cuban coast to trade with the local Indians, seeking precious provisions for the journey ahead. He put to sea after eight days in port, but even as he did so, Columbus could no longer deny the awful truth that his ships were sinking. So much water filled the holds of *La*

Capitana and the *Santiago* that the decks were almost flush with the ocean surface. "I still could not keep down the water that entered the ship, and there was nothing we could do to meet the damage done by the shipworm. I steered the course that would bring me nearest to Hispaniola, which was twenty-eight leagues away, but afterwards I wished I had not done so. The other ship, which was half awash, was obliged to run for port, but I struggled to keep at sea in spite of the weather," wrote Columbus.

In a last-ditch effort to reach safety, Columbus commanded his pilots to change tactics — and course. He ordered the sails set square so that the wind would shove his two-ship fleet due south toward Jamaica instead of Hispaniola. The plan worked. "My ship was almost sinking when by a miracle Our Lord brought us to land," a relieved Columbus wrote. Then, expressing the depths of his joy, he added, "Who would believe what I have just written?"

Columbus named the harbor Porto Bueno. Both vessels arrived safely. It was indeed a good port, a circular enclosure protected from the elements and fronting a lush, mountainous coastline. But no fresh water existed and, thus, no chance to make a life. Columbus knew that his duty was no longer to discover new lands or gold or even navigate the oceans but to provide for his men until a passing ship could come to their rescue. He had to move on.

The waters were a light blue and the ocean flecked with whitecaps as hurricane season once again approached in the Caribbean. On the morning of June 25, 1503, a year after he had sailed so boldly to Hispaniola, Columbus ordered his sinking ships to put to sea one last time, to the coast of Jamaica, in search of a more suitable harbor. In a lifetime of sailing, that day marked the last time he commanded men and ships. Twelve miles down the coast, he discovered a bay that was open to the sea but protected by reefs. Once his crews had miraculously threaded their ships through a gap in that coral barrier, the Admiral of the Ocean Sea ordered *La Capitana* and the *Santiago* to aim straight into shore. The two ships ran aground one hundred yards from the beach and stuck fast. In most inglorious fashion, Christopher Columbus's career as a mariner had come to an end.

CAST AWAY

CHAPTER TWENTY-ONE

Columbus's New World

June–July 1503
Jamaica

Columbus had long railed against Fonseca's policy of letting other explorers sail the Caribbean. The waters of the New World were Columbus's to chart and plunder. But now he was in the ironic position of praying that another explorer would soon sail the coast of Jamaica and come to his rescue. It was either that or spend the rest of his life marooned, likely destined to die of starvation, his recurring illnesses, Indian attack, or at the hands of his men.

Gone was the routine the crew had followed each and every day. Gone were the grommets' morning ditties and turning of the hourglass. Gone, too, were shipboard sounds: the clank of pulleys and the rustle of fabric as sails were raised and lowered, the bellowed course directions, the deck's groan, the hypnotic splash of the ocean against the hull.

And gone, most of all, was movement. The tide rose and fell around the two stranded ships. Waves broke in whispers on the beach. Seagulls soared and dove from the cloud-filled sky. But no longer did Columbus's crew glimpse those vistas like observers, leaning on the rail and gawking at some new sensation or smell as they dashed through on their way to someplace new. Now they saw the same sights and heard the same sounds day after day after monotonous day, with nothing to distract them and nowhere to go.

The ships were wrecked in a bay shaped like a jagged half moon, surrounded by water that was chest-high at low tide and lapped the decks when the ocean rose. It was a wind-blown, though not unpleasant, location, offering a sweeping view of the horizon that would prove vital if a ship passed their way but could just as easily prove disastrous if a hurricane bore down from the north. Columbus named their new home Santa Gloria, giving praise to God for their safety. By first appearances it certainly seemed like a blessed place. Jamaica was a sensual, beautiful land and might have felt like Paradise to the men if it weren't the last place on earth they wanted to be. The riot of vegetation began near the water's edge and carried inland up a series of low, limestone-dotted hills: tall, leafy breadfruit, with its brown-gray bark; cactus; the finger-like red flowers of the white ironwood; poinciana, so massive and broad, with its seed pods and wispy leaves. And vines. Thick like a serpent's middle or as scrawny as a shipworm, vines draped everywhere.

Nearby lived a tribe of Arawak Indians. Other Arawak were scattered all about the island in small bands (their word *xaymaca,* meaning "isle of springs," had given the island its European name). The Arawak were capable of war but largely peaceful. Theirs was a three-tiered class system, with a parallel hierarchy of hereditary chiefs and deities ruling over warriors and slaves. The Arawak fed themselves by fishing and farming cassava, a potato-like tuber common to the tropics. Columbus and his men had little fishing ability and absolutely no farming acumen, so bartering for food with the Arawak would be vital.

Columbus's first order of business was ensuring the crews' safety. He was wary of the Arawak and more comfortable on a ship than on land, so he decided to make a fort of the two vessels. *La Capitana* and the *Santiago* were parallel each other on the sand and so close together that planks could be stretched from one ship to the other, "shoring them up on both sides so they could not budge; and the ships being in this position the tide rose almost to the decks. Upon these and the fore and sterncastles were built cabins where the people could lodge, making our position as strong as possible so the Indians could do us no harm," wrote Fernando. The sails were stripped from the yards and spread across the decks as makeshift floors and tents.

The only possible respite from the monotony lay in the companionship of the Arawak women. Columbus, who personally no longer had much interest in sex, felt that was yet another reason for keeping the men aboard the ships. He was intent on not antagonizing the Indians the way his crews had in Retrete and Santa María de Belen. Columbus understood the more base urges of sailors too long at sea and feared they would "commit outrages on women and children," in Fernando's words, "whence would have arisen disputes and quarrels that would have made enemies of them." Consequently, Columbus developed a system where the men not only needed to ask permission before going ashore, but they were required to sign in and out. He had lost 20 men from the 140 who had begun the journey, and he didn't want to lose any more.

Among the survivors were Columbus's allies Bartolomé, Diego Mendez, young Fernando, and Pedro de Terreros, formerly captain of *El Gallego*. But naysayers had been undermining his authority for some time, led by the *Santiago*'s Francisco de Porras and his brother Diego, the two who owed their place in the voyage to their sister's feminine wiles. Another dissenter was Pedro de Ledesma, the brave pilot who had swum ashore back in Veragua. At sea Columbus's authority was unquestionable. But on land, as was proven so painfully back in Hispaniola, he was a poor leader. The

Admiral recognized this shortcoming and worked hard to ensure loyalty by keeping the men fed and secure. After the calamities of Santa María de Belen, paranoia about indigenous peoples dominated their mind-set. "Here we established ourselves," Diego Mendez wrote of that first week on Jamaica, "though in considerable danger from the natives of the island, who had not been subdued or conquered and who might set fire to our dwellings by night, which they could easily do though we kept careful watch."

Once the ships were fortified, the next order of business was locating food. The hasty departure from Santa María de Belen and the provisions mistakenly left on board *La Vizcaino* were proving costly. The last rations of wine and biscuit were issued before the end of June. The men grumbled about their empty bellies as they lolled about the decks under the blistering tropical sun, but fear of the local Indians made them unwilling to march inland to find more food. Normally it would have been Bartolomé taking on this duty, but he was still recovering from the wounds suffered at Veragua. Columbus, whose invalid condition was all the more noticeable without a ship to convey him, was unable to go ashore. And Fernando was unsuited to leading a foraging party. That left Diego Mendez to take the initiative: "Taking a sword in my hand [I] went with three men into the interior of the island, since no one had yet dared to search for food for the Admiral and his men. By God's mercy I found the natives so gentle they did me no harm. On the contrary they welcomed me and willingly gave me food, and in the village of Aguacadiba I arranged with the chief and his men to make cassava bread, hunt and fish and give a certain amount of food to the Admiral each day."

Mendez roamed far and wide through the mountainous Jamaican jungles, striking accords with all the tribes in a ten-mile radius of the beached vessels. Immediately after coming to an agreement with the ruling cacique to provide food in exchange for beads, combs, knives, fish hooks, and hawk's bells, Mendez dispatched one of his three travel companions back to the ships to fetch those items.

Before long Mendez was alone in the wilderness. He was not scared, though, and was in no hurry to return to the boredom of the ships. Mendez continued his travels through the interior, enlisting two Indians as his porters. One carried the Spaniard's hammock and the other his provisions. With the Indians showing the way, he traveled farther and farther, until he was almost a hundred miles from the ships and as far east as he could trek. He gazed out onto the dark blue sea, knowing that Hispaniola lay just over the horizon — close but so unattainable. While there Mendez recorded of his journey: "Thus I traveled to the easternmost cape of the island, where I visited with a chief, whose name was Ameyro, with whom I swore fraternal friendship, giving him my name and taking his, which is considered a great sign of brotherhood among them. I bought from him a very good canoe, giving him in exchange a very fine brass helmet which I was carrying in a bag, also a coat and one of my two shirts."

The cacique arranged for six of his warriors to paddle Mendez back to the ships. With the westward current at their backs, the journey was brisk. Mendez had been gone so long he was feared dead, and a worried Columbus immediately threw his arms around his young lieutenant and gave thanks to God. The crews were just as thrilled, for they had eaten nothing for days and were dying of starvation. As if by magic Indian canoes laden with food soon surrounded the two ships. The incredulous sailors eagerly bartered with the Indians and ate their first large meals in more than a month. "The Indians of that country, who proved to be kind and gentle people, presently came in canoes to barter their wares and provisions for our truck," wrote a relieved Fernando. "By that time we had nothing on board to eat, for we had already consumed the greater part of our provisions; much had spoiled, and as much again had been lost in the haste and disorder of the embarkation from Belen. We being in such straits, God was pleased to bring us to an island abounding in eatables and densely inhabited by Indians eager to trade with us."

But the Indians worried Columbus. He had no way of knowing how long he would be shipwrecked. Perhaps it would be forever. There was only so much food on the island and only so many beads and hawk's bells that could be bartered before the Indians would come to loathe their new visitors. Columbus began a series of conferences with his captains to find a solution — from *La Capitana,* Diego Mendez; from the *Santiago,* Bartolomé Columbus and Francisco de Porras; from the scuttled *El Gallego* and *La Vizcaino,* Pedro de Terreros and Bartolomeo Fieschi, respectively. Having learned his lessons about unilateral leadership on Hispaniola, Columbus now sought consensus and support. Others, such as the meddlesome Diego de Porras, were also invited to the meetings so that Columbus could avoid alienating his enemies. All agreed that it was unlikely a ship would sail past and just as unlikely that they could build a new ship of their own because they lacked the tools and expertise. Meeting after meeting took place, and ideas were bandied about, as Columbus sought a quick end to their plight. Finally he came up with a solution.

Columbus called Diego Mendez into his cabin in early July. "Diego Mendez, my lad," Columbus began, drawing him into his confidence, "none of my people recognize the danger except you and myself. We are very few, these savage Indians are very many, and we cannot be certain that their mood will not change."

Columbus went on to share his fears that the Indians would come in the night to burn the ships. It would be as easy as firing flaming arrows into the thatch roofs of the makeshift apartments. "It is true you have made this arrangement with them to bring us food every day, and at present they are doing so willingly. But tomorrow the fancy may seize them to act otherwise, and supplies will cease. If they do not choose to bring us food we are not in a position to take it by force," Columbus continued. "I have thought of a remedy about which I should like your opinion."

The plan was the sort of simple, yet audacious, scheme that Mendez himself usually conjured. Columbus needed to get word to Hispaniola about their plight. He requested that Mendez paddle his canoe the forty leagues from the eastern tip of Jamaica to the coast of Hispaniola. There he would travel to Santo Domingo and summon help. If necessary Mendez could purchase a ship on Columbus's good credit and lead the crew back to Santa Gloria. The odds against success were considerable. The wind and currents would be against Mendez the entire way. A sudden hurricane, just like the one they had endured exactly a year earlier, was a possibility. And the distance was enormous for a lone paddler. Yet something had to be done, and the canoe seemed their only option.

"Sir," Mendez answered nervously, "I can clearly see our danger, which may be even greater than it appears. To cross from this island to Hispaniola would in my opinion be not merely dangerous, but impossible. I know no one who would dare to make that passage across forty leagues of sea. For since among these islands the waters are subject to violent currents, and seldom calm, the dangers are only too obvious."

It was the first time Mendez had turned down a request from Columbus. The Admiral, however, was convinced that the journey had to occur, regardless of the danger. He stopped short of ordering Mendez to go, but pushed him to reconsider. Mendez suppressed his growing rage but did not back down. Mendez had been Columbus's favorite for some time and was often ordered on missions that would bring glory to the Admiral. Others in the crew had noticed and resented Mendez's lofty status. They questioned whether he was so quick to show bravery because he cared about the fleet or because he craved Columbus's approval. The attention had begun to make Mendez uncomfortable. "My Lord," he argued cleverly, "I have often put my life in danger to save yours and those of your companions. And Our Lord has marvelously preserved me. Yet many people have complained that your Lordship entrusts all the most honorable responsibilities to me, although there are others in the company who could perform them as well as I."

Mendez called on Columbus to gather the entire crew and ask for a volunteer. If, and only if, no one stepped forward, Mendez would take the assignment, though not happily. "If they all hold back, as they will," Mendez predicted to Columbus, "I shall risk my life once more in your service as I have done many times already." Columbus agreed.

The next morning the Admiral addressed the crew. Barefoot, ragged, and deeply weathered by the elements, the men listened with skepticism to his proposal. Instead of feeling hope, they muttered dejectedly about the foolishness of this one and only plan to get them off the island. They were silent, though, when Columbus asked for volunteers. When the men did speak up, it was to argue about the wind and currents and how even seaworthy caravels had been sunk in the breach between Jamaica and Hispaniola by their ferocity. They scorned the idea of small canoe making the crossing. With great reluctance, but more than a little self-importance, Mendez stood and accepted the mission. "I have only one life but I will risk it in your Lordship's service and for the good of all those here present," he proclaimed grandly. "For I trust the Lord God, that being witness to the motives from which I act, He will preserve me as He has done so many times before."

A thankful Columbus embraced Mendez and kissed him on both cheeks. He had foreseen the outcome of the meeting and wanted to instill his young protégé with confidence. He stated, "I knew very well that nobody here except yourself would dare to undertake this mission. I trust in the Lord God that you will emerge from it as successfully as you have from the other missions you have undertaken."

The embrace and comments were a major blunder on Columbus's part. At a time when he needed to bring about solidarity, he was questioning the bravery of a crew that had endured nothing but calamity since leaving Spain more than fourteen months earlier. It was the sort of animosity that could lead to mutiny if left unchecked, but Columbus was too consumed with the success of Mendez's mission to notice.

Because of Mendez's minimal nautical knowledge, Columbus also requested that *La Vizcaino*'s Bartolomeo Fieschi travel at his side. When the two reached Hispaniola, they were to split up. Mendez was to paddle or walk the remaining 350 miles along the Hispaniola coast to Santo Domingo. Fieschi, on the other hand, was given the dubious honor of paddling back across the strait to Jamaica to bring Columbus the good news.

A courageous Fieschi accepted the assignment, but this too raised eyebrows. The thirty-three-year-old ship's captain, who went by the nickname Flisco, was Genovese, like Columbus. That alone made him suspicious. What the crew didn't know was that Fieschi's family had once been one of Genoa's most powerful. Moreover, Columbus's family was beholden to them for a political favor dating back to 1447, when the Fieschis ran the powerhouse Fregoso political party. The Fregoso party was sympathetic to the French in their struggles with Aragon — the same Aragon now ruled by Ferdinand. At the end of January 1447, the Fregosos took control of Genoa by force, routing a force of six hundred Aragonese soldiers sent by Ferdinand's uncle to guard the palace of the local chief magistrate.

The next week, as thanks for his party loyalty, the Fregosos appointed Columbus's father to a thirteen-month term as warden of the city's new Olivella Gate. This lucrative position gave the lower-class wool merchant a hint of status, allowing him to marry the daughter of a wealthy local landowner. The Fieschis, meanwhile, fell on hard times. They were driven from the city in a civil war in 1459. Flisco was born eleven years later and eventually went to sea to recoup the family wealth. It had been fortunate coincidence that Flisco was in Seville when Columbus was searching for captains to lead the fourth voyage's fleet — a debt repaid.

But now a Columbus was asking a Fieschi for another great favor. And even without knowing the long bond between those families, some members of the crew were angered by the choice. It was no secret that Mendez and Flisco were deeply loyal to the Admiral. Some of the crew suspected the plan was for them to paddle to Santo Domingo and then race onward to Spain. There they would convince the sovereigns to send ships to the gold mines of Veragua, further enriching Columbus. To some extent, these grumblings were correct — as Mendez modified his canoe for the journey, Columbus was composing a letter to Ferdinand and Isabella. But the document, which later became known as the Lettera Rarissima, was not written as a means of endearing himself to the sovereigns. Columbus was a man with nothing to lose, facing the prospect of death on a distant tropical island. His words reflected the frustrations of watching his years of bravery forgotten, his reputation decimated, and his powers and responsibilities stripped, one by one. He finally lashed out about his feelings of betrayal brought on because other explorers were being granted licenses to plunder the New World. "But there is another very important matter," he wrote at the end of the novella-length missive, "inexplicable to this day, which cries loudly for redress. I spent seven years at your royal court, where everyone to whom I spoke of this undertaking said it was ridiculous. Now even tailors are asking for licenses for exploration. Probably they intend to come out and plunder, but the licenses granted are greatly to the detriment of my honor, and to the prejudice of the undertaking itself."

Columbus condemned the sovereigns for his imprisonment and deportation from Santo Domingo, then let fly with a final salvo placing blame squarely upon the two of them. "I came to serve at the age of twenty-eight and today I have not a hair on my head that is not gray. My body is sick and wasted. All that I and my brothers had has been taken from us, down to our very coats, without my being heard or seen, and I have suffered great dishonor. It is incredible that this could have been done by your royal command. The restoration of my honor and of what has been taken from me and the punishment of the man who inflicted this damage on me will rebound to your Highnesses' good name. The man who robbed me of the pearls," Columbus wrote of Fonseca, "and infringed my privileges as Admiral should be punished also. It would be a most virtuous deed and a famous example if you were to do this, and would leave to Spain a glorious memory of your Highnesses as grateful and just princes. . . . I beg your Highnesses' pardon. I am ruined, as I have said; till now I have wept for others. May Heaven now have pity on me and earth weep for me as I wait for death alone, sick and racked with pain."

The letter was dated July 7, 1503. That afternoon Mendez and Fieschi paddled away. Six Indians had been enlisted to help. Mendez had modified the heavy dugout for safety, adding a false keel, mast and sail, and a layer of waterproof pitch. When the eight men, with their rations of water and cassava, were loaded on board, the canoe rode so low in the water that even small waves sloshed over the sides, so Mendez affixed boards to the prow and stern as a barrier. "Certainly courage was required to make this crossing in the only way it could be done, that is, in Indian canoes made by hollowing out a large log. When heavily loaded, these dugouts are three-fourths underwater," wrote young Fernando. "Moreover, the crossing had to be made in medium sized canoes, for the smaller ones were too dangerous and the larger ones too slow and cumbrous for such a long voyage." Slow, cramped, and barely seaworthy, this simple craft was Columbus's last best hope of seeing Spain again.

Fifteen days later, those hopes were dashed when Mendez and Fieschi returned. Things had gone well for them as they paddled along the Jamaican coast, but upon reaching its easternmost tip, Mendez had ordered a halt. The sea was too rough for the crossing, and he was hoping the weather would improve. Feeling restless, he walked along the beach, leaving the canoe far behind. "As I was waiting beside the cape at the tip of the island for the sea to grow calm before beginning my voyage, many Indians gathered with the intention of killing me and taking my canoe and its contents," he wrote. The Indians were a seafaring tribe who roamed the coast like pirates, stealing and murdering with impunity. They led Mendez into the jungle and drew lots to see who would get the honor of slaying him, but the Indians got so caught up in the contest they forgot about their captive. He slipped away and raced back to the canoe. Quickly rousing Fieschi and the Arawak, Mendez put to sea and raised the sail. The wind was at their backs, and the current favored them. The trip back to Santa Gloria was speedy, and the Indian pirates were never seen again. "I told him all that had happened," wrote Mendez of his reunion with Columbus. "And how God had miraculously rescued me from the hands of those savages. His Lordship was very glad that I had come."

But Columbus was, in fact, deeply disappointed. He immediately asked Mendez if he planned to try again. "I would if I could take some men with me to remain at the tip of the island," Mendez replied, fearing another encounter with his kidnappers. Columbus promptly ordered the recovered Bartolomé to lead a large force to safeguard the paddlers' departure. A second canoe was procured for Fieschi, along with another contingent of Indian paddlers. Additionally, six Spanish seamen were added to each crew as protection. Water was carried in gourds, and the Indians procured more cassava bread. Each of the sailors carried a sword and shield. "So Mendez and Fieschi set out down the coast of Jamaica toward the east end of the island, which the Indians call Aomaquique, after the cacique of that province," wrote Fernando. "The distance from Jamaica to Hispaniola being thirty leagues, with only one little island or rock along the whole course, and that some eight leagues from Hispaniola, they had to wait for a perfect calm before starting to cross that great space in such a small craft. By God's favor, this calm soon came."

The wait lasted four days. Mendez, Fieschi, Bartolomé, and the eighty-two other Spaniards spent the time at the cape marking Jamaica's easternmost tip. It was a pensive time. Mendez had the comportment of a man facing execution. As the ocean turned glassy, Mendez and Fieschi sallied forth to meet their fate. "When I saw the seas growing calm I very sadly took leave of my escort and they of me," Mendez wrote.

Bartolomé watched the canoes as they slowly made their way out into the tranquil sea. The sky was cloudless, and the sun's heat intense. He stayed at the cape until nightfall, tracking their painfully slow progress. They still had not made it over the horizon before dark, but in the moonlight Bartolomé was no longer able to see them. He retired for the evening and then lingered at the cape for three more days in case the canoes turned back. Then he began the long march back to his brother and the broken ships, proceeding at a casual pace and stopping at villages along the way to introduce himself and encourage trade, wondering all the while if he had just seen the last of Mendez and Flisco.

CHAPTER TWENTY-TWO

Open Boat

July–December 1503
Jamaica–Hispaniola

The first hours of the paddle to Hispaniola were almost pleasant. Though there was no escaping the sun's burning rays, the sea was calm, and the winds negligible. Mendez and Flisco kept their canoes close together. When the heat grew unbearable, relief was as immediate as a quick dip in the ocean. The Indian paddlers and Spanish seamen did the hard work of pressing their paddles into the water, stroke after stroke, hour after blazing hour. It was up to Mendez and Flisco to navigate, using compasses salvaged from *El Gallego* and *La Vizcaino* before their scuttling.

The paddling didn't end when the sun went down. The currents were so strong that the canoe trip was akin to swimming upstream. Their speed was pitiful — one and a half miles per hour. Any prolonged halt would see the canoes pushed backward, toward Jamaica, negating hours of hard labor. To keep morale up Mendez and Flisco took pulls at the paddles. Hands blistered, tongues dry from thirst, the Indians and Spanish worked through the night in shifts, some sleeping, while others paddled. When it was becoming clear that the Indians were frightened about being so far from land, Mendez and Flisco spoke across the water to each other, agreeing to watch the Indians carefully, lest they attempt to turn back.

The Spaniards kept their water in small casks; the Indians kept theirs in gourds. Before the sun rose to usher in the second day of paddling, the Indians had no more water left. By noon they were exhausted and dehydrated and were accusing Mendez and Flisco of inept navigation. It was common knowledge among the Indians that a tiny island known to them as Navassa was just sixty miles from Jamaica. It was a natural landmark and an ideal resting place. The Indians argued that they had paddled at least that far. They would not be dissuaded from that erroneous belief, even when Mendez and Flisco tried to lift their spirits with food and water.

Unbeknownst to the group, the Indians were all in the throes of dehydration, a most cruel way to die. Lack of water intake dries the mucous membranes of the mouth, nose, and throat, causing the body to experience thirst. As the need for water increases, the body hoards the fluids it possesses, ceasing functions such as sweating and urinating. The person becomes irritable and then sluggish. Eventually, lack of water causes the heartbeat to quicken and blood pressure to lower. The body becomes clammy as it goes into shock. Death follows.

The second night at sea, one of the Indians died from dehydration. Others were so weak they lay in the bottom of the canoe. Those Indians still capable of paddling continued their backbreaking chore. Spaniards and Indians alike had developed the alarming habit of drinking ocean water to stem their insatiable thirst, which was just as deadly as no water at all. With the current as strong as ever but the forward progress slowed by lack of manpower, despair seized Mendez and Flisco. All seemed lost.

As Mendez gazed toward the rising moon, his eyes

seemed to be playing tricks on him. The lower portion of the moon was covered, as if by an eclipse. Yet the shadow was jagged. Mendez squinted at the phenomenon and, in a moment of clarity, realized that it was land — and they were on the verge of paddling past.

Mendez was overcome with euphoria. This was Navassa, the island the Indians had spoken of. He eagerly pointed to the silhouette and ordered the paddlers to alter course and steer there. All the men drank a small ration from the water casks and, refortified, paddled through the night toward the speck on the horizon. At morning they made landfall. The island was barren, rocky, and without fresh water, but the Spaniards and Indians were giddy with delight. They could clearly see Hispaniola in the distance and were able to find pools of trapped rainfall in rocky depressions. "They scrambled from cliff to cliff gathering water in gourds, and found such an abundance of it that they could fill their stomachs and vessels," wrote Fernando.

Mendez cautioned the men against drinking too much after being so deeply dehydrated. Too much water overwhelms the system and can be just as fatal as no water at all. The Spaniards followed orders, as they had been trained after so much time on board ship. The Indians did not. Some vomited the water back up or became so ill they couldn't move. Others died.

Despite the senseless tragedy Mendez and Flisco kept the men focused on the mission. Shellfish were scraped from tide pools and cooked over an open fire. Their stomachs full, the men slept in the sun, finally able to rest. But as the afternoon winds began sweeping across the sea, the two captains knew it was time to leave. A sudden storm might strand them until the next calm, which could be days or weeks hence. Neither man wanted to take that chance. As the sun began to set, the Spaniards and remaining Indians loaded the newly filled casks and gourds into the canoes and shoved off.

The weather stayed calm throughout the long night. The palms of each man were agonizingly raw from the hours of paddling. Their bodies were badly burned from the days in the sun. But with Hispaniola fewer than thirty miles away, and always visible on the horizon, those pains were set aside. Hispaniola meant solid ground and the end of their paddle, and it also meant that their days of being shipwrecked were through. It was like returning from the dead. "The Christians regarded themselves as having been delivered from the whale's belly, their three days and nights corresponding to those of the prophet Jonah," wrote Fernando.

They landed as the sun rose. Cape San Miguel was the southwest tip of Hispaniola and a welcome sight to one and all. "I steered my canoe up a most beautiful river where many natives came to us," wrote Mendez, "bringing us plenty of things to eat, and we remained there two days." Mendez was ill from malaria and seized by violent bouts of fever and sweating, but he was obsessed with completing his mission, as was Flisco, who announced after the two days' rest that it was his duty to return to Jamaica and give the good news to Columbus. He wished to leave immediately.

By this time the sailors had had their fill of deprivation and danger. To a man they refused to get back in the canoes. The Indians did the same. It was agreed that Mendez would hire some local Indians to paddle him to Santo Domingo. Flisco and the sailors would follow in the second canoe when the men were physically and mentally willing. "I then took six local Indians, leaving my own behind, and began to row along the coast of Hispaniola," wrote Mendez, who steered with an oar as the Indians paddled. "It was one hundred and thirty leagues from there to the city of Santo Domingo, to which I had to go since the governor, the comendador de Lares, was there."

But Ovando, the governor and *comendador de Lares,* was not in Santo Domingo; he was in the province of Xaragua, waging war on the local tribes. During his short time in office, Ovando had proven a brutal ruler, imposing a strict discipline on the colonists and rounding up thousands of Indians for slave labor. His foray into Xaragua was meant to subdue the local tribes once and for all, by whatever means possible. A tangential aspect of this mission was to convert the surviving Indians to Catholicism.

The journey along the coast of Hispaniola was unremarkable for Mendez. He and his hired Indians paddled by day and slept ashore by night. He was familiar with the coastline, having seen it during Columbus's outbound journey. Fresh water was collected from streams on shore, and he bartered for food from the coastal tribes. Larger harbors, like the Indian village at Yaquimo, where Columbus had anchored his fleet the previous July, even had an abundance of fresh meats and tropical fruits. If not for his fevers, which ebbed and flowed in four-day cycles, Mendez's adventure would have been incident free.

When he arrived in the harbor of Azua, where Columbus's fleet had anchored after riding out the hurricane, Mendez was just one day's paddle from Santo Domingo. But there he received the news that Ovando was waging war in Xaragua, and that in order to get permission to send a ship to Columbus, Mendez would have to find Ovando.

The journey of more than one hundred and fifty miles was much more demanding than Mendez expected. He traveled on foot with his Indian paddlers, armed with just a sword and buckler. The landscape was mountainous, rocky, muddy, and overgrown. The summer heat was grueling.

Mendez straggled into Ovando's encampment in August of 1503. He was exhausted and ill, but relieved. He had completed his mission — or so it appeared. Having paddled from Jamaica to Hispaniola, paddled half the length of Hispaniola, then marched barefoot into the jungle, he had finally succeeded in finding Nicolas de Ovando. All that remained was to give the governor the news about Columbus. Rescue would be imminent.

But Ovando was cool toward Mendez, just as he had been to Columbus's entreaties prior to the hurricane. He was bemused by the explorer's plight and in no hurry to rescue him. Because of Ovando's heavy-handed, military style of governance, many of the colonists had actually grown nostalgic for the Columbus brothers. The last thing Ovando wanted was for them to return to Santo Domingo. Ovando grilled Mendez about the voyage, learning of Veragua's gold and the tragedy at Santa María de Belen. He also learned that Mendez held a letter in his hand addressed to the sovereigns and that Columbus was constantly ill from rheumatism, gout, and malaria.

These factors placed Ovando in a quandary. He would have been perfectly content letting Columbus die in Jamaica. But once word reached the sovereigns that Ovando had denied assistance to the explorer, especially after the bravery of Mendez and Flisco, there would be grave questions about Ovando's behavior. The sovereigns would want to know why he had ignored Columbus's pleas and why the good news about the gold fields of Veragua had been so slow in reaching Spain.

Ovando was a clever man, wise to the politics of the royal court. Instead of granting Mendez permission to race for Hispaniola and send a caravel for Columbus, he stalled. The war he was waging against the Indians was a holy war, of sorts. The sovereigns would understand. Ovando ordered Mendez to stay at his side until the war was through.

August came to an end, with Mendez still in the wilds of Xaragua. Ovando continued to systematically break the Indians' will to fight by killing their leaders. Before he was done, the region's eighty-four ruling caciques would be burned at the stake or hung.

Day after impatient day, Mendez waited for permission

to travel to Santo Domingo and send a ship for Columbus. And day after impatient day, that permission was withheld. As Christmas 1503 was celebrated with a Mass in Xaragua, Diego Mendez was still Ovando's captive, with no end to the fighting in sight, and Columbus was still shipwrecked with an increasingly restless and furious crew.

CHAPTER TWENTY-THREE

The Porras Conspiracy

January–March 1504
Jamaica

On January 2, 1504, Columbus lay in the stifling humidity of his tiny cabin, crippled by rheumatoid arthritis. His joints were so inflamed that all he could do was stay in bed. No news had come from Mendez and Flisco. The weary Spanish castaways were beginning to think the situation hopeless. If those two were lost at sea, went the talk, then maybe it was time to escape another way. At the very least the men wanted more liberty; living on board the cramped, beached ships was claustrophobic. Sickness was rampant. "Even those who were healthy thought it a hardship to be confined so long to the ships and began to conspire and grumble, saying the Admiral had no intention of returning to Hispaniola," wrote Fernando, who had celebrated his fifteenth birthday in Jamaica. "His true purpose in sending those canoes was not to obtain ships or relief but to enable Mendez and Fieschi to go to Spain to try to fix up the Admiral's business with the Catholic Sovereigns; while negotiations were going on, he proposed to pass his exile right there."

Roughly half the crew was in favor of leaving Columbus. Their plan was to steal or buy canoes from the Indians and then paddle to Hispaniola. Because of Ovando's well-known hatred for Columbus, this act of mutiny would not only be forgiven, they figured, but it would be celebrated. "And when they got home to Spain they would enjoy the favor of Bishop Juan de Fonseca," noted Fernando, reading their minds. "As for the Catholic Sovereigns, they would doubtless look on them with favor, being easily persuaded that it was all the Admiral's fault."

The ringleaders were the Porras brothers, Francisco and Diego — captain of the *Santiago* and comptroller of the fleet, respectively. As the new year of 1504 dawned, they secretly drew up formal articles of mutiny, listing their grievances against Columbus. Forty-eight of the crew's strongest members signed their names to the incendiary document. Those signatures were just names scribbled on a page, though, until they commandeered the ships.

On January 2 the mutineers did just that.

The mutiny began when Francisco de Porras burst into Columbus's cabin. "Senor, what do you mean by making no effort to get to Castile?" Porras demanded scornfully. "Do you wish to keep us here to perish?"

Columbus remained calm, reminding his hotheaded captain that no one wanted to leave more than he but that they were stuck until a rescue ship arrived. However, Columbus reminded Porras, if you have a plan that will get us to safety, present it to the council of the captains.

"There's no more time to talk," Porras stammered. "Either embark or stay with God."

Without giving Columbus time to answer, Porras turned around in the doorway and shouted to his supporters on the deck below: "I'm for Castile. Who's with me?"

"We're with you!" came the cry, and the mutiny was under way. Already armed with swords, lances, and muskets, the mutineers battled Columbus's supporters for control of the ships. Columbus hobbled to his cabin door and beheld the sight of armed mutineers atop *La Capitana*'s best defensive positions: the forecastle and the top of the mainmast. "To Castile! To Castile!" they kept shouting. Three of Columbus's men, fearing he would be cut down, hustled him back into bed.

Bartolomé, meanwhile, was taking on all comers with just a lance. He was finally captured and dragged into Columbus's cabin. Both men were placed under armed guard, and the mutiny was complete. A haughty Francisco de Porras approached the cabin, not knowing what to do next. Columbus coolly reminded him that the murder of the Admiral and his brother was a crime the sovereigns would punish most severely. If the mutineers wished to leave, though, Columbus would not try to stop them.

For all his bluster, Porras saw the undeniable wisdom in Columbus's rationale. "The mutineers took ten canoes which were tied up to the ships," wrote Fernando, "and they set out in them as gaily as if they were embarking from a harbor in Castile. At this, many who were not mutineers but were desperate at the thought of being abandoned by the greater and healthier part of the company also piled into the canoes, to the great distress of the few loyal men and of the many sick, who were convinced they were doomed to remain and perish there. If all had been in good health, I doubt that twenty of those people would have stayed with the Admiral."

As the jubilant mutineers began paddling away, Columbus limped into the sunshine. By the time he turned back inside and collapsed into bed moments later, a change had come over the fed-up Columbus.

From the time he had sailed from Spain until the shipwreck, Columbus's various illnesses had limited his daily activities to navigation and exploration. He spent much time alone in his cabin, reading and praying or just bedridden. His leadership was unquestionable, but he governed from afar, preferring to interact with the pilots and captains rather than the ordinary seamen. After *La Capitana* and the *Santiago* were run aground, he was even more reclusive, rarely venturing on deck or onto the shore. His tendency toward rumination led him into alternating moments of self-pity and self-aggrandizement. With every passing day that Mendez and Flisco failed to return, he was more and more certain he would die in Jamaica.

After the mutiny all that changed. The time had come to display command or risk watching the remainder of his men slip away to join the mutineers. Columbus ignored his afflictions and took full control of the situation.

The sick crew members were the singular burden of Maestre Bernal, an apothecary from Valencia who served as the fleet's lone physician. Bernal had done an excellent job tending to the litany of tropical woes that infested the crew. For all the malaria, dehydration, anemia, parasites, and sun-related maladies, only two men had died by the time of the mutiny. Now, for humanitarian and strategic reasons, Columbus became more actively involved in healing the sick. He owed it to the men to care for them, but he also realized that the fewer men he commanded, the more willing the local tribes might be to attack. Already signs indicated that the Indian food supply was being stretched thin by the Spaniards' unceasing demands. Tension was creeping into the relationship. "After the mutineers departed the Admiral did all he could to hasten the recovery of the sick. He also took care to treat the Indians well that they might continue to bring in provisions for barter. He was so diligent in this work that the Christians presently recovered full health, and for a time, at least, the Indians continued to bring food," wrote Fernando, who then admitted, "we consumed more in a day than they in twenty."

Despite Columbus's labors, the downcast remainder of

his crew was more forlorn than ever, sure their last chance of returning alive to Spain had passed. If they had known what was happening to the mutineers in those early months of 1504, they would have rejoiced.

The Porras brothers were not the leaders they supposed. As they paddled toward the eastern end of the island, they bade their Indian hosts farewell by stealing food instead of bartering for it, telling the Indians to collect payment from Columbus. If Columbus balked, the mutineers assured the Indians, it was all right to kill the Admiral. "They also told the Indians he was hated by the Christians and was the cause of all the misery of the Indians on Hispaniola, and would inflict the same suffering on them if they did not kill him, for it was his intention to stay and settle the island."

When the mutineers reached the eastern tip of Jamaica, they pleaded with local Indians to help them paddle. Then they waited for the sea to calm and began paddling en masse for Hispaniola in their fleet of stolen canoes.

The sea was flat but the weather was not entirely calm. Even as the mutineers paddled their overloaded canoes against the current, the wind shifted directions and speed. Twelve miles from land the winds were so strong the mutineers turned back. Terrified and displaying reproachable seamanship, they watched in horror as their canoes broached in the rough swells and quickly flooded. The mutineers bailed frantically, but the canoes sank lower and lower into the water. In their panic they sought to lighten the boats. The only items not thrown overboard were the Spaniards' weapons and a small supply of food.

And still the wind howled. The current was at their back once they aimed their canoes for Jamaica, but the variable gusts were an unpredictable foe. The mutineers became desperate. In a frantic moment they voted to kill all the Indians and then dump the corpses overboard. The first few Indians were taken by surprise, slain by the sudden and unexpected stabs of swords and lances. The others did not go so easily, boldly leaping overboard and beginning the long swim to shore once they saw their friends slaughtered. The sea, however, was too rough and land still more than ten miles away, so the Indians were soon exhausted. Given a choice between the surety of death by drowning and the potential of Spanish mercy, they swam back to the canoes and clutched the gunwales, keeping their bodies in the water. The mutineers got rid of these new sea anchors by hacking off the Indians' hands. Eighteen Indians were left treading water, their bloody stumps destined to attract sharks.

The exhausted mutineers somehow paddled back to land. There they split into two groups: those in favor of making peace with Columbus and those wishing to paddle from Jamaica again. The latter won out, reminding the others that Hispaniola was the only way back to Spain. In February 1504, after a month of begging food from the tribes Bartolomé and Diego Mendez had labored so hard to befriend, the mutineers paddled for Hispaniola once again. "When a calm set in at last, they made two more efforts to cross, but both failed because of contrary winds. So they gave up that vain attempt and started back westward on foot, very chopfallen and downcast, sometimes eating what they could find and at others robbing food from the Indians, according to the power or show of resistance made by the local cacique," wrote Fernando.

The mutineers resisted the temptation to return to the ships, knowing an angry Columbus might execute them or place them in chains. They roamed the island in small bands, hooligans always in search of a meal or a woman. With their hopes of rescue dwindling, they lived each day with abandon, trying to make the best of a very bad situation — but inevitably making it worse.

Back at Santa Gloria Columbus got word of the mutineers' behavior from the Indians. To them, all Spaniards were alike, and their resentment for the constant demands for food from mutineers and shipboard crew had reached the breaking point. The Indians began squeezing the castaways by lowering productivity but increasing prices. "As a result," wrote Fernando, "they began bringing in less food than we needed. This posed a serious problem, for in order to get food from them by force most of us would have had to go ashore prepared to fight, leaving the Admiral to face great danger in the ships. On the other hand, to depend on their goodwill meant privation and having to pay twice what we had paid before; for the Indians understood our situation and their business very well, and believed they had us at their mercy. So we were greatly perplexed and did not know what to do."

It so happened that 1504 was a leap year, with an extra day appended to February. Columbus knew this. But while studying a book by German mathematician Johann Müller, the man who developed plane trigonometry, he noticed an additional phenomenon scheduled for February 29. *Ephemerides,* as the book was known, predicted that a total eclipse of the moon would take place that night. The moon would darken to a dull red color as it passed through the earth's shadow. To a constant observer of the moon and stars, the eclipse represented a grand distraction from the fading hopes that permeated Columbus's days. But as an admiral responsible for seeing his starving men return to civilization safely, the eclipse represented a grand opportunity. Down through history the sudden obfuscation of the sun or moon had alarmed those unable to explain it. In Persia and China an eclipse was considered to be the moon being devoured by a great dragon. The Greeks believed that the moon was bewitched. The biblical book of Joel spoke of the moon turning to blood "before the coming of the great and dreadful day of the Lord." Columbus gambled that the Jamaican Indians would be just as bewildered.

On February 26, Columbus ordered a messenger to travel throughout the island, inviting the most powerful caciques to a banquet. The messenger spread the word, and two days later the chiefs began arriving on the shores of Santa Gloria Bay. Columbus invited them aboard the tattered remains of his ships. Then the Admiral, through an interpreter, explained that he and his men were Christians "and believed in God, Who lives in Heaven, and were His servants," wrote Fernando. "God rewarded the good and punished the wicked, as he had punished the mutineers by not permitting them to cross over to Hispaniola."

That benign prelude was followed by a powerful threat. Columbus informed the Indians that God was very angry with them for not bringing enough food to the ships — especially food already paid for in barter. He would punish the Indians through famine and pestilence.

The Indians didn't know whether to mock the old man or believe him. Columbus's God had been unwilling to rescue the Admiral. There seemed no reason He would come to his aid now.

Columbus foresaw this and made a bold prediction to convince the Indians he was telling the truth. "God would send them a clear token from Heaven of the punishment they were about to receive. They should therefore attend that night the rising of the moon: She would rise inflamed with wrath, signifying the chastisement God would visit upon them."

The Indians still weren't sure whether to believe Columbus. When he was finished they left him and waited for the moon to rise. "On Thursday, 29 February 1504,"

Columbus wrote, "there was a lunar eclipse. Since it began before sunset I could observe only its end, when the moon had regained its full light, and that occurred two and a half hours after nightfall."

In those two and a half hours, Columbus was in his full glory. As the moon rose higher into the sky, and as sunset cast darkness over Santa Gloria, the terrified Indians raced to his ships. Weeping, sure of the destruction that was about to rain down on them, the Indians dumped loads of provisions on the decks of *La Capitana* and the *Santiago*. They promised to provide Columbus with all the supplies he needed, for as long as he needed, and begged Columbus to intercede on their behalf to his God.

He retired to his cabin with great dramatic flair, promising the Indians only that he would have a talk with God. As the Indians continued to heap more and more food on the decks, Columbus furtively peered out the small window in his cabin door. He was watching the moon. The whole time that the eclipse waxed he stayed in the cabin. But when it began to wane, and the return of normal moonlight was imminent, he opened the door and hobbled into sight. "I have appealed to God," Columbus told the Indians. "I have prayed for you and promised Him in your name that henceforth you would be good and treat the Christians well, bringing provisions and all else we need. God has now pardoned you."

As a token of this pardon, the Admiral went on to assure them, "you will see the moon's anger and inflammation pass away."

The Indians thanked Columbus profusely and studied the moon for signs that Columbus was speaking the truth. "Perceiving that what he said was coming true, they offered many thanks to the Admiral and uttered praises of his God as long as the eclipse continued. From that time forward they were diligent in providing us with all we needed," wrote Fernando.

It had been eight months since Mendez and Flisco departed and two months since the mutiny. Spring was arriving in the Caribbean. Columbus's remaining fifty men were well fed and healthy. He was still optimistic about rescue and making no plans to establish a settlement on shore. But just when Columbus should have been able to lower his guard, another bewildering series of events began to unfold.

CHAPTER TWENTY-FOUR

Civil War

March–November 1504
Jamaica–Hispaniola–Spain

M arch 1504 found Diego Mendez finally marching to Santo Domingo. Governor Ovando's brutal repression of Hispaniola's caciques was complete, and he no longer had any excuse for keeping Mendez in Xaragua. "When the province was pacified," Mendez wrote, "I left on foot for Santo Domingo (which was seventy leagues away) and waited there for ships to come from Castile. None had come for more than a year."

Ovando, like Bobadilla before him, was afraid of Columbus's talents and charisma. He firmly believed that the sovereigns might be so pleased with Columbus's recent accomplishments that they would restore him to office. Consequently, rather than order one of the ships anchored in Santo Domingo's harbor to rescue Columbus, Ovando had stipulated that Mendez must hire a ship outbound from Spain. Mendez passed his days near the waterfront, gazing left like a man with a facial tic, keeping a sharp eye for sails on the southeast horizon. Nothing could be done but wait, knowing that the wait might last months. He told all who would listen that Columbus was shipwrecked and that

Ovando was doing nothing to rescue him. The citizens of Santo Domingo, who had once been so critical of the Admiral, were appalled. Priests began criticizing Ovando's action in their sermons.

Ovando finally dispatched a caravel to Jamaica in order to quiet the grumbling. He also wanted to see if Columbus was still alive. The caravel captain was Diego de Escobar, who had been a rebel leader back when the Admiral had governed Hispaniola. As if that wasn't enough of an affront, Escobar was ordered not to rescue Columbus but merely to deliver a barrel of wine and a slab of salt pork, then sail back and report on the crew's condition.

As the spy caravel sailed on following winds toward Columbus, another conspiracy was being hatched in Jamaica. It involved Maestre Bernal, the fleet's physician. Throughout the voyage he had been just another gentleman volunteer, and a seemingly worthless one at that. During the first six months of being shipwrecked, however, he had been a miracle worker. When so many men had been ill, Bernal had enjoyed a newfound respect, and as long as the crew remained ill, that esteem remained. However, when they got better thanks to Columbus's renewed efforts to secure ample quantities of fresh food, the physician once again became superfluous.

Chafing at the shipboard discipline and stung by his lowered position in the chain of command, Bernal quietly rounded up his favorite former patients and plotted a mutiny. The cramped conditions on board *La Capitana* and the *Santiago* meant that Bernal's every word could be overheard. His plans to seize the ship, kill Columbus, and then paddle canoes to Hispaniola weren't much of a secret, but nearly a year of being shipwrecked had left him beyond caring.

Bernal's plans were interrupted by the arrival of Escobar's caravel. It was the glorious sight for which the men had waited so long. "Our Lord, seeing the great danger the Admiral was in, was pleased to avert it," Fernando wrote with great satisfaction.

The crew rose to their feet and raced to the rail, straining to catch a glimpse of their rescuers. "The Admiral's people were much comforted by the coming of the caravel and covered up the plot which they had been hatching," Fernando noted.

Escobar dropped anchor just inside the reef and rowed over to the stranded ships. He asked permission to come aboard, which was immediately granted. Columbus masked whatever elation he felt, still angry about Escobar's insubordination six years earlier. The two men adjourned to Columbus's cabin to meet in privacy.

The meeting was brief. Escobar dropped off the pork and wine, with the governor's regards, but informed the Admiral that neither he nor his men were welcome on the caravel. It was not a rescue ship. Escobar did, however, give the heartbroken Columbus a bit of very good news: Diego Mendez and Bartoloméo Fieschi had reached Santo Domingo alive. Escobar presented Columbus with a letter from Mendez, detailing his paddle to Hispaniola and explaining the delay in rescue.

Columbus's crew watched in disbelief as Escobar rowed back to the caravel, weighed anchor, and set his sails for Santo Domingo.

Now Bernal's mutiny reared anew. He convinced the crew that Ovando would never allow Columbus to return to Santo Domingo, and because they had the bum luck of being under Columbus's command, the men would suffer the same fate. If Columbus had been dead when Escobar's caravel arrived, Bernal fumed, they would all be on their way to Hispaniola.

Within a matter of minutes, Columbus heard these grumblings. Tackling the problem head-on, he immediately addressed the crew. Columbus cleverly took the blame. "He told them all it had been his doing because that caravel was too small to take them all, and he did not wish to leave without taking them all." Columbus also reminded any prospective mutineers that Diego Mendez was assembling a rescue fleet. It would arrive any day. Columbus's implication was clear: justice would immediately follow the rescue; mutineers would be hanged.

Bernal's plot now out in the open, he backed down. But Columbus had another group of mutineers that needed attending. He didn't like the idea of sailing back to Hispaniola without his entire crew — and that included the remnants led by the Porras brothers. "The Admiral decided to inform the mutineers of what had happened in the hopes of bringing them to obedience. He sent as emissaries two respected persons who were on friendly terms with them; and as proof that the caravel had arrived, he also sent them a portion of the salt pork Ovando had presented to him," wrote Fernando.

By May, when Columbus sent those two men to bargain with the mutineers, he had been shipwrecked almost a year. Columbus offered the mutineers a full pardon if they would return to the ships. From the Indians Columbus knew that the mutineers were in a bad way, always hungry and in ill health. He was willing to let past indiscretions be set aside, for a number of the men had also served valiantly during the fourth voyage. Pilot Pedro de Ledesma, who had swum ashore back in Belen and effected a rescue of the colonists, was one of them. Another was Juan Sanchez, although he was forever fated to be remembered as the man who let Quibian escape. It made more sense to pardon than punish.

Yet when the emissaries met in the jungle with Francisco de Porras, he refused. He demanded that Columbus provide a separate rescue ship for him and his men. "If only one was sent," Fernando wrote, "he should assign half the space to them. Meanwhile, since they had lost at sea all they had gained by barter, he should share with them what he had."

The emissaries thought Porras a fool. They told him the demands were unreasonable. Porras countered that unless Columbus began providing food for the mutineers, they would assault the ships and take them by force. When his followers expressed their doubts about his tactics, Porras reminded them he had friends in the royal court, so Columbus would never dare punish a man such as himself, but the Admiral would be more than willing to punish those crewmen without such lofty connections. In a final act to discredit Columbus, Porras played to the sailors' superstitious side. No caravel had arrived from Hispaniola, Porras told them. Columbus had conjured the ship through his special knowledge of magic. "Clearly a real caravel would not have left so soon," he reminded them, "with so little dealing between its crew and the Admiral's men, and surely the Admiral and his brother would have sailed away in it."

With each sentence damning Columbus, Porras roused hatred in his men's hearts. He reminded them again and again that the men aboard the ships were well fed, even as the mutineers struggled to find food because they had nothing with which to barter. His brother joined in, inflaming the mutineers' sense of injustice. "With such words they hardened their followers' mutinous spirit and egged them on to march on the ships to take by force all they could find and make the Admiral their prisoner," wrote Fernando. The mutineers had already defeated the men loyal to Columbus once, back when they took control of the ships. They were the roughest, most outspoken members of the crew and were confident of winning victory again.

On May 19, 1504, a Sunday, the mutineers marched toward Santa Gloria. Thick greenery covered the low hills, and there were few clearings, so it was easy for them to keep their advance a secret. But the Indians, who much preferred Columbus to the mutineers, sent men ahead to warn him that the mutineers were heavily armed. Columbus realized he was in a bind. The mutineers numbered roughly fifty, and all were sworn to kill him. His followers also numbered roughly fifty, but half of those were fresh off thoughts of their own mutiny. So he did what he always did in times of war: deferred to his strapping little brother. Bartolomé's role during the shipwreck had been to defend the ships. No Indian attacks had occurred, so his services hadn't been needed thus far. When the Admiral briefed him on the coming mutineers, Bartolomé didn't hesitate. Every able-bodied man aboard *La Capitana* and the *Santiago* was issued a sword and buckler. Bartolomé also distributed a limited supply of armor, consisting of a solid steel breastplate and helmet without a face mask. Covering the legs was unnecessary because the men would not be on horseback.

Sunlight glinting off his armor and sweating profusely, Bartolomé and his men waded the hundred yards from the wrecks to dry land. There was no beach. Trees and greenery began just beyond water's edge, the taller trees bent by the prevailing southerly wind, leaning toward the sea. The defenders marched for a half mile over a series of low hills, until the mutineers faced them a hundred yards away. Bartolomé had promised his brother he would attempt diplomacy first, so he assumed a nonthreatening posture. He ordered his men to halt and then sent the two emissaries to speak with the mutineers. "But the mutineers were not at all inferior in numbers to the loyalists, and being for the most part sailormen who held the Admiral's men in contempt as cowards who would not fight, they would not even allow the envoys to address them," Fernando later recounted.

The mutineers and loyalists stood at ragged attention looking over at one another. The Porras brothers had a simple strategy for victory: kill Bartolomé. Five of the toughest men were selected to attack him at once, with Francisco de Porras accompanying them. After Bartolomé was dead the loyalists would have no leader. In the panicked retreat that would follow, the mutineers planned to slaughter the remaining loyalists and then hunt for Columbus. "Kill, kill, kill, kill," the mutineers chanted across to the silent loyalist lines.

Armed Indians watched from a discreet distance. If the battle became so intense that the loyalists and mutineers killed too many of one another, then the Arawak were ready to finish off the survivors and be done with Spaniards once and for all.

The mutineers continued chanting "Kill!" as they sprinted at the loyalists. Bartolomé ordered a charge, and the loyalists raced forward until both lines clashed. The six men designated to attack Bartolomé quickly surrounded him, but while they waited for the proper moment to attack, he struck first. Wielding his sword with precision, Bartolomé dropped five of the six within seconds. The first to go was Juan Sanchez, who had let Quibian escape. The next was Juan Barba, a gunner who had pranced about the ships with his sword drawn on the day of the mutiny. As Bartolomé finished off the others, Porras attacked. His sword thrust so deeply into Bartolomé's shield that the blade became embedded to the hilt. Bartolomé kicked Porras to the ground and placed the tip of his sword to the mutineer's throat.

But he did not kill him. The two men had shared many hours together aboard the *Santiago*. Bartolomé didn't like Porras, but he also couldn't bring himself to slice his neck. He knew it was enough to subdue the chief mutineer. Justice could wait for Santo Domingo, where a proper Spanish court could hear the case.

With Porras pacified, the mutineers broke ranks and fled. Some were taken prisoner. Bartolomé promptly marched them to the ships. "He was joyfully received by his brother the Admiral and those who stayed with him, all offering up thanks to God for this great victory."

Pedro de Ledesma had eluded capture but was in desperate need of medical attention. He had suffered a deep sword wound to the head, exposing his brains. One arm hung limp, nearly severed from his body at the shoulder. Another gash reached from his thigh down to his shin, exposing his tibia. One errant slash had even cut his feet so badly that the sole and bone structure were separated. He staggered through the jungle, losing blood and barely able to stand upright. Finally he tumbled over a cliff and landed in a rocky crevice. It was left to the Arawak to discover his unconscious body. They had never seen the effects of a sword wound before, and so they stood over him, poking sticks into his brain and flesh, gaping at the destruction. "Get away or I'll do you a mischief," he would mumble in random moments of clarity. But the Indians returned when he slipped back into unconsciousness. They were so intrigued they kept Ledesma's location a secret.

When the loyalists finally discovered Ledesma the morning of Monday, May 20, he was carried on a litter to a small hut. The walls and roof were palm thatch. Mosquitoes buzzed around his body as Maestre Bernal cauterized the wounds with oil. The wounds, Fernando wrote, "were so numerous that during the first eight days of his cure the surgeon swore he was always discovering new ones."

Those mutineers still on the lam also returned to the fold on May 20. It was eleven months since the shipwreck, and nearly six since the mutiny. They "sent envoys to plead humbly with the Admiral to be merciful to them, for they were repentant and wished to rejoin his service," noted Fernando. It was a chance for Columbus to lord his authority over the mutineers. He was astute, however, to the politics of shipboard life — and the perceptions of the royal court. If he returned to Hispaniola with a fractured crew, it would reaffirm the negative comments hounding him since 1492. Ferdinand and Isabella would continue to see him as a rogue explorer incapable of managing a colony, "a good Admiral but not a good viceroy," in King Ferdinand's unforgettable judgment. Columbus knew that a passive professionalism would regain him control of Hispaniola faster than harsh treatment of Spaniards. His open pardon was intended for all but one man: Francisco de Porras. Porras was thrown in chains, where he languished in the Jamaican heat as the metal caused his skin to blister and chafe. Even swatting a mosquito meant a heavy clank of his chains and the possibility of bruising himself when those irons impacted upon his skin.

The reunion of the crew was tentative, its success incumbent upon Columbus's diplomacy. The same men who had longed to kill him before could just as easily slash his throat now. As a result Columbus decided it was not yet time for the mutineers to live among the loyalists. "As so many of the new people could not be comfortably lodged and fed and kept at peace aboard the ships, where there was not enough food for even one of the two bands, and as he wanted to avoid the exchange of insults that might revive buried quarrels, the Admiral decided to place the former mutineers under the command of a captain who should tour the island with them, trading with the Indians and keeping them occupied until the coming of the ships, whose arrival was daily expected," wrote Fernando.

That captain was the faithful Pedro de Terreros, of *El Gallego,* and he likely became the last victim of the mutiny, dying mysteriously on May 29, 1504, in the Caribbean interior. The mutineers returned to the ships, feigning ignorance. Columbus was saddened by Terreros's death and questioned the sailors about the lack of a body but had no choice but to accept their explanations and let the matter go. The wounds of the mutiny were still too fresh to push it further.

Meanwhile, back in Santo Domingo, Diego Mendez was overjoyed by the arrival of caravels from Spain. He promptly bought a very small caravel and loaded it "with provisions: bread, wine, meat, hogs, sheep, and fruit. I then sent it to the place where the Admiral was, so that he and all his men might return in it to Santo Domingo and from there return to Castile." His mission complete at long last, Mendez rested. His bold, adventurous role in the fourth voyage was at an end. "I myself went ahead with the other two ships to give the King and Queen an account of all that had happened on the voyage."

As Mendez sailed east to Spain, the little caravel laden with supplies rode the winds to Santa Gloria. To the raucous cheers of Columbus's weary men, captain Diego de Salcedo guided the *caravelon* (a smaller form of the caravel) through the opening in the reefs and dropped anchor. It was a terrible ship, barely more seaworthy than *La Vizcaino* and *El Gallego* before their abandonment. The sails were in tatters from wind, sun, and neglect. The hull was a sieve. Yet she floated, and to Columbus's crew the *caravelon* was the finest vessel they had ever seen. The hogs were promptly butchered and the wine casks tapped. A fire was built on shore, and the feasting began. On Saturday, June 29, after a year and five days trapped at Santa Gloria, Columbus abandoned his cabin on *La Capitana* and stepped aboard the little caravel for the ride back to Santo Domingo. He was too lame to walk without assistance, so boarding the ship was a most difficult task. The Arawak, watching from the shore, wept. Their visitors from another planet, capable of blocking out the moon, were leaving.

During his time in Jamaica, seven more of Columbus's men died, including a ship's boy named Grigorio Sollo, who succumbed between the time the rescue ship arrived and the time it sailed to Hispaniola. The Admiral himself had endured malaria, gout, arthritis, and rheumatism, but much to the chagrin of critics like Porras and Ovando, he was still very much alive. Indeed Ovando did not look forward to the Admiral's return.

Fortunately for the governor, it was hurricane season again. The weather was harsh and winds formidable as the little caravel left Jamaica behind and tacked toward Hispaniola. The crossing had taken Mendez and Fieschi four days in a canoe. Amid the storms and contrary winds, it took Columbus's rescue caravel forty-five days. Leaking and comically overcrowded, the little ship rode low in the water. There were tremendous doubts she would make the crossing. When she did, storms caused her to put in temporarily at the port of Jacmel. The journey was so slow and so terrifying that many of the sailors vowed never to set foot on a ship again if they made it to Santo Domingo.

Many of them went on to keep that promise, but Columbus stayed just four weeks in his former principality before chartering the leaking caravelon and one other caravel for the journey back to Spain. After arriving in Santo Domingo on August 13, Columbus was invited by Ovando to stay at the governor's mansion while the caravelon was refitted and reprovisioned. This warm gesture was extended in the most civil, friendly tone Ovando could manage. The people of Santo Domingo were showering Columbus with affection, forgetting past animosities in a display of admiration for the hardship he had weathered on the fourth voyage. Ovando was merely being politic.

But more privately Ovando showed his true colors by releasing Francisco de Porras from his chains and sending him back to Spain rather than prosecute him in Santo Domingo. Ovando also proposed that the loyalists who had fought the mutineers should be put on trial for murder, with the proceedings to take place in Santo Domingo. Columbus, weary of Ovando's duplicity and eager to return home, quickly produced his letter of instructions from the sovereigns giving him sole authority over his crew. Ovando backed down. "The governor conferred many favors upon the Admiral, but always with a false smile and a pretense of friendship to his face. This continued until our ship was refitted and another equipped, in which the Admiral embarked his relations and servants, most of the others remaining in Hispaniola," wrote Fernando, who had just turned sixteen. He was alluding to the sailors now afraid to put to sea. Though the sovereigns owed those men their two years' salary, Columbus paid them in full from his own pocket, fearful they would be destined for a life of island poverty.

On the morning of September 12, the day after Marco Surjano, a gentleman volunteer from Genoa, died in Santo Domingo and became the fourth voyage's final fatality, Columbus sailed for home. Bartolomé was placed in charge of one ship. Columbus and Fernando sailed as paying passengers on the other. The two caravels floated down the Ozama and let the following winds push them into the blue Caribbean.

But the fourth voyage's travails were not done. Six miles out to sea, the mast of the *caravelon* snapped at deck level. It crashed down to the deck, bringing with it a tangle of yards, sails, blocks, and rigging. The mast was cut away and heaved overboard. Columbus and Fernando immediately transferred to the other ship and the *caravelon* turned and limped back to Santo Domingo. "We in our ship," wrote a relieved Fernando, "continued on our voyage enjoying good weather until we were a third of the way across the ocean."

By that time the caravel was five weeks into the trip home, fighting headwinds the whole way. On Friday, October 18, horrendous weather nearly sank her. Columbus was sick in bed with gout and could only endure the pain and storm. The crew was exhausted and frightened, fearing the worst. Relieved when the sun returned the following day, they let down their guard. This was a mistake, because the winds were still gusting hard. The mast suddenly snapped into four pieces. The sound was like a gunshot, and the men lurched about the heaving decks, desperate to find a place to hide before the timber crashed to the deck. When it had, the ship was dead in the water. Beset by roiling seas a thousand miles from Spain, it seemed destined to bob atop the ocean until the currents forced it back toward the Caribbean. In many ways Columbus was shipwrecked again, but this time at sea.

He was old and sick, but Columbus's ingenuity remained limitless. He took control of the nameless caravel without ever leaving his sickbed, ordering the forecastle and sterncastle demolished and the lumber used to construct a new mast. "A jury mast was constructed from one of the lateen yards and partially braced with ropes and timbers," Fernando remembered. "Our mizzen mast was brought down by another storm, and it was God's will that we should sail in this sorry plight for seven hundred leagues, at the end of which we entered the harbor of Sanlúcar de Barrameda." The date was November 7, 1504. Columbus was finally back in Spain, fifty-three years old and with less than two years to live.

"From there he went to Seville," Fernando concluded his journal of the voyage, "where the Admiral took some rest from the hardships he had suffered."

The fourth voyage was complete.

Epilogue

Columbus always thought the fourth voyage was the pinnacle of his career. But the magnificence of Columbus's first voyage washed over those later voyages in much the same way that the tidal wave in Boca de la Sierpe almost swamped his fleet. The unearthing of *La Vizcaino* is the only tangible reminder that the fourth voyage was his greatest act of discovery and adventure. Or as Columbus fondly named it: El Alto Viaje — "The high voyage."

Until very late in the eighteenth century, it was common knowledge that the New World was discovered by the intrepid Italian explorer Amerigo Vespucci. *Mundus Novus,* the Florentine's travelogue of his voyages to the New World, was proof. "Our ancient forebears thought that there were no continents to the south beyond the equator, only the sea they call the Atlantic," he wrote in 1505. "My voyage has made it plain that this opinion is erroneous and entirely contrary to the truth. For in those regions I have found a continent more densely populated and abounding in animals than our Europe, Asia and Africa. We may rightly call this continent the New World."

Vespucci — hawk nosed, balding, and an acquaintance of Columbus's — was a minor character of minor ambition, possessing great powers of self-promotion. Facts did not cloud his version of events. By the time Vespucci sailed to what was then known as the Indies, in 1499, transatlantic travel was becoming common. He whiled away the three-week crossing as a passenger in the employ of a Seville banker. Even the label "New World," first coined by Spanish courtier Peter Martyr in 1494, was derivative.

Vespucci published *Mundus Novus* in his native tongue. It was later translated into French as well as Latin, then the preferred language of European intelligentsia. He circulated copies throughout southern Europe and had additional copies printed in Augsburg and Strasbourg for northern European intellectuals and royalty. It was an age when mankind straddled the breach between the dank strictures of the medieval world and the fresh air of the Renaissance. The hunger for new knowledge was frenetic. Every thinker worth his salt read Vespucci's world-changing account.

It was only a matter of time before Vespucci's boasting made its way to a quaint French village named Saint-Dié, a hotbed of intellectual thinking. There it inevitably fell into the hands of a thirty-six-year-old Roman Catholic priest and humanist whose given name was Martin Wald-seemüller but who went by his Latin alter ego Hylacomylus (literally — and curiously — "The miller of the lake in the forest").

Hylacomylus was part of a five-man team revising Claudius Ptolemy's epic tome *Geography* — the first such overhaul in twelve centuries. The original world maps, however, were missing from the text. While the other four members of the Saint-Dié revision team, philosophers all, addressed Ptolemy's observations on astrology and music, Hylacomylus drew map duty. As the team's lone cartographer, it was only natural.

Small wonder that *Mundus Novus* also became Hyla-comylus's reading assignment. He pored over Vespucci's text with a focused eye, scrutinizing mentions of latitude and native culture for signs of bluff. He found none. The more he read the more convinced he became of Vespucci's great-ness. Critical observation was replaced by fawning admira-tion, which in turn was supplanted by personal ambition. Waldseemüller set aside *Geography* to become the first man to draw a world map incorporating Vespucci's claims. It would be engraved on wood and broken into twelve sec-tions comprising thirty degrees of longitude, allowing it to be pieced together into a globe.

Hylacomylus then wrote a short tract introducing read-ers to this new worldview. It was published in Saint-Dié on April 25, 1507. The document was divided into two sec-tions. The first featured Hylacomylus's writings; the second was a reprinting of *Mundus Novus*. "Now, really these parts," Hylacomylus wrote of the three known continents of Africa, Asia, and Europe, "were more widely traveled, and another part was discovered by Americus Vesputius (as will be seen in the following pages), for which reason I do not see why anyone would rightly forbid calling it (after the discoverer Americus, a man of wisdom and ingenuity) 'Amerige,' that is, land of Americus, or 'America,' since both 'Europa' and 'Asia' are names derived from women. Its location and the customs of its peoples will be easily discerned from the four voyages of Americus which follow."

Ironically Hylacomylus's map and his role in naming the new continent were soon forgotten. Closer scrutiny of Vespucci's four mentioned voyages would show them to ac-tually number just two. The name, however, took. Within a decade "America" was how Europe referred to the New World. Amerigo Vespucci had become immortal.

The other explorers following in Columbus's wake re-ceived far less glory. After surviving the hurricane of 1502,

Rodrigo de Bastides returned to Spain and was acquitted of all charges brought by Bobadilla. The Crown gave the converso a handsome reward for his bold discoveries and named him governor of all those lands. Bastides returned to Hispaniola in 1504 and started a cattle farm. Twenty years later he started a new colony in Colombia, leading five caravels laden with settlers to the new land. The colonists soon grew disenchanted with their new home and attempted to assassinate Bastides. He was stabbed five times in his sleep but miraculously survived. However, while traveling to Santo Domingo so a surgeon could care for his wounds, sharp currents pushed his caravel off course. He died on the island of Cuba in 1527, but his body was interred in Santo Domingo's cathedral.

Alonso de Ojeda and **Juan de la Cosa** made a final voyage to Paria. Cosa was killed in a battle with local Indians on February 28, 1510, his body shot through with poison arrows. Ojeda escaped to Santo Domingo, only to die in poverty several years later.

Bishop Juan Rodriguez de Fonseca's power flourished throughout the rest of his days. He became wealthy from New World profits and his personal monopolies. By his death, in 1523, he oversaw not just the Americas but had expanded Spain's power to a global level by arranging for a fleet to send Ferdinand Magellan on the world's first circumnavigation.

Diego Columbus, Columbus's firstborn son and recognized heir, had two children out of wedlock after his father's death, the second of which he named Cristóbal Colón. He finally married in 1508. His wife, the daughter of a powerful Castilian duke, bore him seven children. In the summer of 1509, Diego traveled to Santo Domingo for the first time, arriving on July 9. He assumed the role of governor-general of the Indies, the first member of his family to hold the post since his father had been removed from power in October 1500. Diego, who bore a striking resemblance to the Admiral, died in Spain on February 23, 1526. His bones were taken to Santo Domingo for burial.

Diego Mendez was present at Columbus's deathbed. Mendez died in 1536 and requested that the outline of a canoe be carved on his tombstone.

Bartolomeo Fieschi returned to Genoa immediately after Columbus's death and led an uprising against the government in power. He failed and once again left Genoa for a life of exile. He finally returned in 1525 and was given command of a small fleet to fight the French. In 1527 he was named city father, thus restoring his family to local prominence. He died in 1530.

Fernando Columbus was among the crowd at his father's bedside when the explorer died. Observers reported that, of all the relatives and friends who gathered round, it was Fernando who was permitted to stand closest — closer even than Diego, the Admiral's heir. Fernando went on to enjoy a long, satisfying life. He traveled to Santo Domingo with Diego in 1509, marking the final time he would visit the New World. Returning to Spain soon after, he pursued an intellectual life. He wrote, among other works, a biography of his father. Fernando's work as a cosmographer was revered, and his library was one of the world's largest at the time of his death, on July 12, 1539.

Fernando's mother, **Beatriz de Arana,** outlived Columbus. She and the explorer never mended the unspoken rift in their relationship, perhaps brought on by his unwillingness to marry her. He left Beatriz an annuity, which she received until she died, sometime after 1521. Beatriz willed her possessions — which included a house, two orchards, and three vineyards — to Fernando.

Bartolomé Columbus returned to Santo Domingo with his nephew Diego in 1509. Now in his late forties,

Bartolomé had been granted permission from King Ferdinand to undertake a voyage of discovery, but upon arriving in Hispaniola he thought better of that. He was content to hold a secondary position in the local government. He died in the city of Concepción in 1514 and was buried in Santo Domingo.

The wrecks of *La Capitana* and the *Santiago* disintegrated over the centuries. They have never been found, despite a number of archaeological expeditions to Jamaica. The same holds true for *El Gallego,* which settled to the bottom at the mouth of the Belen River. In 1998, American expatriate Warren White was diving for lobster along the Panamanian coast, in a bay known as Playa Dama. He unwittingly snorkeled over a shipwreck that lay in ten feet of water. Spindly *versos* swivel guns and long lombard cannons were visible to the naked eye. When White dove to investigate, he found turtle bones and coconuts — the remains of a meal — nestled in the rotting remnants of the half-buried wooden hull. Almost five hundred years after being scuttled, *La Vizcaino* was found. Most telling, her *versos* guns were still loaded, with the breech pins in position for firing, a reminder that Columbus expected Quibian's attack as he abandoned *La Vizcaino*.

Meanwhile the continent's true discoverer was being written off as a minor Renaissance explorer — when he was remembered at all. Part of this was Columbus's doing. Upon returning from the fourth voyage, he learned that Isabella was on her deathbed. She had been pale and bedridden with fevers since August. Courtiers whispered that she was unable to eat but was consumed by thirst. More ominously, a tumor could be seen protruding from her body. Though Columbus made repeated attempts to visit her one last time, Ferdinand refused to allow it. Isabella died of an undetermined cancer on November 26, 1504. She was fifty-four.

Even if he had been summoned to her bedside, Columbus would have been hard-pressed to make the trip, for he was in failing health himself. The fourth voyage had caused his maladies to go from bad to worse, particularly his rheumatoid arthritis and ophthalmia. He could no longer walk or write and could barely see. Whatever fantasies he once maintained about returning to the gold of Veragua were forgotten. Yet in 1505, for the sake of his sons and brothers, he undertook one last journey, a grueling five-hundred-mile horseback ride from Seville to Valladolid. His aim was an audience with King Ferdinand. Columbus was a wealthy man and the purpose of the journey was to garner royal approval of a perpetual trust for his heirs. Ferdinand granted that request. Columbus died shortly thereafter, on the night of May 20, 1506. A large crowd of family and friends clustered around his bedside when he died, among them Bartolomeo Fieschi — the courageous "Flisco" — that old family friend from Genoa.

Columbus's funeral was in the parish church of Santa María la Antigua, in Valladolid. He was first buried at the Franciscan cemetery in Valladolid, but in 1509 his body was moved to the Carthusian Monastery in Seville. In 1523, at the behest of his son Diego, who had become governor of Hispaniola after the end of Ovando's reign in 1509, Columbus's body was moved to the Las Cuevas monastery in Spain. In 1541 Columbus's remains were disinterred one more time and moved to Santo Domingo, where they were buried in the city's cathedral.

After France took control of Hispaniola in 1795, Spanish authorities, desperate to keep Columbus's remains on their own soil, moved him to Havana. In 1899 they were returned to Seville and interred in its cathedral.

The seeds of controversy were sown in 1877, when the

cathedral in Santo Domingo (built during Ovando's reign, it is still the oldest cathedral in the New World) was being refurbished. Workers found a wooden box engraved with the name "Admiral Christopher Columbus," containing a collection of bones (though not a full skeleton). Based on that authorities there claimed that the Columbus whose bones had been whisked off to Cuba must have been a distant relative instead of the explorer. Columbus's remains, they insisted, had never left their island. Today the Dominican Republic (the modern-day name for the eastern half of Hispaniola) claims that the body of Christopher Columbus rests inside a lighthouse-shaped mausoleum they specially constructed to serve as his tomb.

The dispute remained a historical uncertainty until the summer of 2003, when Dr. Jose Lorente at Spain's University of Granada received special permission to open Columbus's Seville sepulcher and perform DNA testing on the bones inside. The Dominican Republic was initially reluctant to allow DNA samples to be taken from the remains in Santo Domingo but relented in principle in January 2004 — although they never actually opened Columbus's tomb and turned over a sample (perhaps all too aware that Columbus's remains are one of their primary sources of national pride and the tomb a key tourism site).

The DNA verification process involves comparing the bones exhumed in Seville and Santo Domingo with the DNA from other bones known to belong to Columbus's relatives. A sample was taken from the bones of his brother Diego and from his son Fernando, both of whom were buried in Spain. The results were unveiled with much fanfare in Madrid on October 1, 2004. Although Dr. Lorente was almost certain the small assemblage of bone chips that ʾstituted the Seville remains belonged to Columbus, the ˙ere inconclusive.

Columbus had never been a favorite of King Ferdinand's and became even less so as his heirs filed an annoying series of lawsuits against the Crown, citing the Capitulations of Santa Fe as a means of claiming all the New World riches due the explorer's estate. Ferdinand reacted to these *pleitos* by systematically discrediting Columbus and his achievements until it was clear the Genovese explorer had discovered nothing at all. When Ferdinand died, in 1516, and was succeeded by Charles V of Austria, it was decreed that the name of Columbus should never be uttered. When his heirs began selling off his maps and letters, destroying whatever legacy remained, Columbus's historical anonymity was complete. Vespucci reigned as the New World's discoverer.

Even Columbus's admirers contributed to his misrepresentation. A 1519 portrait by the renowned Venetian painter Sebastiani del Piombo bears the inscription, *"Haec est effigies liguris miranda Columbi antipodum primus rate qui penetravit in orbem"* — "This is the likeness of the Ligurian mariner Columbus, the first in the world who penetrated the antipodes." The painting, which industrialist J. P. Morgan donated to New York's Metropolitan Museum of Art in 1900, shows a surly, fat, middle-age man with thick lips and a flat nose. Columbus looked nothing like that.

Piombo was just twenty-one when Columbus died. He had never been to Spain, let alone set eyes on the Admiral. And Columbus never had his portrait painted or likeness sketched during his lifetime. Yet Piombo's career was ascendant in 1519. He was working in Rome and was close friends with Michelangelo. The world accepted the painting as a true likeness of Columbus. There was no reason not to.

Art historians would later discover that the inscription was not part of the original painting but was added years later by an unknown hand. They would also surmise that the painting was not created in 1519, but as many as fifteen years afterward. Most damning, the subject was definitively identified as an Italian cleric.

Working separately, but with such effectiveness that they could have been acting in concert, Vespucci and Piombo had transformed Columbus into a historical cipher.

Luckily for Columbus there existed four published accounts of his voyages — three of them written by eye-witnesses. The fourth was penned by Peter Martyr, who interviewed Columbus after his return from the first voyage. With the passage of time, these works were given greater credibility.

The French Academy sponsored an essay contest in 1792, asking whether the discovery of America had been helpful or harmful to world history. The inquiry spawned a spate of research. In 1828 Washington Irving wrote the first English-language biography of Columbus. Its popularity led King Philip VII of Spain to order all documents relating to Columbus unearthed from the nation's archives. It soon became clear that Columbus, not Vespucci, had discovered the New World.

Still, a precedent had been set. Piombo — or whoever etched the Latin inscription atop the fat Bolognese cleric's black hair — began a tradition that would span the centuries. Pre-Renaissance artists had attempted to capture the elusive face of Christ. Post-Renaissance painters invested similar energy reinventing Columbus. An exhibition of seventy-one paintings of Columbus at the 1893 Columbian Exposition in Chicago — the World's Fair — bears this out. All were purported to be originals, many allegedly drawn with the subject in attendance. Yet some showed him obese, some showed him thin. Some showed him blond, some of dark complexion. He was portrayed, by turns, as jowly, bearded, clean shaven, olive skinned, and even dressed as a monk. Not a single image matched eye-witness descriptions.

Columbus has been alternately venerated (the Catholic Church proposed him for sainthood in 1866) and vilified (his insistence on enslaving the Indians for personal gain rather than converting them to Christianity quashed beati-fication as quickly as it began). In ceasing his role as cipher, he became a lightning rod for controversy. Those who viewed Europe's global expansion as inevitable saw him as the visionary who led the way. Others, preferring to believe that Columbus's discoveries begat a genocide against the New World's peaceful indigenous people, uniformly vilify him — as if he had orchestrated the atrocities himself or as if the indigenous tribes hadn't already been waging war on one another (an ironic offshoot of Columbus labeling those tribes "Indians" occurred during World War II, when Ger-man pilots termed their Allied adversaries *Indianes* — Indi-ans — all because they came from a land to the *west*). Still others invest themselves in the pointless argument that Columbus was not the New World's discoverer — for it's certain that he wasn't. The Irish, Vikings, and perhaps even the English and Chinese were there first. Columbus's claim to fame isn't that he got there first, it's that he stayed.

No matter their merit, arguments will follow Colum-bus forever. History does not know what to make of the Admiral of the Ocean Sea or how to categorize the ramifi-cations of his discoveries without passions of one kind or another intruding. The explorer will always remain some-thing of an enigma. He was Italian, yet claimed the New World for Spain. He was a compassionate Christian, yet con-sidered slavery a viable form of commerce. He was a man of great charisma whose passion sometimes turned others against him. He was an explorer — a wanderer, really — who fancied himself capable of great bureaucratic skills. His advocates marveled at his daring and tenaciousness, persevering so long in his quest for funding and then defying conventional wisdom to sail across an uncharted sea. His detractors thought him brutal and weak. The only certainty about Columbus is that, for better or worse, he chose to live a bold life rather than settle for mediocrity.

Notes

I was inspired to write about Columbus by a *Los Angeles Times* story (June 23, 2002) documenting Warren White's discovery of *La Vizcaino,* and the subsequent furor over whether the vessel found off Panama truly belonged to Columbus (although evidence points overwhelmingly toward the affirmative, marine archaeologists are divided). This book, as I imagined it, would focus on *La Vizcaino,* the circumstances surrounding its demise, and that controversy. But in the course of my research, it became obvious that the fourth voyage's other calamities deserved equal weight — as did the enigmatic Columbus. Instead of focusing my research in Panama, the book became far-flung, taking me throughout the Caribbean and across Europe. The world has changed a great deal over the last five centuries, but many of the places Columbus visited and the sights he saw remain the same. Those first-person observations by Columbus and others led to many of the descriptions in this book.

On a more academic note, an exhaustive number of books have been written about Columbus. I pored over a great many of them, but have limited my bibliography to those that assisted me most when it actually came time to sit down and write. Washington Irving and Samuel Eliot Morison's works on Columbus were indispensable, as was Gianni Granzotto's elegant biography. As with the travel aspects of writing, no substitute exists for first-person narrative, so whenever Columbus or Fernando could describe a scene in their own words, I stepped back and let them.

I am deeply grateful to Dr. Jose Lorente for taking the time to keep me abreast of his DNA experiments in Spain. It was always nice to start my working day here in California by reading an overnight e-mail from Granada, informing me of the latest on Admiral Columbus and his exhumed bones. For a guy who's been dead five centuries, Columbus was very much a physical presence as I wrote this book, thanks to Dr. Lorente.

The core of this work, then, is the compilation of journals, biographies, and personal travels. Writing this book was like detective work, or a treasure hunt, with bits of information gleaned here and there to create a fact-filled narrative. A detailed guide to references by chapter follows.

PROLOGUE

Morison's *Admiral of the Ocean Sea,* Irving's *The Complete Voyages of Christopher Columbus,* Granzotto. Bedini's comprehensive Columbus encyclopedia was invaluable and thorough. Also, thanks to Dr. Matthew Dugard for the insights on the pains associated with ophthalmia, rheumatoid arthritis, and gout.

CHAPTER ONE

Kamen and Thomas's recent volumes on Spanish history were enormously helpful here, as was Bedini. Durant's exhaustive volumes on the history of civilization provided valuable background on Europe, the papacy, and the medieval mind-set.

CHAPTER TWO

Mandeville, Tuchman, Bedini. An excellent primer on the history of cartography is Wilford's *The Mapmakers*. He turns a potentially dry subject into a page-turner.

CHAPTER THREE

The subject of spices was a fascinating tangential avenue of research. The December 17, 1998, issue of *The Economist* featured a riveting travel piece on the Spice Islands called "A Taste of Adventure." Schivelbusch was also an excellent source.

CHAPTER FOUR

Morison's *Admiral of the Ocean Sea,* Granzotto. For background on Ferdinand and Isabella, the works of Durant and Rubin. William Manchester's *A World Lit Only by Fire* offers a sometimes irreverent peek at the medieval and Renaissance worlds that makes them come to life in a way that few history books ever have.

CHAPTER FIVE

Despite his overarching influence on the development of a Spanish empire in the New World and his venomous disdain for Columbus, Fonseca has become a relatively obscure historical figure. Even Morison, gatekeeper of all things Columbus, gives him short shrift. I relied heavily on Bedini, Kamen, Irving (*Voyages and Discoveries*) and Thomas to piece together a portrait of this most Machiavellian character.

CHAPTER SIX

Joyner's excellent biography of Magellan gives a fascinating background on Portuguese sailing and details about the caravel. Da Gama's journey is still the subject of national debate in Portugal, for no one has ever proved his exact course between Lisbon and the Cape of Good Hope, particularly the roundabout early miles, when he nearly made landfall in South America. I relied on Bedini and *The Catholic Encyclopedia* for particulars. A sidebar to the Portuguese journey to India was that Bartolomeu Dias, who made the first journey around the tip of Africa, thus crushing Columbus's hopes for funding from King João, was also the first European to greet Columbus after his first voyage to the New World. As a tattered *Niña* limped along the Portuguese coast, Dias was on the vessel that boarded the *Niña,* demanding to know its business. In this way the two explorers met in neatly ironic fashion. Dias drowned on May 23, 1500, when his ship sank in a storm.

Chapter Seven
Morison's *Admiral of the Ocean Sea,* Cohen, Colon.

Chapter Eight
Morison (*Admiral of the Ocean Sea*), Cohen, Colon, Irving (*Columbus*).

Chapter Nine
Morison's *Admiral of the Ocean Sea*), Bedini, Irving's *The Voyages and Discoveries of the Companions of Columbus.* Irving actually lived for a time at the Alhambra during the nineteenth century. He provided exhaustive insights into the Spanish court and the manipulations of Ojeda. They are profound — if a little catty, for Irving was an unabashed supporter of Columbus — in nature, even nearly two hundred years after their writing. For the terrifying descriptions of the Caribs, thanks goes to Dr. Diego Alvarez Chanca, Ferdinand and Isabella's personal doctor, who traveled as fleet physician on the second voyage. His observations about the people and places in the New World are keen and lucid. They can be found in Cohen's *Four Voyages.*

A historical footnote to Bastides's voyage was that Vasco Nuñez de Balboa sailed as a crew member. He would go on to discover and name the Pacific Ocean, in 1513. The year after that great triumph, in a scene reminiscent of Columbus's battles with Bobadilla, Balboa was arrested on charges of treason and executed. The order was given by a royal administrator sent to investigate troubles in Spain's colonies.

CHAPTER TEN

Kamen, Morison's *Admiral of the Ocean Sea,* Granzotto, Thomas, Bedini. The Library of Iberian Resources confirms that Bobadilla was *maestresala,* or captain of the royal guards, in Córdoba in July 1488 and chief magistrate from January 1495 to February 1497.

CHAPTER ELEVEN

The specifics of Columbus's voyage from Hispaniola to Spain and subsequent appearance in Granada have become a source of confusion over the centuries. Some believe Columbus landed in Cádiz in late October, while others insist it was not until November. After studying the dates that Columbus and the sovereigns traveled on their different routes during those months, I believe he arrived in Cádiz in late November and appeared in Granada on December 17, as I have written it. Also, though having visited the Alhambra on several occasions and standing in the understated throne room where Columbus fell to his knees and wept, it wasn't until reading Irwin's excellent *The Alhambra* that the myths and cobwebs perpetrated in the various guidebooks were swept away.

CHAPTER TWELVE

Kamen, Bedini, Thomas. Also, for a glimpse of Ovando's physical features, look no further than the statue towering over the cafés of Santo Domingo's colonial section.

Chapter Thirteen

Colon, Morison's *Admiral of the Ocean Sea,* Bedini. For life aboard ship, Joyner. For information on Caribbean currents, *The Caribbean Current,* by Joanna Gyory, Arthur J. Mariano, and Edward H. Ryan (http://oceancurrents.rsmas. miami.edu/caribbean), was most helpful. The National Oceanic and Atmospheric Administration (NOAA) Web site (www.nhc.noaa.gov) offers detailed analysis of hurricane conditions, tropical cyclone terminology, and a list of the deadliest Atlantic hurricanes from 1492 until modern times.

Chapter Fourteen

Morison's *Admiral of the Ocean Sea,* Colon, Cohen, Joyner.

Chapter Fifteen

Colon, Bedini, Joyner, Morison's *Admiral of the Ocean Sea.*

Chapter Sixteen

Irving's *The Complete Voyages of Christopher Columbus,* Morison's *Admiral of the Ocean Sea,* Bedini, Colon.

Chapter Seventeen

Colon, Cohen, Morison's *Admiral of the Ocean Sea,* Morison and Obregon's *The Caribbean as Columbus Saw It,* Bedini, Granzotto. The United States Department of Defense contributed via a U.S. Navy survey of all DOD lands in Panama. This exquisite environmental report offers details on the tropical forests of the Panamanian coastline and discusses bird migration, flooded forests, marshes, mangroves, and evergreen seasonal forests. In its own dry way, it is very evocative reading.

CHAPTER EIGHTEEN

Colon, for the journal entries. McCullough for the Panama Canal and Columbus's location. Bedini, Thomas, and Cohen for insights into Mendez. "Eastern Panamanian Montane Forests," which can be found on the World Wildlife Foundation Web site (www.worldwildlife.org), is another fine peek into the dense world of Panama's jungles that sheltered the Indians of Veragua. This land that Columbus was unable to colonize has remained virtually unsettled for centuries, despite the efforts of treasure hunters searching the hillsides for the legendary gold mines found by Columbus.

CHAPTER NINETEEN

Colon, Morison and Obregon's *The Caribbean as Columbus Saw It*. Bedini's work includes a comprehensive crew list from each voyage, making it possible to pinpoint which sailors were slaughtered by the Guaymi. To this day the mouth of the Belen is as Columbus left it. Aerial photos still clearly show the sandbar and the broad river mouth. However, no traces whatsoever of the structures that formed Columbus's fledgling colony remain.

CHAPTER TWENTY

Christian Miller's June 2002 piece in the *Los Angeles Times* pinpoints the wreckage of *La Vizcaino* and the items left behind. Salvage efforts were under way, but due to the potentially lucrative nature of excavating *La Vizcaino*, factions within the Panamanian government have temporarily stopped all work. Panama's National Institute of Culture and Ministry of Economy and Finance are at odds over salvage rights. Panamanian officials have even gone so far as to declare that *La Vizcaino* discoverer Warren White, who once spent his energies proving that the wreck he found belonged to Columbus, did not find *La Vizcaino* first, thereby denying him salvage rights (*The Panama News,* vol. 10, no. 14, July 18 and August 7, 2004).

CHAPTER TWENTY-ONE
Colon, Morison's *Admiral of the Ocean Sea.* The site where Columbus's vessels were shipwrecked is now known as St. Ann's Bay. It can easily be accessed off the A-1 highway on Jamaica's north coast, two hours east of Montego Bay. However, no signs point to the site, and it is not listed on any map.

CHAPTER TWENTY-TWO
As part of his will, Mendez wrote a gripping and detailed account of his open-boat journey, in Valladolid, Spain, on June 6, 1536. The witnesses were all servants of Diego Columbus's widow. The text, in its entirety, can be found in Cohen.

CHAPTER TWENTY-THREE
Colon, Granzotto, Bedini, and Morison's *Admiral of the Ocean Sea.* The battlefield is also off A-1, though on the inland side of the road. Unmarked and overgrown, the general area is private property.

CHAPTER TWENTY-FOUR
Colon, Kamen, Thomas, Bedini, Morison's *Admiral of the Ocean Sea.*

Selected Bibliography

Arciniegas, German. *Caribbean: Sea of the New World*. New York: Alfred Knopf, 1958.

Bedini, Silvio, ed. *The Christopher Columbus Encyclopedia*. New York: Simon and Schuster, 1992.

Bergreen, Laurence. *Over the Edge of the World: Magellan's Terrifying Circumnavigation of the Globe*. New York: HarperCollins, 2003.

Bishop, Patrick. *Fighter Boys*. London: HarperCollins, 2004.

Boorstin, Daniel J. *The Discoverers*. New York: Vintage, 1983.

Brown, Jonathan. *The History and Present Condition of Santo Domingo. Vol. 1*. London: Frank Cass, 1971.

Cohen, J. M., transl. *Christopher Columbus: The Four Voyages*. London: Penguin, 1969.

Colon, Fernando. *The Life of the Admiral Christopher Columbus*. Translated by Benjamin Keen. New Brunswick, NJ: Rutgers University Press, 1992.

Curtis, William Eleroy. *The Relics of Columbus: An Illustrated Description of the Historical Collection in the Monastery of La Rábida*. Washington, DC: William H. Lowdermilk, 1893.

Deagan, Kathleen, and Jose Maria Cruxent. *Archaeology at La Isabela: America's First European Town.* New Haven, CT: Yale University Press, 2002.

———. *Columbus's Outpost among the Tainos.* New Haven, CT: Yale University Press, 2002.

Durant, Will. *Story of Civilization.* Vol. 4, *Age of Faith.* New York: Simon and Schuster, 1980.

———. *Story of Civilization.* Vol. 5, *The Renaissance.* New York: Simon and Schuster, 1980.

———. *Story of Civilization.* Vol. 6, *The Reformation.* New York: Simon and Schuster, 1980.

Fernandez-Armesto, Felipe. *Columbus.* New York: Oxford University Press, 1991.

Fuson, Robert. *The Log of Christopher Columbus.* Camden, ME: International Marine/McGraw-Hill, 1992.

Gardner, William J. *A History of Jamaica.* London: Frank Cass, 1971.

Granzotto, Gianni. *Christopher Columbus.* New York: Doubleday, 1985.

Heat-Moon, William Least. *Columbus in the Americas.* Hoboken, NJ: John Wiley and Son, 2002.

Irving, Washington. *The Complete Voyages of Christopher Columbus.* Boston: Twayne, 1981.

———. *Voyages and Discoveries of the Companions of Columbus.* Boston: Twayne, 1986.

Irwin, Robert. *The Alhambra.* London: Profile Books, 2004.

Joyner, Tim. *Magellan.* Camden, ME: International Marine/McGraw-Hill, 1992.

Kamen, Henry. *Empire: How Spain Became a World Power 1492–1763.* New York: Perennial, 2002.

Kelsey, Harry. *Sir Francis Drake: The Queen's Pirate.* New Haven, CT: Yale University Press, 1998.

Lopez, Jose Bermudez. *The Alhambra and Generalife: Official Guide.* Granada: Editorial En Su Mano, 1999.

MacCulloch, Diarmaid. *The Reformation*. New York: Viking, 2004.

Madriaga, Salvador. *Christopher Columbus: Being the Life of the Very Magnificent Lord Don Cristobal Colon*. Westport, CT: Greenwood, 1979.

Manchester, William. *A World Lit Only by Fire: The Medieval Mind and the Renaissance, Portrait of an Age*. Boston: Back Bay Books/Little, Brown, 1992.

Mandeville, Sir John. *The Travels of Sir John Mandeville*. New York: Penguin, 1983.

McCullough, David. *The Path Between the Seas: The Creation of the Panama Canal, 1870–1914*. New York: Simon and Schuster, 1977.

Morison, Samuel Eliot. *Admiral of the Ocean Sea: A Life of Christopher Columbus*. Boston: Atlantic–Little, Brown, 1970.

———. *Christopher Columbus: Mariner*. London: Faber and Faber, 1956.

———. *The Great Explorers: The European Discoverers of America*. New York: Oxford University Press, 1978.

———. *Journals and Other Documents on the Life and Voyages of Christopher Columbus*. New York: Heritage, 1963.

Morison, Samuel Eliot, and Mauricio Obregon. *The Caribbean as Columbus Saw It*. Boston: Little, Brown, 1956.

The New International Version Study Bible. Grand Rapids, MI: Zondervan Publishing, 1995.

Noyce, Wilfrid. *The Springs of Adventure*. New York: World, 1958.

Nunn, George E. *The Geographical Conceptions of Columbus: A Critical Consideration of Four Problems*. New York: American Geographical Society, 1924.

Pastor, Xavier. *The Ships of Columbus*. London: Conway Maritime Press, 1992.

Pellerano, Jacinto Gimbernard. *Historia de Santo Domingo*.

Segunda Edicion. Santo Domingo: Editora de la Universidad de Santo Domingo, 1966.

Peters, Edward. *Inquisition*. Berkeley: University of California Press, 1983.

Phillips-Birt, Douglas. *A History of Seamanship*. New York: Doubleday, 1971.

Richardson, Bonham C. *The Caribbean in the Wider World, 1492–1992*. Cambridge: Cambridge University Press, 1992.

Rubin, Nancy. *Isabella of Castile: The First Renaissance Queen*. New York: St. Martin's, 1991.

Sauer, Carl Ortwin. *The Early Spanish Main*. Berkeley: University of California Press, 1966.

Schivelbusch, Wolfgang. *Tastes of Paradise: A Social History of Spices, Stimulants, and Intoxicants*. New York: Vintage, 1993.

Taviani, Paolo. *Columbus, The Great Adventure: His Life, His Times, His Voyages*. New York: Crown, 1991.

Thomas, Hugh. *Rivers of Gold: The Rise of the Spanish Empire, From Columbus to Magellan*. New York: Random House, 2003.

Tuchman, Barbara W. *The March of Folly: From Troy to Vietnam*. New York: Ballantine, 1984.

Villiers, Alan. *Men, Ships and the Sea*. Washington, DC: National Geographic Society, 1973.

Weber, Benton F. *Semi-Tropic California: The Garden of the World, Including a Concise History of Panama and the Panama Canal*. Los Angeles: Benton, 1915.

Wilford, John Noble. *The Mapmakers*. New York: Vintage, 2000.

Williamson, David. *National Portrait Gallery History of the Kings and Queens of England*. New York: Konecky and Konecky, 1998.

Yewell, John. *Confronting Columbus*. Jefferson, NC: McFarland, 1992.

Index

About the Author

Martin Dugard's previous books include *Chasing Lance: The 2005 Tour de France and Lance Armstrong's Ride of a Lifetime; Into Africa: The Epic Adventures of Stanley and Livingstone; Farther Than Any Man: The Rise and Fall of Captain James Cook; Knockdown: The Harrowing True Story of a Yacht Race Turned Deadly;* and *Surviving the Toughest Race on Earth.* His dispatches have appeared in *Esquire, Outside, Sports Illustrated,* and *GQ.* Dugard lives in Orange County, California, with his wife and three sons.

Reading Group Guide

THE LAST VOYAGE *of* COLUMBUS

*Being the Epic Tale of the Great
Captain's Fourth Expedition, Including
Accounts of Mutiny, Shipwreck, and Discovery*

by Martin Dugard

A conversation with Martin Dugard

How did you first learn about Columbus's final voyage?

I was in the midst of researching a book on African exploration when the *Los Angeles Times* ran a story about the discovery of Columbus's *Vizcaino* off the coast of Panama. At the time, I knew Columbus had made more than one voyage to the Americas after that first voyage of 1492, but I didn't know how many or what their purpose was. I was intrigued, however, that the remains of that ship had been found after so long and mentally catalogued it as something to research at a later date.

It was almost two years before I got around to reading more on Columbus and his fourth voyage. What I found totally blew my mind. It was one of the most adventurous voyages in history, if not the most adventurous. Everything that could go wrong did go wrong: hurricanes, shark attacks, mutiny, waterspouts, and so on. And somehow Columbus persevered. That told me a lot about his character and led me to believe he was something more than the historical opportunist that modern history portrays him to be. One thing led to another, and soon I was immersed in telling the story of that fourth voyage.

A lot has been written about Columbus. What made you think that his life deserved further treatment?

No one had ever written a book specifically about the fourth voyage. It was one of history's long lost stories. There are a lot of great untold tales in the annals of exploration, but it struck me as odd that someone like Columbus, whose life has been examined again and again, had this great gap in his life's history. The fourth voyage was Columbus's favorite. It was a journey of redemption where he showed once and for all that he was one of the world's greatest mariners. A story like that needed to be told.

Of all the remarkable struggles that faced Columbus on that final voyage, what stands out in your mind as the most grueling?

That year of being shipwrecked. Everything else was relatively short-term: the few days enduring that hurricane off Hispaniola, the long hours battling the Indians in Belen, and even the hundred days tacking into the wind and rain off the coast of Central America. But that year off the coast of Jamaica had to be excruciating. Columbus could barely move because of his gout and rheumatism, the sweltering Caribbean heat and humidity were omnipresent, his crew had mutinied, his remaining men were constantly complaining, and there was that cloud of uncertainty hanging over it all. Were they ever going to be rescued? It seemed very unlikely. To top it all off, his youngest son was at his side. How must Columbus have felt, knowing that his teenaged son might be fated to spend the rest of his life on a remote jungle island? It must have been a daily mental grind.

What was the biggest challenge you faced in trying to tell this story?

The biggest challenge was getting inside Columbus's head. He edited his journal entries and personal letters so thoroughly that it was hard to figure where the man ended and his self-made legend began. Anytime you write history, it's like being a detective. The goal is to piece together a comprehensive story using the clues that person has left behind.

In Columbus's case, that process began by traveling to all the spots vital to the story: Spain, Portugal, the Caribbean. Meanwhile, I read the works of his biographers, all of whom seemed to paint a different picture of the man. Then I added the peripheral stuff, like researching daily life in the Spanish court, or the types of food and clothing that might be found aboard a caravel. Then I roughed out the book, writing it from start to finish so I could see the story on paper and find the holes. That's when I dug even deeper into Columbus and his life, looking for more and more detail so I could understand him and his times more clearly.

It was only then, after a year of thinking about Columbus almost every minute of every day, that I began to get a clear mental picture of that enigmatic man. The key to Columbus, I realized, is that he was a genius at sea, but that his personal life was a train wreck. He was enigmatic and bold and selfish and many other things that aren't easily summarized in one sentence. Yet all those traits prepared him for the uncommon challenges of the fourth voyage. It was like some great summation of his life.

How did reading Fernando's personal journal broaden your understanding of the private life of Columbus?

It saddened me a little, because I could sense the distance between Columbus and his son. They had been apart so many years that it soon became clear that the two barely knew each other. However, Fernando kept a brilliant journal. He recorded temperatures, conversations, sea conditions, and many other vivid aspects of that fourth voyage. His work was indispensable.

In your research, did you visit the places that Columbus visited?

I always make it a point to travel to each spot I'm writing about. It's one thing to read a description of the Alhambra, it's quite another to wander through that great palace on a rainy autumn morning, just like Columbus did when he was seeking permission for the fourth voyage. When you visit a spot you can write about how the air smells, what the temperature feels like on your skin, what sorts of grasses and trees and birds make the place special. All those things are vital to making the story rise up off the page and transporting the reader back five centuries. You can't get those descriptions by reading about them in someone else's biography or by scanning the Internet. I had to go there and take in all the sensations, then insinuate them into my consciousness so that it would become impossible to write about a certain setting without those sights and scents and sounds being synonymous with that place in my mind.

Did you try sailing?

My original goal was to sail down the coast of Central America, tracing Columbus's path. But once I began the research and learned exactly how foul conditions could be at sea there, I decided against it. However, I do sail, and I had the privilege of sailing from Genoa (Columbus's birthplace) to Spain aboard a tall ship as part of my research. Having said that, it's one thing to sail the same waters that Columbus did. It's quite another to do so aboard a caravel. They were small, foul ships with very little room for privacy or personal space. The crew didn't even have bunks.

Columbus is a somewhat controversial figure these days. Indeed, some people blame him for the decline of the indigenous population. What do you think about the dark side of his legacy?

I think that's a matter of blaming the messenger. Columbus is blamed because he got to the Americas first. If he hadn't been first, then it's certain that a Portuguese or British mariner would have come along not long after. Columbus was no saint, and he certainly has a lot to answer for, but the subjugation and brutality against indigenous Americans that would go on for the next five hundred years were not his doing. He didn't hold the indigenous people of the Americas in lofty esteem for very long once he arrived. But throughout history, that's what happens when cultures collide. One side tries to get the upper hand over the other. It seems ludicrous to associate Columbus with such atrocities as the U.S. government's nineteenth-century policy of genocide against Native Americans.

Columbus has been elevated to legend status, and a lot of people have misconceptions about him. What did you learn about him that differed from your preconceptions of him?

I always thought of him as a cartoon character, thanks to the "In fourteen hundred ninety-two, Columbus sailed the ocean blue" ditty I learned in grade school. When I was older, that was replaced by this image of him as the oppressor and enslaver of indigenous cultures. What most surprised me was that he was neither. He was a man of humble origins trying to make his mark on the world. He didn't sail in search of wealth, as most people believed. He was in search of the potential that the New World offered. In the strict class system of Europe, he saw the New World as a place where he could make his mark. He was tall, with red hair and freckles, and something of a ladies' man. But most of all, he had an unrelenting ambition and a brilliance as a sailor that has long been forgotten by history.

Columbus's final voyage took place more than five hundred years ago. Still, the story has a remarkable immediacy. What do you think makes this centuries-old tale feel so relevant?

We all need a shot at redemption from time to time. And that's what Columbus was hoping for with the fourth voyage. Unfortunately, it's the classic story of very good intentions gone horribly awry. But in the end . . . in the end, Columbus succeeds through perseverance and sheer will. There's something timeless about that. Even as I wrote, I could feel the emotional resonance of those themes loud and clear.

Questions and topics for discussion

1. It is quite possible that no historical figure has been more written about than Christopher Columbus. Some historians have asserted that he was a great hero, while others have painted him as a greedy villain. How did reading *The Last Voyage of Columbus* affect your view of him?

2. Christopher Columbus claimed that his fourth voyage was his greatest. Do you agree? Why or why not?

3. Columbus knew about the Inquisition and all of its attendant horrors, but he remained loyal to Ferdinand and Isabella. How would you characterize his relationship with them? How did his relationship with the king differ from his relationship with the queen?

4. Many Spanish people of Columbus's time looked upon men of Genovese extraction with great suspicion. Indeed, foreigners were seen as a "destabilizing influence." To what degree did this prejudice contribute to Columbus's fall from grace? Are there any modern-day equivalents to this scenario?

5. *The Last Voyage of Columbus* may be a "swashbuckling history," but it also features a very personal look at Columbus and his son Fernando. Did Fernando change throughout the voyage? How did his relationship with his father evolve?

6. "The Admiral of the Ocean Sea" was a good captain, but he made several questionable decisions on land. Would you characterize Columbus as a great leader? Why or why not?

7. To what extent were Columbus's travails the result of poor decision making, hubris, or greed? To what extent were they the result of bad luck or meddlesome outside forces?

8. In 1495, Fonseca decreed that Columbus would no longer be the only explorer in Spain's New World. Furthermore, he demanded that all individuals — including Columbus — obtain special governmental clearance. Columbus wasn't happy, of course, as he had a proprietary feeling about the territories that he had discovered. Was Columbus justified in thinking he should be given special treatment in the New World?

9. Martin Dugard writes that, unlike Ojeda's, "Columbus's voyages had some measure of curiosity and purity." Do you agree with this assessment? Why?

10. Dugard writes that the only certainty about Columbus is that "for better or worse, he chose to live a bold life rather than settle for mediocrity." Did you find the tale of Columbus's final voyage inspiring?

Martin Dugard's suggestions
for further reading

1. *Admiral of the Ocean Sea: A Life of Christopher Columbus* by Samuel Eliot Morison
Exhaustive and informative, if sometimes a little slow. The definitive take on Columbus's life.

2. *A World Lit Only by Fire: The Medieval Mind and the Renaissance, Portrait of an Age* by William Manchester
Perhaps the best book on the medieval mind and the pre-Reformation popes. Funny, bawdy, and very informative.

3. *The Story of Civilization* by Will Durant
Probably best digested in small chunks, this multivolume series is revealing and concise.

4. *The Life of the Admiral Christopher Columbus* by Fernando Colon
This book is written by Columbus's son, who sailed as a teenager on his father's fourth and final voyage. It provides the best first-person reportage of any of Columbus's trips.

5. *Christopher Columbus and the Age of Exploration* by Silvio A. Bedini
This is not a narrative, but an encyclopedia pertaining specifically to Columbus's life and times. I kept it within arm's reach at all times while writing *The Last Voyage of Columbus*.

6. *Rivers of Gold* by Hugh Thomas and *Empire: How Spain Became a World Power, 1492–1763* by Henry Kamen
   These two books are very similar in scholarship and focus, and read very well. The telling details of Spain and Columbus made them both great nightstand reading.

7. *The Springs of Adventure* by William Noyce
   This book was written by a British mountain climber and offers the best insights into the minds of explorers and adventurers that I have ever come across. A fine combination of quotes and anecdotes.

8. *The Life of Captain James Cook* by J. C. Beaglehole
   Admittedly, this exhaustive text can be a sleeping pill. But there is no better way to understand an explorer's relevance than by seeing his impact on subsequent generations. Beaglehole's details on life at sea and the ways of exploration are a fine companion to Morison's work on Columbus.

9. *The Alhambra* by Robert Irwin
   This slim, elegant history of the most pivotal castle in world history dispels many myths and illusions perpetuated in scores of guidebooks and online travel guides. Well-written, with beautiful photography.

10. *Bury My Heart at Wounded Knee* by Dee Brown
    An eloquent, heartbreaking narrative on the policy of genocide perpetrated against Native Americans by the United States government.